MIRRORED IMAGES

MIRRORED IMAGES

American Anthropology and American Culture, 1960–1980

SUSAN R. TRENCHER

BERGIN & GARVEY
Westport, Connecticut • London

Library of Congress Cataloging-in-Publication Data

Trencher, Susan R.
   Mirrored images : American anthropology and American culture,
1960–1980 / Susan R. Trencher.
      p.   cm.
   Includes bibliographical references and index.
   ISBN 0–89789–673–4 (alk. paper)
   1. Anthropology—United States—History.   2. Anthropology—United
States—Philosophy.   3. Ethnology—United States—Philosophy.
4. United States—Civilization—1945-   I. Title.
GN17.3.U6T74   2000
301'.0973—dc21   99–36904

British Library Cataloguing in Publication Data is available.

Library of Congress Catalog Card Number: 99–36904
ISBN: 0–89789–673–4

First published in 2000

Bergin & Garvey, 88 Post Road West, Westport, CT 06881
An imprint of Greenwood Publishing Group, Inc.
www.greenwood.com

Printed in the United States of America

The paper used in this book complies with the
Permanent Paper Standard issued by the National
Information Standards Organization (Z39.48–1984).

10 9 8 7 6 5 4 3 2 1

Copyright Acknowledgments

To our parents

Contents

Preface

Several of the readers, known and unknown, who read this work before it reached this stage commented on the absence of my own point of view explicitly stated and placed within the text. As one anonymous reviewer put it: "Surely given her subject matter (reflexivity) she cannot get away with this." I (and hundreds of others) do not consider myself even obliquely subtle, and I assume that much of my own position is evident throughout. The effort here is to provide a reasoned and reasonable introduction to some of the issues which have stimulated and troubled American anthropology for the last three decades, and insofar as explicating my own views in broad terms is useful, I took the critique seriously enough to include some thoughts on the genesis of this research and overall positions which permeate it.

Since the 1960s, discussions about, arguments over, and references to that time have occupied an exceptional share of American attention and space. But then, the 1960s has been regularly perceived and announced as an exceptional time. Certainly this has been true among American academics and by some of the now aging participants in that time. I include myself in both these groups. Thus, although this work was specifically motivated by anthropological interests in both American culture and American anthropology, the interests themselves were formed in the middle of the 1960s, when I began my undergraduate education. On reflection I am sure that the particular moment in American anthropology which I selected for study was significantly, albeit at first silently, generated by my own experience in the 1960s. It was part of the extended effort of many Americans, including the authors of the works examined here, to make sense of what being American

meant and how it shaped perception and experience of and in the world in
a time of turmoil and culturally cogent self-examination.

I started with a naive question: How does being a member of one culture
(American) impact on studying another? Embedded in the question were
my interests in American culture and anthropology, as well as an assumption
that there was an impact. The question was not whether, but how. This
seemed to me entirely reasonable as an anthropological question, since as
part of my undergraduate education and most powerful socialization in Anthropology I did not struggle with notions of positivism and pure objectivity. This was not because I was unaware of them, but because my professors,
members of the generation above mine (academically speaking) but of various generations otherwise, did not (in current vocabularies) essentialize
their own views or those of their students. They taught that anthropology
was a science and talked about their own work, written and in the field, in
ways that made it clear that they neither assumed nor demanded rigid definitions. Disparate definitions and theories of culture were part of course
assignments without requiring the choice of one or any of them as truth or
disembodied authority. On the contrary, such diversity, along with the peoples we studied, were presented as the fundamental opportunities of anthropology. (This seems a good place to thank my early mentors in
anthropology, Ruth Krulfeld and Patrick Gallagher, and in philosophy the
incomparable Thelma Lavine.) Thus the generalized experience in anthropology as a discipline described in the primary works in this study was unfamiliar and a subject for further research, as is the critique of anthropology
which came later and is to be pursued elsewhere.

I do see the splash of personal interest, life experience and interpretations,
through which they are produced and which produce them as sometimes
inextricably merged and as relevantly raised in works which grappled with
anthropology and ethnographic presentation. But humans do have tools,
among them the talent for reflexivity that provides the lens through which
we imperfectly but sufficiently give primacy to one aspect of self over another. Thus we are able to get on with the job of anthropology, just as
others get on with their jobs. And in many cases it is the imperfect but
much-maligned processes of objectification and objectivity which allow us
and them to do that. Positioned, albeit incomplete, objectivity can have its
uses. Do we after all really want our physicians, for example, to share our
embarrassment during examinations (what good if both of us turn away?),
sob with us over our diagnoses (although we don't mind the celebration of
them), or provide us with their own medical history? And for myself, I do
not want them making up their credentials, nor inventing test results in that
blend of fiction and autobiography which is sometimes heralded as better
ethnography. I have offered interpretations, based on what I have taken as
evidence, of the material I have gathered. The effort in the social sciences,
as I see it, is to produce interpretations that have an empirical grounding

and make reasonable sense. That I hope that these are elements of the work that follows goes without saying, but it will come as no surprise to people who know me to see that I have said it anyway.

Specifically, I sincerely thank the anthropologists Paul Rabinow, Jean-Paul Dumont, Gerald Berreman, and Dell Hymes, who were formally interviewed for this work and who were uniformly generous with time, past memories, and present insights.

Producing this work has been, as family, friends, and colleagues know full well, very much a shared project. It is one of the great fortunes of my life to be surrounded by generous and decent people. I thank my colleagues in the Department of Sociology and Anthropology at George Mason University, who have all in one way or another offered support and encouragement. I particularly thank Kevin Avruch, who was generous enough to sit on "the" committee and continues to offer good advice and assistance. I thank family, including colleagues as friends and friends as family—Louise Rappaport, Laura Morrison, Barbara Obrentz, Maggie Morton, Jim and Roberta Gottlieb, Mark and Erica Jacobs, Linnie and Art Robinson, Alice Klein, Barry Park, Sarah Amsler, Irene and Donald Rabinovitch, and Michael Smith—for their interest, enthusiasm, and often their patience. Without Eleanor Gerber on the first "go-round" I would still be going around. Bhavani Arabandi and company performed miraculous deeds with good humor. And finally, to all of the following, without whom I would still be searching for the next reference, the better phrase, and my glasses: Thank you straight from my heart to colleagues, mentors, and friends, Joe Scimecca, Karen Secrist, and John Stone. If good works count, they have earned a place in heaven. A special salute to John, "He Who Must Be Obeyed," before whom I break with tradition and bend my knee and bow my head. Thank you to our children, Emily, Julie, and Dan, who bathe the world in light and keep it shining. And a life thank you to Billy Trencher, always the man of the "our."

CHAPTER 1

Introduction

> Therefore, anthropological analysis must incorporate two facts. First that
> we ourselves are historically situated through the questions we ask, and
> the manner in which we seek to understand and experience the world,
> and second, that what we receive from our informants are interpreta-
> tions, equally mediated by history and culture. (Rabinow 1977:119)

One of the hallmarks of American anthropology over the past fifty years is
the extent to which its own practice has been the subject of assertion, questioning, and criticism by anthropologists themselves. This work has been
shaped by this discussion and by two primary anthropological (and Anthropological[1]) interests: (1) the mediation of anthropological practice by its
own cultural milieu and (2) American culture.[2] Brought together through
a focus on a particular form of written Anthropological practice (referred to
in the work as "fieldworker ethnographies") and an exploration of the
American and Anthropological milieu in which it emerged, this work is simultaneously part of this ongoing self-examination as well as a study of it.[3]
Viewed as culturally mediated through temporal context and "typically
American constructs," including and especially ideas and assumptions about
the individual and equality (see Varenne 1984; Lipset 1996; Kammen
1997), American Anthropological practice is taken as an anthropological
subject for study which simultaneously acts as a heuristic device for the
investigation of American experience and culture.

FIELDWORKER ETHNOGRAPHIES IN THE FIELD

In the late 1970s, part of a generation of neophyte anthropologists, struggling to set their professional feet on the ground, wrote accounts which

reflected on and represented their participation in the Anthropological project and rite of passage—fieldwork. These ethnographers of fieldwork (*sic* fieldwork ethnographers) produced works in which anthropologists turned their own experience in the field and their interpretation of it into the subject of their ethnographies, and in so doing produced works that were significantly about the fieldworker. "Fieldworker" here refers to a significantly cultural construct. That is, although aspects and experiences of ethnographers as individuals appear (the ethnographies were after all produced by individuals), the salience of these ethnographies is in the practice, not the persons. Specifically, the focus is on the ways in which these works present and represent significantly American comprehensions and interpretations. *Reflections on Fieldwork in Morocco* (Rabinow 1977), *The Headman and I* (Dumont 1978), *Tuhami: Portrait of a Moroccan* (Crapanzano 1980), and *Moroccan Dialogues* (Dwyer 1982) were selected for detailed study primarily on the basis of their "early" (1977–1982) arrival in what was to become a sea change in American anthropological practice. These works rejected the epistemology of science and replaced it with interpretation. In reflection, they claimed reflexivity as the primary Anthropological method for revealing culture. In so doing they presented and represented important, internally linked changes and to some degree circular changes in the Anthropological enterprise which encompassed both subject and method. The subject of these ethnographies shifted from culture to fieldwork. The method through which these ethnographies were produced shifted from fieldwork (as participant observation) to reflection on fieldwork. And reflection was linked to the abandonment of the objective observer and its replacement with the subjective participant.[4] Taken together, these shifts ultimately produced ethnographies which were about the fieldworker—a look at what Rabinow (1977), author of one of the ethnographies selected for study, has called the "cultural self" relevant to enculturation and the shifting world of history and experience.

FIELDWORKER ETHNOGRAPHIES AT HOME

In the years since their publication, fieldworker ethnographies have regularly and often been the subject of comment and critique. While their significance here initially resides in the overt claims made in these works about their own practice and method, they are also worth Anthropological exploration as works which have been grouped together and referred to by a range of American anthropologists with diverse views on their underpinnings and presentation. Anthropologists commenting on and critiquing fieldworker ethnographies have often disagreed over their derivation, meaning, and value, but they have agreed that they represent a change in practice, some elements of which have in the last twenty-five years been more ubiquitous than anomalous.

For example, these works were being cited by Marcus and Cushman (1982), in their review of "experimental ethnographies,"[5] as representative of "philosophically informed reactions" to standard ethnographic forms. For Ortner (1984:143), *Reflections on Fieldwork in Morocco* and *Tuhami* exemplified "recent works that question philosophically whether we can ever truly know the 'Other.' " By 1988, Geertz (1988:91) characterized the relevant works by Rabinow (1977), Crapanzano (1980), and Dwyer (1982) as "I witness accounts," the throes of "the Diary Disease" caught through exposure to the publication of Malinowski's diary in 1967. Seen as a kind of epidemic by the late 1980s, Geertz categorized them as examples of "the journal-into-work mode of text building and the literary anxieties that plague it" (Geertz 1988:91). In the same year, Sangren (1988) characterized these works as "postmodern" and included as part of their genesis the shrinking job market for young anthropologists at the time, rather than the epistemological challenges claimed to be engaged in by their authors. Mascia-Lees, Sharpe, and Ballerino-Cohen (1989:9) also saw these works as "postmodern,"[6] in this instance as generated in part by the struggle to maintain Western hegemony, including the struggle of white males to maintain their traditional position of dominance in contemporary society.

What follows in this work is not an effort to supplant or deny previous interpretations, but to add to them in an effort to situate Anthropology in the "real world" (Fox 1991:13). That is, to make sense of them in the cultural (including economic, political, and social) context of their production. But first I take a preliminary and critical look at the smaller professional lineage relevant to their emergence.

STREAM OF SELF-CONSCIOUSNESS

Understanding the significance of contemporary interests as in part related to older ones enriches our understanding of fieldworker ethnographies as part of an Anthropological current of interest running under and through the discipline. (And unable to escape the reflexive rebound, it helps to situate the present work.) In the following brief history, a context is provided for fieldworker ethnographies as well as the interests of the present study.

At the end of World War II, when American anthropologists began questioning Anthropological practice during and in the aftermath of the war, the questions they raised and the concerns which accompanied them had different emphases, but were neither unique nor original. For instance, anthropologist Paul Radin had directed himself to versions of these questions in *The Method and Theory of Ethnology*, first published in 1933.[7] But following World War II, public comment by some anthropologists had a particularly political and condemnatory edge, which re-emerged with added vitriol in the 1960s. American anthropologists simultaneously asserted cultural influence and doubly decried it; that is, argued it as a presence which was negative in both its content and its impact on practice. But in so doing they often failed to illuminate the cultural setting and its relationship to their own work. For instance, after World War II, Embree (AA 1950:430–434)[8] and Henry (AA 1951:134–135), in a series of letters to the editor published in the *American Anthropologist*, argued that work by anthropologists in a major project in Micronesia (made possible by political and economic relationships at that time) was ethnocentric—a product of American values and experience. According to these anthropologists, the crisis of war had engendered a particular kind of Anthropological thought and practice already "familiar" in Western activity. Embree (AA 1950:431) argued:

The twentieth century American anthropologist is voicing the views and sentiments of the nineteenth century foreign investors, convert-seeking missionaries, and writers such as Kipling, singing the praises of the docile brown man—when ruled by western man. . . . When the crisis of war arose and we found ourselves attacked by an Oriental nation which we had thought in the usual popular way to be "progressive" some of us seem suddenly to have lost our objectivity and decided that those objectionable little people must have an evil, a "pathological" or at best an "adolescent" culture.[9]

Henry (AA 1951:135) particularly noted the imposition of American interests on choice of subject matter, citing national character studies done during the war years (i.e., Benedict 1946; Gorer 1943; LaBarre 1945) as primarily "studies of the enemy."[10] During the 1940s and 1950s, arguments over the grounds and terms of Anthropological practice were generally atheoretical, and expressed in letters sent to professional publications (the *American Anthropologist* and publications for professionals, i.e., the *Fellow Newsletter* [now the *Newsletter*]) and sent to members of the American Anthropological Association. As letters rather than articles they were neither conceived nor presented as empirical studies, and were most often exchanged as views of professional conduct by members of the profession rather than as professional documents.

In the 1960s through the 1970s, this "edge" reappeared in broadly based and sometimes empirically investigated assertions made by anthropologists positing a link between the milieu in which Anthropology and Anthropological work were produced, became part of the Anthropological discussion with increasing regularity, and began to be published as articles. One of the ways in which this emerged was through an increase in interest in the history of Anthropology. Rowe's (1965) now well-known work on "The Renaissance Foundations of Anthropology" reflected a growing interest by anthropologists in examining the genesis of Anthropology, its relationship to historical setting, and the history of the discipline (see for example Kuper 1973; Darnell 1974; Evans-Pritchard 1981). Bennett's (1966) article referred to Rowe's and argued that there was evidence that social theories and cultural analysis were present in earlier works in Islamic and Oriental

thought (thus implying that Rowe's work was too narrowly framed in Western history). According to Bennett, culture theory and descriptive ethnography could be traced to the work of Ibn Khaldun and actually preceded
Renaissance Anthropological concerns by one to two centuries.

A third (seldom cited) analysis by Hoffman (1973) looked not only at
the emergence of anthropology, but also overtly critiqued Rowe's work, in
terms more consistent with politicized discussions in Anthropology of the
late 1960s and early 1970s (see Part II). Hoffman (1973) argued not only
a different and older source of Anthropology, but also critiqued Rowe's
work for reflecting a "Western bias." Hoffman claimed that "the unwar-
ranted extension of our ideas about the Western European medieval world
led to several problems in many recent treatments of the historical emergence of anthropological inquiry" (ibid.:1347). Using Byzantine sources,
Hoffman contended that the postulated medieval break in the Western intellectual tradition was actually almost nonexistent. He argued that the idea
of a break had been overemphasized in order to leave out the larger soci-
ocultural non-Western milieu in which the anthropological tradition had
developed. Rowe's omission of the Eastern origin of men like Herodotus
and other comparative and ethnographic historians whose work was situated
in the Hellenization and Romanization of the Mediterranean, was, according to Hoffman, a manifestation of bias. The "accepted" view (Rowe's article was widely cited in positive terms at the time) in Anthropology of its
origins was thus itself argued as culturally biased and a consequence of the
"attempt to restrict the definition of the Western intellectual tradition in
time (i.e., the 'Classical' Period of antiquity) and space (i.e., to Western
Europe) without accounting for the great variation in it" (ibid.:1335).

Rowe's work became a classic in the field, the others did not. The differential reception to these works (Rowe's was the most widely cited and
praised) is itself interesting in retrospect, particularly as part of questions
salient here regarding the cultural mediation of Anthropological practice.
Specifically phrased, they are part of more general anthropological questions.
For example: Was the reception of Rowe's work the product of superior
research? Was the reception evidence that there were biases among anthropologists, which made it more likely to be accepted? What were the cultural
strands in the production and reception of Rowe's work? Of Bennett's? Of
Hoffman's? Whatever the responses to these questions, the works themselves
have significance in American Anthropology as they represent the turns,
interests, and tenor of the times in which they were produced. At a mini-
mum, they provide evidence for interest by anthropologists in their own
history (see also Hallowell 1956), an interest which anthropologists in the
1980s have variously taken for granted and argued as unique or original.
Further, the interest in their own discipline has, as Hoffman's work demonstrated, been Anthropological as well as historical.[11]

For example, nearly twenty-five years after Embree and Henry raised the issue of racism in Anthropology, Hsu (1973:7), a Chinese-born American anthropologist, cited work in the field and argued, in "Prejudice and Its Effect in American Anthropology: An Ethnographic Report," that American anthropologists regularly devalued or ignored work produced by "non-whites." No longer written as a letter to the editor, as Embree and Henry's had been, Hsu's work was an ethnographic look at American Anthropology as part of American culture. Hsu argued that racial prejudice by American anthropologists framed researcher focus as a matter of culturally engendered interest (see also Bennett 1946 on the Redfield–Lewis debate and Washburn 1963 on race) translated through culturally relevant racial categories (i.e., "whites" and "non-whites"). According to Hsu, deep-seated cultural prejudices were reflected in (1) the research questions Anthropologists asked, (2) the race of the anthropologist, and (3) in the kinds of material Anthropology the dominant population of "white" anthropologists accepted as adequate Anthropological knowledge (ibid).

Hsu's practice, in which he assumed racism as part of general American life, was consistent with many of the works examining Anthropological practice in the late 1960s and early 1970s, which focused on a largely unspecified cultural tradition with which it was assumed the audience of anthropologists (being Western, specifically American) would be familiar. The ethnographic effort was directed at Anthropology, while the cultural side was asserted but unexplored. Consistent with Hsu's work, many minority anthropologists began to look at the significance of their own social identity and that of (other) anthropologists. In the same year that Hsu raised the issue of racial bias, Magubane, an African-born anthropologist living in the United States, took up the question of the effects on analysis (rather than choice of subject) of the observer's view and undertook a more broadly cultural investigation. Magubane (1973:1701–1715) argued that the concepts used by social anthropologists of change working in a village in Africa represented ambiguities in the relationship between method and theory which, consistent with Hsu's observations, Magubane argued as rooted in a lack of understanding by investigators about the construction of cultural as well as intellectual frames.

Drawing on philosophical works of Mills and Lukacs, Magubane used a then new vocabulary (cf. Frantz 1968; Wolf 1972) in Anthropology—"colonial" and "colonized"—to describe the field relationship. He argued that the questions asked by investigators and their "intellectual problems" were "relevant to the public issues of their time and to the private troubles of individual men and women" as well as relevant to the inability of observers to transcend the primacy of facts which are falsely reified in the capitalist tradition (Magubane 1973:1712). The "facts" observers took into account were "as much if not more, the products of political considerations as of their scientific utility" (ibid.:1714; cf. Kuhn 1962). This argument harks back to Bennett's (1946) similar but unpoliticized analysis of the Redfield–

Lewis debate, in which he argued that different conclusions by anthropologists working in the same culture were the result of individual observer focus. The letters and articles above, and others like them, form part of the foundation for fieldworker ethnographies—not in their particularity but in their production and their publication. They raised questions about Anthropology and its context, and were themselves produced in particular temporal, including social, political, economic, and intellectual, settings.[12] By the time fieldworker ethnographies were written, not only the interests, but many of the claims of these earlier works were taken for granted. Western bias was simultaneously assumed and rejected as part of Anthropological practice.

This work combines the critical and historical interests evidenced in the works described above, but it also simultaneously includes them as part of its subject matter. Rather than taking their claims for granted or looking at them solely as part of the history of Anthropology, they are taken as a means to illuminate elements of the Anthropological and American "lifeworld" in which they were produced. (I am drawing here both from phenomenological definitions of "lifeworld" as taken for granted definitions and understandings that are part of our activity in the "everyday world" as well as Habermas's [Honneth et al. 1989] "reminder" that the lifeworld is "so unproblematic that we are simply incapable of making ourselves conscious of this or that part of it at will.") From this point of view, works *in* the history of the discipline, are produced in part *by* the history of the discipline which in turn is permeated and produced by the events and the interpretations of them which surround it. I take as my starting point Scholte's (1972) "hypothesis" in *Reinventing Anthropology* (a seminal work for the present project), that: "Intellectual traditions are culturally mediated and relative. If anthropological activity is culturally mediated, it is in turn subject to ethnographic description and analysis" (431).

THE OBJECTIFICATION OF THE STUDY

In part because this work so easily circles in on itself, and because in the 1980s and 1990s questions and assertions concerning methods and theory considered appropriate to Anthropology have multiplied (thus dividing anthropologists), I take a moment to briefly set out my intellectual position in this work.

To study Anthropological practice as an anthropologist (that is, to see the project as a contribution to an anthropology of Anthropology) requires a certain detachment. Drawn from a critical philosophical base, primarily through the work of Juergen Habermas, the present "spokesperson" for that point of view, I use reflexivity as a reasoned, "distanced" reflection back and forth, in order to study self-proclaimed reflexive works. My view of the social world is phenomenological (cf. Schutz 1971; Berger and Luckmann 1967). In capsule form, I start from the premise that there is a reality out there. But in cultural research what ultimately matters about that reality, in Anthropological terms, is the sense that is made of it by "natives," and by those who seek to make sense of how "natives" make sense. Here I draw from Geertz's (1973) articulation of the work of an anthropologist as providing (at best) second-order constructions of the first-order constructions of natives. From this point of view, I claim that anthropologists can grasp meaning sufficient for practical purposes—in this case, a sufficient understanding of the significance of what is attended to by Others (variously defined), and to see its meaning. "Sufficient" is understood as adequate for practical purposes. It makes no claim to be native or some form of particular or universal truth. The claim is of a grasp of at least some of the grounds of taken-for-granted reality and meanings that identify natives as natives and differentiate them, at least for analytic purposes, from non-natives. From this point of view, Anthropology relies on a critical questioning of empirical data and shares elements of both science and interpretation.

Thompson (1990) sets forth a critical and hermeneutic base (depth hermeneutics) which provides some methodological guidelines for this research.[13] Briefly, the value of depth hermeneutics is that it encourages different kinds of analysis ("socio-historical," "formal or discursive," and "interpretation") which support and legitimate each other and which reveal that particular modes of analysis may illuminate certain aspects of a phenomenon rather than others. Interpretation (or re-interpretation) builds on the previous two stages and moves beyond them as it "uses socio-historical analysis and formal or discursive analysis to shed light on the social conditions and structural features of a symbolic form, and it seeks to interpret a symbolic form in this light, to explicate and elaborate what it says, what it represents, what it is about" (Thompson 1990:23).[14]

Further, similar to arguments in Anthropology itself that a reflexive and critical look at Anthropology includes putting it in its social and historical context, Thompson (1990:12) argues:

this emphasis on the symbolic character of social life must be complemented by an emphasis on the fact—not always evident in the writings of Geertz—that symbolic forms are embedded in structured social contexts. This dual emphasis defines what I call the "structural conception" of culture. Cultural phenomena on this account, may be seen as *symbolic forms in structured contexts*. (emphasis in original)

Cultural analysis thus "may be regarded as the study of meaningful constitution and social contextualization of symbolic forms" (Thompson 1990: 12).

Fieldworker ethnographies are used in this work as "symbolic forms" which "say something of something" (Geertz 1973; ff. Ricoeur 1971), but what they "say" can be discerned only by attending to the social contexts within which they occur (cf. Thompson 1990:145). I have used the American Anthropological Association[15] as a cultural, as well as a professional, venue for intellectual, political, and economic events and discussion of them, salient to Anthropology and relevant to the production of fieldworker ethnographies. These discussions simultaneously provided access to the broader American cultural milieu of the time.

WITHIN LIMITS: THE TERMS OF THE STUDY

In order to pursue a "critical exegesis of the text" within the particular times, places, circumstances, constraints and opportunities (cf. Helm 1984a) in which they were produced, I focused on three questions: (1) Briefly, what was the disciplinary grounding and practice preceding fieldworker ethnographies? (Part I, Chapter 2 and 3); (2) What were the articulated and interpreted terms of fieldworker ethnographies? (Part II, Chapters 4–7); (3) What were the socio-historical and intellectual contexts in which these ethnographies were constructed? (Part II, Chapters 8–11).

I began this project interested in how American culture influenced practice in American Anthropology. This interest led to one in philosophical conceptions of reflexivity and then to works in Anthropology which were argued by ethnographers (including Rabinow, Crapanzano, Dwyer, and Dumont) and identified by others (i.e., those writing about ethnography, e.g., Marcus and Cushman 1982; Fabian 1983) as reflexive. My working definition of reflexivity at the outset of the project was: critical reflection by the anthropologist on his or her own practice, included as part of the intention in ethnography.[16] Broadly, it can be argued that all anthropologists are involved in a reflexive project. Reflexivity in these terms refers to the involvement of an investigator with the subject of investigation, a sense of interaction which is (to varying extents) inevitable in the process and practice of Anthropology. But more specifically, *Reflections on Fieldwork in Morocco* (1977), *The Headman and I* (1978), *Tuhami* (1980), and *Moroccan Dialogues* (1982), included within them specific claims about reflexivity and specifically used reflection. Authors of these works claimed to explicitly place their interaction with the subject of study in an investigative foreground and make it into their subject or concern themselves with that interaction as a phenomenon. The foregrounding of this interaction was intended to create or expose a "dialogue" between investigator and subject which acted as a means for the anthropologist to reflect on the categories of understanding and experience constructed through enculturation—the "cultural self" (Rabinow 1977). These works were, in an important sense, "self-identified" for this study, through the authors' stated intent in their ethnographies.

As a strategy for linking fieldworker ethnographies, I created an ad hoc group based on "family resemblances" (cf. Needham 1975; ff. Wittgenstein 1953) in which conventional definitions of a conceptual class based on its

members sharing certain properties is not a logical necessity.[17] "Family resemblances" indicate "a logical network of similar overlapping and criss-
crossing; sometimes overall similarities, sometimes similarities of detail,"
which may exist among the members of a class (Needham 1975:350). The
fluidity of family resemblances denies reification of this group as a category
of individuals or works, allowing them their similarity but precluding the
necessity of seeing the anthropologists or their works as permanent or reified
representatives of a single or perpetual viewpoint.[18] The notion of family
resemblances was also useful because individuals producing these works did
not share and did not need to share a wholly consistent notion of Anthropology, nor do they comprise a fixed membership. This view was corrobo-
rated by Rabinow (1989), who, when asked to identify his relationship and
that of his work to other authors and works specified here, described it as
one of "family resemblance." "I don't think of us as a group. I think . . .
the best phrase is Wittgenstein's 'family resemblance' . . . we shared a set of
experiences . . . some broad perspective on how to do things and what the
world was like."

Relevant family resemblances were not limited to the terms of ethnographic practice, but also included features of biographical situation relevant
to socio-historical context. For example, fieldwork ethnographers were engaged in fieldwork and out of the United States during the height of the
protests and turmoil associated with the war in Vietnam (1968–1969). In
the same year, there was also an abrupt shift in employment opportunities
in academia (starting in 1969) as government monies for universities became
less available (see Chapter 10). Fieldwork ethnographers returning from the
field found themselves writing dissertations and looking for employment in
a job market which was shrinking for the first time since World War II. After
finishing their dissertations, three of these anthropologists participated in
(by then and into the 1990s) expected professional practice in Anthropology
by reframing their dissertations into first books. In their second books, fieldworker ethnographies, these anthropologists articulated but ultimately broke
with other intellectual traditions and ethnographic practice common in Anthropology.

Certain similarities in the biographies of these anthropologists are taken
here as significant. As Varenne (1984) pointed out in his study of the representation of the individual and of culture in American Anthropological
conversation, what is of significance is the "cultural representation" in their
conversation. Varenne included British-born and -trained anthropologist
Gregory Bateson, who had been working in the United States, "precisely
because he was not born or raised in the United States"; I include French-
born and -raised anthropologist Jean-Paul Dumont, who received his undergraduate education in France and his graduate education in the United
States. Dumont, like Bateson, "is an American figure to the extent that his
work has been incorporated into the American conversation" and his work,

like Bateson's, provides a different but relevant perspective on that conversation (Varenne 1984:282). For example, unlike the indigenous American fieldworker ethnographers, Dumont's work framed positivist and confessional works as two "extremes" which he sought to bridge (rather than dismiss), and further, drew more from and credited the work of earlier anthropologists. While the setting up of the two "extremes" may be in part attributable to Dumont's understanding of binary opposition and Hegelian dialectic through his early teacher and influence in Anthropology, Claude Levi-Strauss, the latter's influence extended to American Anthropology as well (as does an interest in dialectics in general). More significant here is Dumont's attention to the history of previous practice and his explicit sense of his own work as part of that history, while the American fieldwork ethnographers rejected past practice and denied their work as related to it. (In Chapter 11, the ahistorical set of the American fieldworker ethnographies is "typically," albeit certainly not exclusively, American).

In keeping with the nature of family resemblances, although dialectics are significant in all of these works there are variations in the dialectical framework employed. For example, tripartite (dialectical) division was in part intentionally produced by the authors of these works as part of their understanding of their work as itself a dialectical process. Rabinow's organization of *Reflections on Fieldwork in Morocco* was intentionally Hegelian since as a young anthropologist he had "high ideas" about mirroring the form of *The Phenomenology of Spirit* (Rabinow 1989). Dwyer's work is more Marxist (through Lukacs and Goldmann) than the others, Crapanzano's is more Freudian. Dumont, as noted, relied most heavily on Levi-Straussian dialectics. In these works there is an emphasis on written ethnography as a means to resolution through constitution of a professional self. But while Rabinow, Dumont, and to a lesser extent Dwyer, specifically address the shift from the neophyte to the professional state, Crapanzano, the only one of the group with a regular teaching position at the time of the publication of his fieldworker ethnography, focused more on the psychological self than the professional one.

Also salient to the present study is Varenne's observation that focusing too narrowly, or giving too much emphasis to the biography of the individual can make it easy to dismiss any work which proposes to "generalize" biographical experience. "It is . . . easy to argue against the usefulness of *any* cultural model on the grounds that individual experiences by definition are the product of unique biographies and thus cannot be reduced to any generalizing statement" (Varenne 1984:283). The phenomenological viewpoint which informs this work argues that people experience a set of embedded contexts in which they change over time as part of the "biographical situation" as well as shared cultural experience (Schutz 1971).

Thus, in analyzing fieldworker ethnographies as mediated by cultural context, I ultimately seek what is cultural about them as visible through the analysis within them, which from this point arises in part, and in significant ways, from the doxa of Anthropological settings "at home" ("Doxa" here is used consistently with Habermas's view of "lifeworld," seen above, as well as with Thompson's "an interpretation of the opinions, beliefs and understandings which are held and shared by the individuals who comprise the social world." Also see Bourdieu 1990a:20). It was "at home" that these ethnographers reconstructed, reflected, and wrote—separated from field-work by time, space, and their own previous analyses in the form of disser-tations—first books and related articles. From this viewpoint, central constructs of fieldworker ethnographies identified in Chapter 4 as experi-ence, confrontation, and power and domination,[19] "say something" about, and were linked to, American settings. Within fieldworker ethnographies, the experience of ethnographers in proximate American contexts was taken for granted and projected backward into the analysis of field experience. This backward projection generalized particular experiences interpreted through asserted terms of power and domination which allowed other cul-turally salient assumptions to go unchallenged. Thus, in fieldworker eth-nographies the fieldwork encounter was presented as fraught with tension and permeated by struggles for power and domination assumed by these ethnographers as characteristic of the experience of all ethnographers and of Western and American interaction with Others.

HOW IT FITS TOGETHER

Part I is a backdrop for the rest of the work. Since fieldworker ethnog-raphies were part of an on-going conversation in Anthropology, Chapters 2 and 3 provide particular and proximate elements which help to make sense of Parts II and III. Chapter 2 presents a brief overview of epistemologies (science and interpretation) as relevant to disciplinary underpinnings and practice. Chapter 3 focuses on particular shifts in epistemology and practice more proximate to fieldworker ethnographies in "early works" (disserta-tions, articles, first ethnographies) by their authors. This chapter is filtered through a discussion of the "interpretive science" of Clifford Geertz as spe-cifically significant in the production of these works. Part I thus sets the stage for Part II, "An Interpretation of Fieldworker Ethnography: Crisis in the Field" (Chapters 4–7). In Part II, fieldworker ethnographies are ex-amined within the terms of the works themselves. What claims are made about anthropological practice? What problems of theory and method do their authors identify? What are the resolutions proposed? Chapter 4, "All in the Family," sets out some of the specific intentions and claims made by fieldworker ethnographers in and about their own work. Three family re-semblances are extrapolated from these claims, each one of which forms an entry for succeeding chapters. They are: (1) privileging of experience over observation, (2) concern with power and domination, and (3) depiction of fieldwork as resolution.

In Chapters 5–7, these claims are explored and critiqued within the works themselves and interpreted as inversions of earlier ethnographic practice. Chapter 5 focuses on "The Ethnographic Experience," and the form of fieldworker ethnographies as produced by the privileging of experience over observation as the foundation for Anthropological knowledge is explored. The focus in Chapter 6, "Confrontation, Power, and Domination" is on the terms in which fieldwork is claimed as a series of confrontations in which power and domination played defining roles. Depicted by fieldworker ethnographers as a series of encounters between individuals informed by global encounters between West and non-West, these works are analyzed as including within them particular encounters by these ethnographers which invert their own specific and generalized claims about field interactions. Specifically, fieldworker ethnographers asserted themselves as dominant in the fieldwork encounter by virtue of their "Westerness," yet in their specific descriptions of everyday interactions revealed that the ethnographer's agenda and activity were often dominated by the informant. These ethnographies thus contained within them the inverse of their own claims about domination, which were "resolved" in the written account by the imposition of the ethnographer who transformed himself into the dominant partner through a distanced interpretation rather than through an immediate experience, a resolution explored in Chapter 7, "Come the Resolution." Here the focus is on the claim of fieldwork experience as inevitably disruptive to the ethnographer's sense of self, reconstituted through a reflexive negotiated dialogue in the field. This claim is analyzed as significantly produced through a dialectical process at home. Fieldwork ethnographers reflected on past experience with Others, in the absence of Others thus producing a monologic and linear reconstitution (a one-way reflection back) rather than the dialogic and dialectical resolution for which they sought.

In Part III, "An Interpretation of Culture: Crisis at Home," intellectual, political, and economic crises in American experience are partially reconstructed, specifically as available through Anthropological discussion, including activities and debates within the American Anthropological Association (AAA). The focus is on what "being an American" meant as derived from published arguments among anthropologists, as available through professional documents and documents by professionals. A sense of crisis permeated these discussions in which central questions about the nature of the discipline, the roles and responsibilities of anthropologists as citizens and scientists, and the terms of the future of the profession were publicly debated and in the relevant time frame increasingly vehemently argued.

In Chapter 8, "We Hold These Truths to Be Self-Evident," some of the public, especially political, issues of the time considered salient to Anthropological practice through the discussion of them in the Association and elsewhere are presented. Chapter 9, "Anthropologists Go to War . . . with Themselves," links fieldworker ethnographies to the economic conditions and professional settings to which these anthropologists returned as the first generation of anthropologists since World War II to face a constricting economy and narrowed professional options. Chapter 11, "Intellectuals Shift," explores the links among shifting intellectual grounds of Anthropological practice to other aspects of the cultural world as the paradigm of science was challenged by interpretive modes of understanding and analysis which presaged those of fieldworker ethnographies. Finally, Chapter 12, "Reflections on Fieldworker Ethnographies," contemplates the emergence of fieldworker ethnographies and their particular terms and situates them as incipient postmodern practice relevant to postmodern conditions and as relevant to such conditions consistent with other analyses, including the "legitimation crisis" of late capitalist societies (Habermas 1975).

A NOTE FROM THE FIELD

In the American and Anthropological climate of incivility (itself a subject for Anthropological investigation, but beyond the purview of this work) of the late 1990s, I note again that although this book focuses on particular works, obviously authored by individuals, it is neither a study nor an assessment of individuals. As Varenne (1984:282) has put it, "In this perspective persons who act in the most diverse fashion can be understood as products of identical forces, the identification of these forces being considered the primary goal of social scientific inquiry." It is these "forces," not the persons, the ethnographies, not their authors, which are the focus of this book.

Finally, this work is not a history, but has elements of it as a study of particular work produced in the past as well as the past in which they were produced.[20] I have stressed this by using the past tense when writing about them, although they clearly exist as present works (still in publication) and works in some way relevant to the present. This raises a second point. These works have been identified by others (e.g., Mascia-Lees et al. 1989; Sangren 1988) as "postmodern," and in the final chapter I consider them as early works in the postmodern turn but otherwise refrain from referring to them in the body of the book as postmodern. This has been intentional. When these works were published the term "postmodern" was not in use and in any case, I see these works as incipient to, rather than examples of, postmodern practice. (Like fieldwork ethnographers by their own account, when they first returned from the field, neither here nor there.) It is also useful to separate postmodern practice as (like other practice) an ideological enterprise from the experience of the postmodern condition and its fragmentation, argumentation, alienation, and elevation of the individual. This book is part of the process of placing Anthropology (1960–1980), including its turn as part of the postmodern condition, in perspective.

NOTES

1. "Anthropology" is used to mark the specific focus in this work on anthropology as both a discipline and a profession in its American setting, rather than as a more generic enterprise (anthropology).

2. I rely on definitions of culture, which include social elements often left out of ideational definitions of culture. This is consistent philosophically with Habermas's claim in *Knowledge and Human Interest* (1971) that concepts and ideas are not simply derived from experience; they are constituents of it, and further, that all knowledge is mediated by social experience. In Anthropology I agree with Goody (1994) that separating social action (and its products) from culture (meaning) into two fields is probably unnecessary. As Goody says:

I find it difficult to distinguish two such fields. They act and interact in ways that may allow one to discern beliefs, symbols, and values, but these are intrinsic to their interaction; social action must include such a dimension and would be meaningless without it. The statement of beliefs, the use of symbols, the "expression" of values, these are part of "the ongoing process of interactive behavior." Any more separable notion of "framework" emerges from the analytic perception of the observer rather than from the action perspective of the actor. That does not make it wrong, but it may make it unnecessary.

3. Others, outside the field *per se*, for instance, George Stocking trained in history and, more recently, James Clifford in literary studies, have also been part of this discussion. While these authors are frequently misidentified as anthropologists, their primary training and socialization in other disciplines makes their effort a distinctly different one from the standpoint of this work. That is, they use Anthropology as the subject of study, as others in their fields might choose the Russian Revolution or Conrad's *Heart of Darkness* (which Clifford [1986] has compared to Malinowski's diary). While the boundaries of discipline and profession have always been permeable in Anthropology (i.e., Kroeber's "half history, half anthropology" [1935] and Wolf's [1964] "half science and half humanity"), their work is not taken here as a self-study, as professionally and disciplinarily defined. They are, from this point of view, much like the description by many anthropologists of their own work among others, perpetual outsiders, of a sort. In like fashion, their presence in this discussion in Anthropology has been fostered by the ongoing interest of anthropologists who variously encouraged, argued, debated, and accepted and rejected their work, thereby providing a platform for it.

4. While as depicted in these works the participant was always and inevitably and appropriately privileged over the observer while in the field, there is no opportunity for analysis of that assertion in the immediacy of fieldwork. Thus, the present analysis is of the written account; the present work focuses on and refers to "ethnography" in its original meaning in Anthropology as a written representation.

5. When the Marcus and Cushman's article "Ethnographies as Texts" was published in 1982, Dwyer's book was not yet available. They included in their discussion two articles in *Dialectical Anthropology*: "On the Dialogic of Fieldwork" (1977), and

"The Dialogic of Ethnology" (1979), which formed part of the basis for *Moroccan Dialogues* (1982).

6. Mascia-Lees et al. also termed these works as part of the "new ethnography," a term which to my knowledge had not been used for these kinds of works prior to that time, but which at the 1995 meetings of the American Anthropological Association was commonly used in a variety of sessions. The term "new ethnography" to refer to these works is itself interesting, since its use is consistent with an ahistorical outlook in American Anthropology and culture (see Chapter 10). A generation earlier "new ethnography" referred to work by ethnoscientists.

7. Although in intervening years Radin's (1933) interest was often seen as marginal to the field, the reissue of the work in 1966 attested to the upsurge of renewed interest by anthropologists in looking at their own work as part of an Anthropological problem and a potential problem for anthropologists at the time.

8. Professional correspondence and information to members, which appeared in the *American Anthropologist* (AA) in the 1940s and 1950s, and in the professional newsletter (Newsletter) of the American Anthropological Association (AAA) beginning in the 1960s, are cited within the work rather than set out separately in the bibliography. Names of the authors of the letters are included within the surrounding text or as part of the citation.

9. Embree here is presumably referring to studies by anthropologists including Geoffrey Gorer, Margaret Mead, Gregory Bateson, and Ruth Benedict, for the Department of the Navy, during World War II.

10. While other anthropologists working in Micronesia at the time denied this view, and held that Anthropology was an objective science, they sometimes (presumably unwittingly) provided evidence for it. For example, well-known anthropologist George Peter Murdock, while working in Micronesia, claimed a scientific objectivity for Anthropology but exposed his own cultural grounding in ways apparently unnoticed by him in *Science* (1948) when he wrote: "The Palauns are progressive and eager to adopt American ways."

11. *Reinventing Anthropology* (Hymes 1972b), a work which argued for (and in sections attempted) an Anthropological study of Anthropology, particularly American Anthropology, was produced in this time line. This work has particular relevance to the inception of the present work, as well as salience to fieldworker ethnographies. See the discussion later in this chapter and in Part II.

12. The work of Pierre Bourdieu provides a special and relevant focus consistent with the effort of this work, in which he emphasizes the independent role of educational and cultural factors. Bourdieu's use of "field," "cultural capital," "reproduction," and "habitus" is particularly pertinent as a means to address some of the interests of this work, but requires a different focus on material and analysis than the one undertaken. However, work undertaken through Bourdieu's body of work would provide a more profound understanding of the ways in which fieldworker ethnographers have parlayed their careers through university and other professional networks. As noted later in the work, fieldworker ethnographies are disengaged from the civic realm, but their authors (especially Crapanzano and Rabinow) have been heavily engaged in the professional realm. This activity has been less evidenced in activities of the Association (typical of generations of earlier Anthropologists) than through activities in positions of professional power, including professional retreats (especially those sponsored by the School of American Research in New Mexico),

and their membership on the boards of professional publications. These latter include (at one time or another) "American Anthropologist," "Cultural Anthropology," "Representations," "American Ethnologist," and "Humanistic Anthropology," the "History of Anthropology" series, among others.

13. Habermas also refers to depth hermeneutical inquiry in *The Theory of Communicative Action* (1984). However, while I agree with Habermas's effort to look beyond the underlying themes of interaction to particular reasons for the emergence of those themes, I am less convinced by Habermas's theory of communicative rationality, which governs his effort in this respect.

14. In Thompson's methodological framework, (1) "socio-historical analysis" is concerned with the social and historical conditions of production, (2) "formal or discursive analysis" is "concerned with the internal organization of symbolic forms . . . structural features, patterns and relations" (Thompson 1990:23), followed by "interpretation" (or re-interpretation). The sequence presented here is the one suggested by Thompson. My own analysis moved back and forth. I assume that variations in the sequencing of investigation and analyses of any subject will impact on the interpretation of texts and contexts, but I am unable to say how. My understanding of Thompson's method is that such variation is consistent with his own framework, which seeks to include rather than exclude methods. It is worth noting and underlining here that Thompson suggests that all modes of investigation have their limits and are best regarded as "partial stages" within a larger methodological approach (Thompson 1990:21). I would extend "partial" to include unfinished—that is, any and all analyses which seek to investigate such complex, interlocking, and ongoing phenomena are by their nature not only partial but incomplete as well.

15. The American Anthropological Association is the largest society for anthropologists in the United States, and publishes the journal *American Anthropologist* as well as a professional newsletter for its members. The Association currently serves as the umbrella organization for more than twenty other professional societies for anthropologists. The professional newsletter of the Association is used here as an entree to (some of the) issues significant to Anthropology and anthropologists in the time frame of this analysis. It is on the other hand, a necessarily limited instrument for this purpose. Research indicates that from the late 1960s to mid-1970s, elements of interest in American political and economic contexts were widely discussed and argued in a somewhat anomalous way (which itself reveals the tides of the time). That is, in these years there was a convergence and collision of cultural and professional spheres, which contrasts sharply with the immediately prior and following decades. Anecdotally, I would argue that in the 1950s such discussions were difficult and potentially professionally dangerous in the climate McCarthyism engendered. (For instance, see discussions in the *Fellow Newsletter* in which anthropologists quietly grappled with how to deal with fellow professionals accused of membership in the Communist Party.) As argued later in this work, the 1980s are marked by a withdrawal from the public, political realm by many anthropologists, which "began" with the ascendance of Richard Nixon to the American presidency. Further, beginning in the early 1970s, economics became a focus of discussion in the Anthropology Newsletter (the name changed from *Fellow Newsletter* to *Anthropology Newsletter* in 1968, following an opening of membership to new classes, including and especially students), while within the decade political and social issues largely disappeared. For instance, there is no discussion for instance of the Watergate debacle. I take the

inclusion and absence of material as revealing something about the broader cultural milieu in which Anthropologists found themselves.

Finally, in using the Association in this way, I am *not* suggesting that authors of fieldworker ethnographies as individuals or as a group were involved in or otherwise privy to the particular debates or activities highlighted in the Association or my analysis during this time. Rather, these debates and activities are seen as here, and assimilated by "natives" as part of the "lifeworld."

16. I use "his" here specifically, since the works included here are all by male anthropologists. As cited above, Mascia-Lees et al. 1989, and other anthropologists writing from a feminist perspective (i.e., Hartsock 1987), these works are in part a reaction by males to their loss of dominance in society. Rabinow when asked about the absence of such works produced by female members of a group of "ex-patriot" Chicago anthropologists meeting in New York in the 1970s (which included at one time or another the male authors, excluding Crapanzano), replied that they (i.e., Karen Blu, Sherry Ortner, Daisy Dwyer, Nancy Foner) "just weren't interested in the subject." More recently, female ethnographers have included such a project in their work (i.e., Behar 1992), but its appearance has taken a different form which I find interesting in its contrast, but which is a different investigation than the one undertaken here.

17. Throughout this study I focus on examples from fieldworker ethnographies, which emphasize their similarities—the "family resemblances" which I argue link these works and take them out of the realm of the idiosyncratic and make them cultural. However, these ethnographies are also autonomous entities. It could certainly be argued that they are as different as they are similar; however, I undertake no such examination of them here, as such an effort would represent a different analytic enterprise from the one undertaken in this work.

18. For example, while these ethnographies continue to be published in the 1990s (generally with new forewords or introductions), the anthropologists who wrote them have moved, if not entirely away, on—to different interests, approaches, and projects. (See for example, Dumont's introduction to a new edition of *The Headman and I* [1993].)

19. I use "power and domination" as a single construct rather than separate them as "power" and "domination," since in fieldworker ethnographies the terms arise as inseparable in the claims that fieldworker ethnographers make about them, and in these works, one assumes the other. This is not, of course, an inevitable assumption.

20. This project circles back on itself in a number of ways, some of which I am aware of, and some which no doubt escape me. The ones I am aware of I conceive of as "dilemmas." (In *The Political Context of Sociology* 1967), Leon Bramson makes an interesting and relevant distinction between "dilemma" understood by Europeans as something which remains problematic, and by Americans as something to be solved.) Some of the dilemmas represented by this project are that it seeks to examine a situated form of practice, which arose in the "same" milieu as this work. Further, I employ reflection as a means to study ethnographies which claim themselves to be reflective, thus constituting a project which seeks to be reflexive about claims to reflexivity. My own use of reflection as a method follows Habermas ("A Postscript to *Knowledge and Human Interest,*" *Philosophy of the Social Sciences* 3, 1973: 157–189, see p. 161). I note that Habermas's work, which is used throughout this study, itself emerged as significant in American social science, and in Anthropology in par-

ticular, within the time frame under study (see for example, the work of Diamond, Scholte, Hymes, and Berreman in *Reinventing Anthropology* (1972b). Taylor's (1979) warning about the hermeneutic circle has not gone unnoticed, but the escape hatch is a transitory and incomplete abstraction. This is good news since getting above oneself is all too easy and getting outside oneself is cold comfort.

PART I

Boas Redux

CHAPTER 2

Science Times

At the beginning, the two seedlings of early modernity—science and interpretive understanding—were able to coexist more or less peaceably and without mutual recriminations; but harmony soon gave way to antagonism. (Dallmayr and McCarthy 1977:2)

THE LOGIC OF EPISTEMOLOGICAL DECISIONS

Briefly, since Aristotle, science as a pre-eminent means to know the world has been promulgated as having as its object the investigation of four questions, the last of which has become the most essential for defining the endeavor. These questions, relevant to the things humans experience around them are: "Do they really exist?" "What is their essence?" "How are they?" "Why are they such?" The last question, as the pre-eminently scientific one, seeks certain explicative knowledge of causes. Thus, these answers regularly require a proof of certitude, some means to demonstrate the validity of explanations.[1] Moreover, these explanations will (ideally) form a system of connected truths. This latter feature has, since antiquity, grown in significance, so that, in positivist versions of science, these systematic connections have been considered as the most essential characteristics of science. Among the fundamental features of scientific method is the role of the scientist as an objective observer-analyst. Ideally, the researcher is objective in the process of study, and neutral about its product. Objectivity, and its "by-product" neutrality, are taken for granted in large part because in the natural sciences, the subject of study is logically taken as an object insofar as the phenomena of scientific study are not understood to have a subjectivity.

As part of the method of science, objectively derived findings are combined to form generalizations. In turn, generalizations are the foundation for generating hypotheses through which scientists experimentally confirm or disconfirm their hypotheses and ultimately formulate theory.

OLD DOGMAS AND NEW TRICKS

> The rhythms of development have been different but during the twentieth century each of the social sciences has passed through a decline of speculative and philosophical reflection, and a rise of optimism about results to be expected once a firm scientific and empirical foundation was achieved. (Bernstein 1979:ix)

American Anthropologists, subject to the same tides and turns as other social scientists, have repeatedly grappled with the identity of Anthropology as science, humanity, or social science. Anthropology in the mid-twentieth century was informed by and reflected ideas claiming the ascendancy and certitude of the natural sciences as a model for Anthropological work. But as in the other social sciences in which the mainstream view held science as the appropriate epistemological underpinning (cf. Bernstein 1978), this claim in Anthropology was not monolithic.

In Anthropology, students of Boas who formed the first generation of American anthropologists, took for granted that Anthropology was a science. This science was grounded in and modeled on the natural sciences. But while methods of data collection and analysis included those found in the natural sciences, the hallmark of the viewpoint of the first generation of American anthropologists (referred to in this chapter as "Old Science") was its inclusion of analytic methods outside the "positivist" version of science. Introduced in sociology by its "father," Auguste Comte, positivism held that no matter what the phenomena studied, success was to be found in the unity of the sciences in method and goal—that such methods would produce "positive" knowledge.[2] The methods and ends of Old Science were consistent with interpretive epistemological framings which generated "understanding" rather than explanation and prediction, and were more familiarly used by the humanities, particularly history and literary criticism. Boas, educated in Germany, had roots in this epistemology as well as those of science, through its intellectual antecedents in German philosophy introduced by Dilthey and refined by Rickert.

Dilthey argued that there were essential differences between the natural sciences (*Naturwissenschaften*) and the "mental sciences" (*Geistewissenschaften*), or as Rickert later called them, the "cultural sciences" (*Kulturwissenschaften*). Dilthey characterized the differences between *Naturwissenschaften* and *Geistewissenschaften* on the basis of the kind of phenomena they studied (i.e., by virtue of their subject matter). While the former studied the natural world, Dilthey recast the "mental" world by transforming the concept of

Geist (spirit) from a metaphysical to an empirical concept comprising entities including language, games, poems, religions, institutions, and so on. From this perspective, these products of human activity are the objectifications of *Geist*.

For Rickert, the method, not the subject, was the basis upon which disciplines were properly classified. Thus, Rickert distinguished between the monothetic (generalizing) and idiographic (individualizing) sciences. The former includes the "systematic" sciences that aim at establishing general laws (e.g., the "natural" sciences), while the latter include studies which are concerned with the discovery and exploration of individual facts (i.e., history). Rickert's distinction cuts across the physical and human disciplines, since the study of individual phenomena in the physical sciences ultimately leads to the establishment of general laws (therefore these sciences are generally monothetic); while the human sciences are largely idiographic since, in general, they deal with individual phenomena. The goal of the focus on the understanding of individual phenomena is not the production of general laws, but the understanding of the particular. "Since only through their relation to normative values could historical events acquire significance, Dilthey's approach was recast by Rickert under the label of 'cultural sciences' " (Dallmayr and McCarthy 1977:4).

By contrast, the hallmark of New Science, the prevailing view of science in Anthropology in the decade following World War II, was its agreement with positivist views that the strict methods and goals of science, and *only* those methods and goals, were adequate to produce knowledge. The goal of inquiry from this perspective was explanation and prediction based on the formulation of nomological (law-like) statements derived from empirical evidence. Thus there was significant divergence among anthropologists holding Old and New Science views. What they held in common was the shared view of Anthropology as a science and the assumption that *objective* research and analysis was the basic requirement of any scientific Anthropological research.

Thus, from the introduction of Anthropology into American academic life at the turn of the twentieth century, through the 1950s, anthropologists regularly referred to themselves as scientists and to Anthropology as a science. However, while both Old Science and New Science perspectives claimed science as the epistemological and professional basis of Anthropological theory, method, and practice; underlying their claims were divergent assumptions as to what constituted a science. This included differences over the appropriate methods of science, particularly analysis, and the grounds of scientific objectivity. Differences in Old Science and New Science views and their impact on the discipline were accessible in an exchange which took on the elements of a debate, on the subject of the contribution and significance of Franz Boas, the "father" of American Anthropology.

In Anthropology, Boas as a real and symbolic figure has been argued as scientist (Herskovits 1953), failed scientist (White 1945; Murdock 1949), half humanist–half scientist (Kroeber 1943), and humanist (Stocking 1960; Wax 1956:71). For purposes here, Boas's contribution to Anthropology as a point of contention among anthropologists revealed underlying assumptions relevant to terms of science which informed Old and New Science conceptions. In Old Science, Boas's collection of literary and other texts, his lack of theoretical development, and the barrier his work erected against such development by others did not exclude his work as science. Not so for the New Scientists in Anthropology who, in the 1950s, vehemently argued that Boas's work failed to meet the standards of science. To make sense of these differing interpretations of both science and Boas, we go back to the "beginning" of Anthropology in the United States, when Boas sought to establish Anthropology as a science.

SCIENTIFIC DISCIPLINE

Trained as a physicist during a period of radical empiricism in Europe, Boas saw science as a "holy vocation" (Wax 1956:64). From this standpoint, the appropriate effort of the social sciences was the emulation of the natural ones. In the early 1900s, during the formation of the American Anthropological Association, Boas used the mantle of science to give Anthropology legitimacy as an academic discipline and a profession. Focusing on the training essential to the work of the scientist, that is, objective observation and recording of data, Boas sought to differentiate the work of anthropologists-as-scientists from the work of laymen-as-anthropologists. The professional, scientifically trained anthropologist was thus separated from the interested, even experienced, layman. Science provided not only the method, but the authority for the young discipline.

The differentiation between scientist and layman was significant to Boas, who revealed in this effort his view that to be other than a scientist was to risk one's consideration as part of an academic discipline which could yield reliable knowledge. During the struggle besetting the beginning of the American Anthropological Association in 1898, Boas wrote:

The greater the public interest in a science and the less technical knowledge it appears to require, the greater is the danger that meetings may assume the characteristics of popular lectures. Anthropology is one of the sciences in which this danger is ever imminent, in which for this reason, great care must be taken to protect the purely scientific interest. (quoted in Stocking 1960:8)

Boas thus believed in the power of science, and sought to extend that training and credibility to entrench Anthropology as a scientific discipline. However, by the late 1950s, differences of opinion over Boas's role in American Anthropology, privately debated for years, were being publicly aired.

To understand the basis of the disagreement between Old and New Science perspectives it is useful to examine assumptions of anthropologists claiming to deny Boas's place in establishing Anthropology as a science. The review of a book written by Boas's student Melville Herskovits and subsequent professional comment help to elucidate these issues. Ultimately, the difference in opinion was less over what Boas did than over the sense each "side" made of his activities.

SPEAKING OUT OF TURN

The title of the book, *Franz Boas: The Science of Man in the Making*, proclaimed the relationship between Boas and Anthropology as a science held in Old Science. Boas, the scientist, was credited with establishing Anthropology and anthropologists in a scientific framework, both procedurally and professionally. By contrast, a review of Herskovits's book by Ray (1955), chastised him for failing to mention discussion "not infrequently heard among anthropologists that Boas 'held up' the development of anthropology by one to three years" (Ray 1955:131). These criticisms had commonly been made by anthropologists holding New Science perspectives that required nomological statements as the goal of science. From this perspective, Boas's science was inadequate science because in positivist terms it could not produce adequate (positive) knowledge.

Described within New Science as an "unsystematic theorist" (Murdock 1949), Boas was charged with neglecting the nomological goals central to definitions of science (White 1945). Critics argued that Boas's failure to generate theory, and his habit of attacking theories proposed by others, acted as a barrier to the development of cultural laws, and actually ran counter to strategies of practice central to science in which disconfirmation was used to refine rather than discredit theory.

But conceptions encompassed by Old Science included less strictly defined means and ends of scientific purpose. Rather than refuting Boas's critics on the grounds of their charges, Old Science anthropologists (primarily Boas's students) did not offer a defense of Boas's science, but, consistent with their own quasi-interpretive Anthropological practice, offered a rebuttal of criticisms in the form of an explanation of Boas's work, based on his personality, education, method, and contribution, in context; in short, an interpretation of Boas which sought an understanding of him and his work. For example, Lowie (1956:156) agreed that Boas failed to develop theory in Anthropology, but argued that his methods had to be examined in the context of *his* (Boas's) time, not measured by standards and practices of the present. (Lowie here seems to be drawing on a form of temporal relativity, consistent with ideas about cultural relativity in Anthropology.)

Kroeber acknowledged the conflict in Boas's work, but viewed it not as an epistemological or methodological question, but one of personality and education. Kroeber argued that through Boas's training in mathematics and physics, "Boas imbibed standards of 'objectivity' or demonstrability guarding against the subjective—intuitive or empathetic" (1956:157). Although Boas's collection of grammars and corpuses of texts were "pure humanist by the then usual reckoning . . . the performance had something incongruous about it" (ibid). Kroeber's analysis concluded that Boas's incorporations of native texts were presented without interpretation due to Boas's "perverse dread of unscientific subjectivity" (ibid.:158). Kroeber further asserted that the "only explanation" he could find for the collection of these texts in the first place was that the "aesthetic component" in Boas was stronger than he, himself, realized. According to Kroeber, "I do not know whether he [Boas] ever had any impulses to creative literary production. If he did, presumably he soon realized that his intellectual analytic faculties were much stronger and he turned to science in fact, at first, to the 'most scientific' of the sciences" (ibid.). But these efforts to situate Boas and his science in his own time did not impress New Science anthropologists, although they did continue to agree with Boas and Old Science anthropologists on one central issue. A requirement for both Old Science and New Science was observer objectivity.

THE OBJECT WAS OBJECTIVITY

Newtonian, or classical physics, as the model for all other sciences, assumed observer objectivity. In view of its nonhuman subject matter, it was largely assumed that objectivity could be largely taken for granted. Although by the 1940s and 1950s, many physicists, especially theoretical physicists, had already begun moving toward the mid-point on the division between subject and object, the social sciences were still modeling themselves on the earlier assumptions of classical physics. From this viewpoint, if observer objectivity cannot be claimed, there is no basis for assuming genuine empirical knowledge of an external reality; therefore, there is no means by which to claim adequate knowledge. Science, in the framework of positivism, not only "demanded" objectivity, it logically *required* it. Thus, a key aspect in the delineation between the natural sciences on one end of the continuum, and the humanities on the other, was the position of the scientist *cum* observer.

In mainstream social science, objectivity was also attained primarily by assuming it. This assumption was consistent with the (positivist) philosophical claim that the logic of inquiry is the same in natural science and the human sciences. But within Anthropology, there was no theoretical basis for this claim in the New Science of the 1950s and no logical basis for it in Old Science views. What defined objectivity in Anthropology was disciplinary practice. The scientist-observer assumed that interaction with the subject of research (defined as an object) did not affect the collection of objective data, rendering the scientist's data descriptive or factual rather than interpretive. In Anthropology, the role of the researcher, described as "participant observer," was common to all versions of science in Anthropology. But in view of the human subject(s) of Anthropological research, and the facet of direct interaction in the role of participant, objectivity became problematic. Various strategies were employed to bolster claims of objectivity.

Anthropologists who held New Science views in the 1950s claimed their objectivity through a metaphorical identification of their own role with what they perceived to be the role of physicists. Taking their own position from a positivist conception of science, they did not question whether such objectivity was necessary or possible. New Science work tended toward the development of large theoretical frameworks, also consistent with natural science practice. This led to a less individuated anthropology that set aside the view of the anthropologist as a "lone traveler" whose individual subjectivity or that of the people studied, might influence research. To some extent, this focus controlled the choice of relevant subjects for study. Rather than the more "subjective" topics favored in Old Science, for example, culture and personality or early child training, New Science focused on the development of broad theoretical systems examining structure, function, comparative kinship, and ecology.

Within Old Science, objectivity could not be *assumed* as it was within New Science, in part because Anthropology was not comprehended as a unified science. The Old Science conception of Anthropology consistent with interpretive separations between *Naturwissenschaften* (natural sciences) and *Geistewissenschaften* (cultural sciences) could not claim objectivity through analogy to the natural sciences. Thus, objectivity had to be acquired by the positive action of the investigator. Such acquisition, although problematic, was considered possible by Old Science anthropologists based on quasi-scientific models, for example, psychiatry. Margaret Mead (1952:345), for example, argued:

A . . . requirement . . . [in the training of anthropologists] should be the acquisition of a disciplined awareness of our own cultural position. . . . Just as the psychiatrist who is to explore the intra-psychic processes in other individuals' needs to take part in such an exploration of his own psychological processes before he can trust his own perceptions in the psychiatric situation, so the anthropologist needs to have brought into awareness his own idiosyncratic version of his culture in order to be objective.

Mead's position was consistent with claims in Anthropology by both revisionists (see Chapters 8 and 10) and fieldwork ethnographers, who argued the significance of reflexivity as a method within an interpretive frame.[3] While there is no evidence that anthropologists at the time rallied around Mead's particular call for "cultural psychoanalysis," not inconsistent with the views of fieldwork ethnographers it was generally consistent with another, more commonly used strategy en route to assumed objectivity in Old Science, the invocation of cultural relativity.

OBJECTIVE RELATIONSHIPS

> Insofar as "... (cultural relativism) guards against making value judgments about a culture founded upon the values of our culture, it is undoubtedly a pre-requisite for responsible field work and cultural analysis. Boas had great influence in making this attitude a common-place in anthropology." (Kardiner and Preble 1962:133)

The use of cultural relativism as a means to minimize ethnocentrism (which was understood as a form of subjectivity) has been ascribed to Boas. In this view of Anthropological method, assumptions of cultural relativity acted as a basis for claims to objectivity. At least ideally, by limiting the anthropologist's own cultural subjectivity through the awareness of other "cultural subjectivities," objectivity could be "acquired." And limited cultural subjectivity comprehended as objectivity was considered essential to the discipline. Although Old Science was not tied to unity of method claims, it did incorporate the position articulated by Boas that value judgments (evidence of lack of objectivity) were a threat to the discipline's claims to knowledge.

Specifically in Anthropology, ethnocentrism, the condition of viewing other cultures from the perspective of one's own, was held to pose a fundamental threat to the scientific legitimacy of all Anthropological research. Objectivity, from this point of view, can be redefined as the absence of ethnocentrism. Cultural relativism as the barrier to value judgments by anthropologists, was essential to the Anthropological enterprise if it was to lay claim to adequate knowledge and achieve the status and prestige of the sciences. Cultural relativism was adopted as a canon of the discipline, one which was to enable anthropologists to overcome ethnocentrism and simultaneously lay the foundation for claims of researcher objectivity and knowledge. Thus, although Old Science encompassed a broader spectrum of method, both Old and New Science embraced objectivity. The methods of science, including distance from the subject of study, were understood in both views as necessary to legitimize research and produce adequate knowledge. Objectivity was an epistemological necessity.

The use of interpretation in Old Science specifically, and in the framework of practice generally, was increasingly marginalized through the 1950s as the new generation of social scientists in all disciplines began to turn to science and its positivist version to lay claim to "adequate" knowledge.[4] But in the 1960s, public intellectual discussion (e.g., see Barzun 1961; Toulmin 1961) and "studies" of science (especially Kuhn's argument of paradigm shift in physics)[5] grappled with objectivity, and later in the decade became part and parcel of the debates among anthropologists over events and activities in the social and political realm. Whatever its multiple significant antecedents, by the 1960s, when fieldwork ethnographers began their education, they were already immersed in the interpretive turn, especially as interpreted by Geertz.

NOTES

1. In the sciences, social sciences, and humanities, "explanation" is generally used in conjunction with the natural sciences, as a product of its empirical methods, while "understanding" is associated with the forms of inquiry relevant to the social sciences and humanities. "Explanation" is customarily relevant to the epistemology of science, and "understanding" with interpretation.

2. See *Consilience: The Unity of Knowledge* (1998) by Edward O. Wilson for a recent restatement of these claims. See also in that work the interestingly conflicted background to these claims in Chapter 1 ("The Ionian Enchantment"), in which Wilson reflects on his own experience as part of the formulation of his view of the continuities between religion and science (both of which he sees as an effort to make ourselves significant in the universe). Wilson generalizes his own experience and asserts, "To wit, people must belong to a tribe; they yearn to have a purpose larger than themselves. We are obliged by the deepest drives of the human spirit to make ourselves more than animated dust, and we must have a story to tell about where we came from, and why we are here" (Wilson 1998:6). Since the evidence for these claims is, insofar as they exist, available in Anthropology, not biology (Wilson's discipline), and the methods by which such evidence has been produced more diverse than those consistent with "unity of science" claims, it is clear that Wilson has succeeded no better than Comte in grounding his claims in his own method. Rather, the use of his own experience as a base for his interpretation of the relationship between science and religion serves as an example of interpretive understandings. In that case, there may be grounds for unity of method claims, but they are the reverse of those traditionally made.

3. One of the ways in which it differed from fieldwork ethnographers' claims for reflexivity is that, in the latter works, objectivity was neither seen nor valued as the outcome of their awareness. Instead, their awareness would make them better at engaging in dialogue and negotiation.

4. See, for example, Coser (1984) for a discussion of the influence of a "new" (and stricter) version of positivism (logical positivism as articulated by the Vienna Circle) in the United States, through its primary spokesperson Rudolph Carnap. Carnap was at the University of Chicago when other refugee scholars in America holding views more consistent with those of Dilthey and Rickert were turned down for such positions at Chicago, but offered positions at The New School for Social Research in New York. The positioning and networks which produce and are the product of such placements are beyond the purview of this work, but clearly have relevance to the larger project in which it is located.

5. Kuhn's work, *The Structure of Scientific Revolution* (1962), with its contention that paradigm shift in the social sciences is as much a product of social network as scientific finding, was a point of marginal discussion in physics, the discipline on

which it focused. But it became enormously significant in the social sciences insofar as it "unclothed" the emperor physics, in a way which social scientists, often tired of being the younger sibling of science, found promising as a basis for the explanation, and at times the justification, of their own practice.

CHAPTER 3

The Dissertation Re-Bound

While ethnographies produced in the first few decades of the 1900s were directed at describing "whole" cultures, dissertations and first ethnographies by fieldwork ethnographers fell into a category of accepted ethnographic practice in which the project of ethnography had been reduced from that of earlier Boasian and Malinowskian models.

(The) . . . all-purpose ethnographic monograph is less common today. . . . Many anthropologists . . . believe . . . that no culture can be adequately described in a single monograph. They therefore, prefer more specialized monographs on kinship, religion, economy, social organization or the like, although the emphasis often remains holistic with the subject seen in context and in relation to other aspects of culture. (Edgerton and Langness 1974:66)

For the most part, "early works" (dissertations, articles, and first ethnographies by fieldwork ethnographers) "looked like" standard ethnographies. In general, standard ethnographies focused on culture and were presented through the third-person narrative of the ethnographer. Like other writings commonly produced in Anthropology at the time, these early works focused on culture covered particular "problems" (unlike the "whole world" monographs of the past), and were written in the third person with the occasional reference to the ethnographer himself. But these works actually incorporated significant shifts in the underlying epistemology of anthropological practice, although its manifestation in the written account remained subtle. This chapter focuses on these works and on the pervasive intellectual influence of Clifford Geertz as a means to locate some seminal ideas in

generation of the process and product of fieldworker ethnographies as part
of the interpretive turn in Anthropology.

THE EARLY WORK CATCHES THE TURN

> Believing with Max Weber that man is an animal suspended in webs of
> significance he himself has spun, I take culture to be those webs and the
> analysis of it to be therefore not an experimental science in search of
> law, but an interpretive one in search of meaning. (Geertz 1973:5)

> Anthropology is an interpretive science. Its object of study, humanity
> encountered as Other is on the same epistemological level as it is. Both
> the anthropologist and his informants live in a culturally mediated world,
> caught up in "webs of signification" they themselves have spun. (Ra-
> binow 1977:5)

Of the various interpretive programs posited by anthropologists in the
late 1960s and early 1970s, the one outlined by Geertz (1973) provided
the most powerful influence for the work by fieldwork ethnographers which
preceded fieldworker ethnographies, and which contained the seeds of that
form. The intellectual flow traced above, from Weber through Geertz to
Rabinow, briefly illustrates the assimilation of perspectives and the foundation of an analysis, which was already significantly and primarily interpretive:
what Geertz contended, citing Weber, Rabinow asserted, without citation.[1]
The point is not one of academic "negligence," but is evidence that Rabinow, along with other fieldwork ethnographers, took these terms for
granted. An examination of Geertz's work and influence while these scholars
were researching and writing their early works in graduate school, illuminates significant steps in the evolution of fieldworker ethnographies.[2]

Geertz's influence in the intellectual life of American fieldwork ethnographers came through a network of academic, personal, and professional
relations before, during, and after their fieldwork experience. Despite their
varied intellectual backgrounds and interests, these anthropologists cited
Geertz and acknowledged his assistance in their work. In part, this was due
to the location of their fieldwork in Morocco where Geertz, already a senior
scholar, was engaged in a research project. But the network neither began
nor ended there.

For example, Geertz was Rabinow's advisor at the University of Chicago
and guided his dissertation research in Morocco as well as its write-up at
"home." Rabinow cited Geertz as a major theoretical influence in *Symbolic
Domination* (1975:102), "My theoretical orientation is drawn most obviously from the work of Clifford Geertz, Jean-Paul Sartre, and Max Weber."
Rabinow also acknowledged Geertz as helpful while he was writing *Reflections on Fieldwork in Morocco* (1977).

As a graduate student at Columbia University, Crapanzano undertook his doctoral research in Morocco, and in *The Hamadsha* (1973), his ethnography based on that research, acknowledged Geertz's assistance. Rabinow remembered being briefly introduced to Crapanzano when he went to Geertz's house in Sefrou. Crapanzano also spent a year at the Institute for Social Research at Princeton, Geertz's academic "home," after leaving the University of Chicago.

As a graduate student at Yale, Dwyer had contact with Geertz in Morocco, and cited Geertz's work in economics to interpret his own data on entrepreneurial activity (Dwyer 1974:12). Dwyer's acknowledgments thanked Geertz for reading early drafts of various chapters in *Moroccan Dialogues* (1982) and his dissertation credited Geertz with an important role in introducing hermeneutics in Anthropology:

Hermeneutics, the study of the nature of interpretation has its roots in the general theory of signs, beginning with Aristotle, to the exegesis of religious texts (Ricoeur 1969:7). Recently, this study has been brought to bear upon the more generalized understanding between different cultural systems . . . and has thus become explicitly relevant to anthropological concerns. Turner (1957) and Geertz (1973) are anthropologists who have first fully employed hermeneutic concepts. (Dwyer 1972:334)

Thus, in explicit statements and citations, American fieldwork ethnographers acknowledged and incorporated Geertz as a significant influence in their own work. The full-blown opposition to key terms of science found in fieldworker ethnographies was an extension of, but consistent with, the terms of practice articulated in Geertz's *The Interpretation of Culture* (1973), specifically as illuminated in his version of anthropological practice in "Thick Description: Toward an Interpretive Theory of Culture."

AN INTERPRETATION OF "INTERPRETIVE SCIENCE"

Geertz's (1973:1–33) first essay in *The Interpretation of Culture* sets forth his version of the nature of interpretation and the mission of anthropology as an "interpretive science." But in this essay, Geertz abandoned all but one of the central efforts and methods of prevailing Western conceptions of science, and certainly central elements of both Old and New Science, as described in the last chapter. Grounded in an interpretive epistemological framework, Geertz drew from philosophy and related disciplines, including symbolic (Langer), phenomenological (Schutz), analytic (Ryle), and literary (Burke and Ricoeur) perspectives. Geertz argued that anthropologists "do" science, but do not "do" natural science:

Anthropological studies are not "scientifically" tested and approved hypotheses. They are interpretations or misinterpretations . . . and the attempt to invest them with the authority of physical experimentation is but methodological sleight of hand. Ethnographic finds are not privileged, just particular. (Geertz 1973:22)

Thus, for instance, in the natural sciences, particular examples of the subject of study, seen as an object, are combined to form generalizations. In turn, generalizations are the foundation for generating hypotheses through which scientists confirm or disconfirm, by experiment, their hypotheses and ultimately formulate theory. It was this understanding of the goals and methods of science which primarily informed standard ethnographies in Anthropology. Although as also noted earlier, in Anthropology as well as the other social sciences, views about the standards of science were not monolithic or entirely homogeneous. They shared the position that generalization, hypotheses, and the formulation of laws and theories, which seek causality and enable prediction, provided the best foundation and future for Anthropological practice.

But in Geertz's view, while anthropologists observed everyday behaviors enacted in cultures under study, the anthropologist recorded these activities as part of an interpretive enterprise, as an effort *to make sense of them*, rather than to predict or formulate laws relevant to their occurrence. Geertz thus sought to *interpret* matters at hand, rather than "project future outcomes of experimental manipulations or deduce future states of a determined system" (Geertz 1973:25).

The work of the anthropologist then was to generate "thick description" (cf. Ryle 1949)—a description which allowed behavior to be recorded within a particular cultural system and note the consistency with cultural relativity, but one which ultimately sorted and interpreted meaningful behavior from behavior without meaning. Culture was thus understood as a set of symbols whose import must be discovered, rather than a set of facts, the truthfulness of which was to be established through objective empirical activity.

Generally, then, Geertz abandoned the defining tenets of science. Whereas science sought generalizations, laws, theory, and causality, "interpretive science" generated no generalizations, tested no hypotheses, formulated no laws, produced no theory, and did not address causality. For Geertz culture could be understood not through some nomothetic science seeking causal explanation of nomological laws, but through understanding the way in which man experienced culture, in particular places, in particular ways.[3] Thus, the aim of Geertz's interpretive science was not prediction of the action of phenomena, but, consistent with epistemological interpretive aims, making sense of phenomena as action. But although activity was understandable, how was the anthropologist to interpret it? Geertz (1973:364) himself argued:

What is needed is some systematic rather than merely literary or impressionistic way to discover what *is* given, what the conceptual structure embodied in the symbolic forms through which persons are perceived actually is. What we want and do not have is a developed method of describing and analyzing the meaningful structure of experience (here the experience of persons) as it is apprehended by representative members of a particular society at a particular point in time—in a word, a scientific phenomenology of culture.

Primary methods Geertz proposed, to "discover what *is* given," included (1) "rescuing" activity (social discourse) from its "perishing occasions" (sic); that is, writing it down, thus, "fixing" it so that it can be interpreted;[4] and (2) interpreting the action from the "actor's" viewpoint; that is, the point of view of the "native." Thus, the description of other lives and the understanding by others of those lives written into ethnography was the job of the anthropologist. As Geertz stated: "This description in the form of ethnography, is produced by writing down "the flow of social discourse," and through its inscription, "trying to rescue the 'said' of such discourse from its perishing occasions and fix it in perusable terms" (Geertz 1973: 20).

Borrowing from philosopher Paul Ricoeur's notion of the "inscription of action" what writing fixes is not the event itself, but the *noema*—the meaning—of the event. Social action, recorded by the anthropologist as participant observer, is written into a *text* by the anthropologist as writer. Geertz thus argued the role of writer as central not only to the ethnographic project but as a defining characteristic of the entire Anthropological enterprise as a science. Geertz essentially privileged the anthropologist as writer:

If you want to understand what a science is, you should look in the first instance not at its theories or its finding . . . you should look at what the practitioners of it do. . . . In anthropology, or anyway social anthropology, what the practitioners do is ethnography . . . "What does the ethnographer do?" he writes. Or, again, more exactly "inscribes." (1973:5, 19)[5]

Second, according to Geertz, what the anthropologist "inscribes" and how it is understood is as a "text," a "fictio," specifically, as "something made"—a construction of the construction of the native viewpoint (Geertz 1973:14).

Geertz used the viewpoint of the native as a means to render not an objective account of reality but one which was "constructed." How then do these ideas of interpretive science become significant in the "standard ethnographies of sorts" which follow dissertations and precede fieldworker ethnographies?

In central respects, key points of Geertz's preliminary theory are taken up and used as assumptions of practice in early works. Just as Geertz used philosophical arguments and turned them from abstract discussion into a "practical" basis for doing Anthropological work, salient terms of Geertz's work were similarly assimilated and asserted in fieldworker ethnographies. In this way both Geertz and fieldworker ethnographers appropriated theories and used them as a foundation, or perhaps more concisely, as facts.

Thus, early works by fieldworker ethnographers bore the stamp of Geertz's influence. Dissertations and first ethnographies by these anthropologists included culture defined as a symbolic system, and sought no generalizations, hypotheses, predictions, or laws. Instead, empirical data used to form generalizations in standard ethnographies was used to "break down" phenomena, to "make sense" of it. Dumont serves as a reminder that although the particular focus here is on American ethnography, interpretation in the mode of French structuralism, especially through Levi-Strauss, was also part of the intellectual "conversation." Dumont wrote: "[cultural] analysis consists therefore in breaking the code in order to build a model of a given structure. It does so by starting from the empirical data collected in the field" (Dumont 1976:15).[6] Analysis in early works separated events, interactions, and symbols rather than using relevant aspects of them to constitute some larger framework in which they could be included (e.g., religion, economics, etc.). Analytic categories became tools of interpretation rather than ends in themselves. Standard aspects of traditional ethnographies were already shifting. But the shift was not so readily apparent. That is, the use of material as part of an interpretive, rather than scientifically framed analysis, was submerged under the style of presentation in these works which, as we will see, in surface respects significantly mirrored that of standard ethnographies.

Consistent with standard ethnographies, the focus of early works by fieldworker ethnographers was the group. Crapanzano (1970, 1973), Dwyer (1974), and Rabinow (1971, 1975) focused on the representation of *a* group within a larger cultural group. Dumont, (1972, 1976), trained at the University of Pittsburgh in a less interpretive program, again provides an interesting exception, since he offered a study of *the* group (the Panare). Crapanzano and Rabinow focused on particular religious groups in Morocco; Crapanzano defined his group through a particular religious practice (the Hamadsha), while Rabinow's group was identified by virtue of their claimed kinship to a religious figure. Dwyer's dissertation focused on a group of rural Moroccans as a means to study entrepreneurial orientations, including, for example, their attitude toward the taking of risks (this became a central theme in Dwyer's fieldworker ethnography as he re-interpreted his fieldwork experience as a "wager").

While ethnographies produced in the first few decades of the 1900s were directed to describing "whole" cultures, dissertations and first ethnographies (especially by American fieldworker ethnographers) fell into a category of accepted ethnographic practice in which the project had been "reduced" from the "all purpose" account to the specialized one. This "smaller" project of ethnography was actually consistent with scientific practice in which

a first step was the stating of a particular problem within a broader phenomenon to be researched as the subject of study. In addition, as in science,
particular aspects were seen as having significance to the broader phenomenon. Focus on a particular group or practice was accepted in the discipline
as also a work about the larger group.

Further, in dissertations and ethnographies under discussion, broad cultural settings remained a subject of study through a general discussion of
history as a context within which there was a particular focus. However,
within the similar form of the presentation of the group in these early works,
there was a shift in the fieldworker ethnographer's "intention." In standard
ethnographies, the group was used as a means to discuss generalized or
abstracted patterns.

The ethnographer's account does not evoke for his readers a sense of life in the
society as he actually witnessed it, because the anthropologist is writing about an
abstract and generalized cultural pattern derived from these real-life events. . . . Individuals disappear into "statuses," "groups" and "classes" of various types. (Edgerton and Langness 1974:65)

By contrast, although informants and anthropologists continued to "disappear" in dissertations and first ethnographies by fieldwork ethnographers,
there was a shift from the description of abstracted patterns to accounts of
the group from a collective vantage point articulated as an "actor-oriented"
perspective, as suggested by Geertz (1973). Rabinow wrote:

The method I employ is actor-oriented and what has been called progressive-
regressive. An actor-oriented method attempts to understand the actor's view of his
own social world. It involves analysis of the symbols which give meaning and through
which understanding is possible, as well as the social and economic conditions within
which these symbols operate; in other words how experience is organized. (Rabinow
1975:6)

Dumont (1976:1) described an effort and intention similar to Rabinow's:
"We shall not be interested in the individual philosophy of a particular 'I',
but in the common philosophy of a collective 'we' . . . to give an account
for (an account of) the way in which the Panare think of themselves. In
other words, this study is an excursion into Panare philosophy as manifested
in their culture." Dwyer (1974:13) examined narratives of Moroccan entrepreneurs and announced his intention thus: "I will look at these narratives
as personal expressions by individuals in particular situations, of their cultural
systems."

Thus, there had been a change in position from the objective observer
assumed in science, to one from the perspective of the cultural "actor," and
a related shift from description of a cultural system by that observer to an

articulation of meaning from the point of view of "a" subject. However, there were no subjects present in these works. Written as a third-person narrative and written from an actor's point of view, in these ethnographies there were still no actors. They continued to "look" like standard ethnographies as the convention of the "unintrusive presence of the anthropologist" (Marcus and Cushman 1982) in the work remained largely intact.

For example, in *Symbolic Domination* (1975) Rabinow made a brief "appearance" with an informant: "After an unproductive account on my part to draw out a further theory of 'shurfaness,' one of my informants told me the following story." This slight reference is the only 'personalized' one in the body of the work. Within the terms of his actor-oriented approach, Rabinow continued to seek an unsubjective presence, one consistent with researcher objectivity and the third-person narrative at the level of presentation.

As observers of another culture, we cannot negate our presence as outsiders, nor do we wish to. Our cultural distance provides us with an external vantage point from which we can see and understand certain results, unintended consequences and the weight of past circumstances in the lives of the people we are observing. (Rabinow 1975:4)

Thus, Rabinow introduced himself as "present" as an "observer" and maintained the claim that the "distance" provided by the lack of the anthropologist's participation in the everyday world of the Other set the anthropologist apart in an analytically useful way. The view that the anthropologist using this perspective can see "more" than the native was also consistent with Geertz.

Early works by Crapanzano, Dwyer, and Dumont incorporated their own presence to a greater degree than Rabinow's, as they more openly grappled with some of the dilemmas of objectivity. Crapanzano (1970,1973) injected himself as an eyewitness in *The Hamadsha* through his firsthand account of a Hamadsha performance. The work begins:

The square in front of the tomb of Sheik Al-kamal in Meknes was just beginning to fill up with townsmen, families from the nearby shantytowns, and a few Berber and Arab tribesmen when we arrived at 2:45 on a Friday afternoon in January. We were immediately surrounded by children—whom we had to fend off, sometimes violently as they gaped and grabbed with curiosity at us. (Crapanzano 1973:xi)[7]

Although Crapanzano remained largely absent from the rest of the work, he did explicitly record his presence in the field, and struggled with claims of objectivity:

My interview of the Hamadsha as essentially curers not only influences my own perception of them and the questions I asked them but also the manner in which I have chosen to present the collected material. Naturally, I have tried whenever and wherever possible to compensate for this bias, but it would be foolish to claim that I have overcome it. The Boasian ethnography must always remain in the realm of the ideal. (Crapanzano 1973:9)

The "bias" Crapanzano left unanalyzed became an important focus of fieldwork ethnographies. In later work, discussion of "bias" as a problem was extended, but an analysis of its content was not. Dumont (1972, 1976) also openly grappled with his own presence in his dissertation and first ethnography based on his doctoral research on the Panare. He explained his use of "I" and "we" in his work as follows: "The reader may find it curious to be confronted at times with an 'I' and at times with a 'we.' These two words have not however, been employed at random. 'I' is used when I refer to my personal experience of the field; 'we' is reserved for our common analytical adventure" (Dumont 1976:5). The specific details included were not claimed as the product of an objective scientist, but the selection of a particular observer.

The topics discussed in this chapter are directly relevant to the further understanding of our analysis. In addition, other information is presented that should help the reader gain a more complete view of Panare culture. In other words, were it not for its brevity, this chapter based on direct observation, could be in itself an ethnographic report. But the reader should bear in mind that there is always an element of arbitrariness in which it is presented, since the observer sees mostly what he is prepared to see. (Dumont 1976:29)

Dwyer (1974) most overtly wrestled with the presence of himself as observer in his work, including the issue of observer objectivity. Observer objectivity, assumed and required by science as a means to constituting adequate knowledge, was argued by Dwyer to be impossible, and further to be a barrier to knowledge. Using Heisenberg's (1927) "Principles of Uncertainty" in physics, and Kuhn's (1962) discussion of theory-laden fact, Dwyer argued that the barrier of the objective observer had been removed but must in turn be treated as significant for the study itself. "Thus in both the natural and social sciences, the relationship between the observer and the observed, between the investigator and his object of study is itself an important variable in the study" (1974:122).[8]

The ethnographer and issues of objectivity were explicitly addressed in early works by fieldworker ethnographers, but overall, these references were sporadic rather than systemic. Resemblance to the form of standard ethnographies again remained largely intact. Nevertheless, they also represented a move away from standard ethnographies and a move toward the upheaval of, or down the road to, fieldworker ethnographies. Relinquishing the objective scientist linked to the third-person narrative was the ground upon which the inversion of the standard form was built.

FIELDWORKER ETHNOGRAPHERS "LEAVE HOME"

In the 1960s the intellectual paradigm informed by science was challenged by that of interpretation. In the 1970s, these paradigms were seen by fieldworker ethnographers and others as increasingly incommensurable.[9] What began as a turn toward interpretation and away from commonly accepted ideas about science as the sole model for Anthropological practice became a full-scale rejection of science in fieldworker ethnographies. This included its methods and the means for representing knowledge in written form. Especially significant in the change in written form which fieldworker ethnography represented was the rejection of objectivity as these scholars sought to overcome the subject-object splits they saw as intrinsic to science, and intrinsically harmful to the Anthropological enterprise.

As fieldwork ethnographers reflected on their experience in the field, and constructed their second ethnographies based on their dissertation research, their references were drawn less from Geertz than through Geertz, although it could be argued that even their own experience as a subject of study was in part "suggested" by Geertz who, in keeping with the times, sought to "describe and analyze" the "meaningful experience" of "persons." They drew less from the theory of Anthropology informed by philosophy and literary theory, and more from philosophy itself. They drew less from the work of others in Anthropology, and more from each others' work.

Thus, where Geertz's "text" was constructed to "fix" action for Anthropological interpretation, Dwyer's "text" was constructed to make the experience "public"—to take it beyond his personal boundaries and give it a "critical function."[10] According to Dwyer (1982:xviii):

My aims could only be carried forward by finding some way to make the experience concrete, to turn it into a text, and make it accessible to people who had not participated in it. Otherwise, the experience would remain a purely personal one, which however, worthwhile to the Faqir and myself, would serve an extremely limited critical function.

While Geertz used Paul Ricoeur (1971) as the authority for the Anthropologist "inscribing" a text as meaningful action; Rabinow drew on Ricoeur to define the problem in his book as "hermeneutical." In *Reflections on Fieldwork in Morocco* (1977:5), Rabinow stated: "The problem of the book is a hermeneutical one, and the method I employed is a modified phenomenological one. . . . Thus, following Paul Ricoeur, I define the problem of hermeneutics . . . as 'the comprehension of self by the detour of the comprehension of the other.' " Where Dwyer (1974) credited Geertz with introducing hermeneutics into Anthropology, Rabinow (1977) took his hermeneutics straight from Ricoeur.

Early works by fieldwork ethnographers already included, in varying degrees, concern with the problems of objectivity. But where the objectivity of the anthropologist, however attained, had been seen as essential to the discipline's ability to generate knowledge, viewed as "truth" and "reality," the "actor-oriented" method proposed in Anthropology by Geertz began to shift the terms of objectivity. In writings by Geertz and in "early works" the change went unaddressed. According to Geertz, "we begin with our own interpretation of what our informants are up to, or think they are up to and then systematize those." The natives may not be up to what they "think" they are up to, which required the anthropologist-as-analyst to make sense by, in part, assessing the sense the native has made. Geertz engaged in this sort of interpretation, for instance, in his paper on the Balinese cockfight (1973:448–542), in which he "saw" what the Balinese do not say. "For it is only apparently cocks that are fighting there. Actually it is men" (1973:417). The model built here is not only one of interpretation; it is one of accretion, as the anthropologist struggled to (following literary critic Kenneth Burke) "say something of something" (Geertz 1973:448). The interpretation thus becomes a "re-interpretation"—an elaboration on the *anthropologist's* understanding which may or may not resemble the native's.

This problem is submerged in early works and in fieldworker ethnographies by the weight of the anthropologist's "last word" (see Chapters 6 and 7). Simply put, in order for the actor's point of view to be represented, the actor must write the text. Although Geertz argued that "what is needed is a 'scientific phenomenology' one which is systematic rather than merely literary or impressionistic" (Geertz 1973:16), he did not produce a method to suit the proclaimed "need." Without such a method, the point of view presented through the actor-oriented method must inevitably and ultimately be that of the anthropologist, albeit not in isolation from the actor. It is the anthropologist, in Geertz own account, who "imagines" and "constructs" the actor's "construction." But how is the actor's point of view represented? How would you know if it were? The implicit assumption and active contradiction in Geertz's work is that the anthropologist was "left" as objective, acting as a conduit for the actor's point of view, despite Geertz's own assertion that the anthropologist was actively constructing. In "early works," claims to absolute objectivity were relinquished but not acted upon—its loss had no effect on the form of presentation. The subject-object split between anthropologist and informant—the "distance" between them, was preserved.

These works incorporated and reflected the divisions, as well as some of the terms of continuity, in earlier debates about the terms of science. While the use of interpretive, including literary, methods in Anthropology was not new (see for example, Kroeber 1943, Benedict 1948), their use as the exclusive model for practice *was*. To use the language of the form, analogy turned to metonym, as "culture *as* text," got read as "culture *is* text."[11] Perhaps ironically, then, the effort to resolve the "distance" of science, inherent in the subject-object splits it was seen to engender, contributed to a different division within Anthropology itself. Thus the subjectivity of the ethnographer's position became the authority for knowledge and anthropologists informed by different paradigms for practice became increasingly distanced from each other.

In 1988, Geertz described American fieldwork ethnographers as "Malinowski's children" (Geertz 1988:91). However, in significant respects they are Geertz's, and consistent with Western expectations of "children" they pushed the limits of the generation before, often overturning them in the process.

NOTES

1. The intellectual antecedents in German philosophy for interpretive science in the version promulgated by Geertz are not dissimilar from Boas's, although extended through a longer chain. Detailed investigation of these sources is beyond the immediate purview of this book, but is relevant in locating Geertz (and often his students) intellectually. For example, webs through which Geertz's viewpoint may be traced include the influence of Parsons, one of Geertz's mentors at Harvard, who in turn was a "spokesman" for Weberian sociology. Weber's work itself has been examined as a manifestation of the postulated split in German philosophy between the natural and social sciences. According to Dallmayr and McCarthy (1977:4): "The bifurcation of natural and cultural science became a cornerstone of Weberian sociology" (These distinctions were those discussed in Chapter 2 as relevant to the natural, mental, and cultural sciences). Rickert's work in particular can be identified in Weber's 1904 essay "Objectivity in Social Science and Social Policy," where Weber presented sociology as a "cultural science" defined as "those disciplines which analyze the phenomena of life in terms of their cultural significance" (1977:27). Geertz's science can thus be set within established (although not universally accepted) differentiations proposed by Dilthey and reframed by Rickert. Thus, in general, Geertz's description of science is most consistent with the terms of *Kulturwissenschaften* as understood by Rickert. Geertz's interest (e.g., see *The Interpretation of Culture* [1973:1–33]) in the "particular" in which he seeks to build an idiographic theory; "the essential task of theory building here is not to codify abstract regularities . . . not to generalize across cases but to generalize within them" (Geertz 1973:26). It is worth pointing out, however, that consistent with Parsons, Geertz did not adopt Dilthey's method of *verstehen*, which sought understanding as the means for interpreting cultural phenomena (see also Rudolph A. Makkreel, "Wilhelm Dilthey and the Neo-Kantians: The Distinction of the *Geistewissenschaften* and the *Kulturwissenschaften*," *Journal of the History of Philosophy* 7 (1969):423–440.

2. The analysis here is not intended to produce or suggest any kind of direct causality. But as will become clear in this chapter and elsewhere in this book, Geertz's

work is taken as part of the seminal body of work influencing the views of fieldwork ethnographers at the time, and the eventual production of fieldworker ethnographies.

3. This is familiar in Anthropology because despite the differences in the philosophies informing Geertz's ideas, they are familiar, if not entirely similar to Boas's views on, "historical particularism."

4. Thompson (1990) questions this aspect of Geertz's program as grounded (as referenced by Geertz) in the work of Paul Ricoeur. According to Thompson (1990: 133):

Geertz suggests that cultural analysis is concerned with texts in the sense that the practice of ethnography is the production of texts; the texts we are dealing with are *ethnographic texts* which "fix" the "said" of social discourse. Now there can be no doubt that writing ethnography involves the production of texts. But where are the arguments to support the claim that what ethnographic texts are doing, or should seek to do, is to "fix" what is "said" in the social discourse of the subjects who form the object of ethnographic inquiry? The arguments cannot be found in the writings of Ricoeur, whose proposals concerning the fixation of meaning have nothing to do with the relation between the social scientific researcher and the subject/object of his or her research.

5. It is also in this work that Geertz opens the door to literary analysis as the pre-eminent means to analyze and evaluate Anthropological works, as argued by literary critic James Clifford and an array of anthropologists, specifically Crapanzano, among fieldwork ethnographers, as part of the postmodern turn. As an Anthropological question the excitement generated by these ideas in American Anthropology is of interest in a work of this sort. Of course, all scientists write (to some extent), especially social scientists. If we are then all writers in the "first instance," we "must" all be doing the same thing. But we are not. There is clearly something that anthropologists ought to be doing before they start writing—for instance, observing and/or participating (from an Anthropological point of view). At a conference on Malinowski held in New York in 1984, I asked James Clifford (who was as yet unknown in many Anthropological quarters), what the difference was between a novel and an ethnography. Clifford had given a talk at the meetings in which he compared Malinowski and his work to Joseph Conrad's *Heart of Darkness*—a comparison variably received by the audience at the meeting. He responded that it was not his job to figure it out. I think many anthropologists have figured it out. Geertz (1973) stated that the anthropologist produces "something made"—I think that's close enough. The novelist produces something "made up." The difference is enough to set the two apart, sufficient for practical purposes.

6. Among American anthropologists, Levi-Strauss particularly informed the interpretive analysis of Schneider, who offered a theoretical framework that "competed" with that of Geertz.

7. The presentation here is similar to that of Geertz's in his description of the Balinese cockfight. It also bears some similarity to, for example, Dwyer's attendance at the *Amouggar*, described earlier. However, the form is still incipient here.

8. This is consistent with discussions of the effects of observer focus on research discussed by other anthropologists, including Bennett (1946), Kroeber (1959), and Washburn (1963). This is discussed in more detail in Chapters 8–10.

9. Ideas of incommensurability are consistent with Kuhn's influential work, *The Structure of Scientific Revolution* (1962 [1970]). However, incommensurability of

paradigms as described by Kuhn has been challenged by other authors who insist that the strands of relationship are strong, despite the turning over of paradigms.

10. Fieldworker ethnographies, although a break with Geertz, may have been in some ways suggested by him. For example, prior to the appearance of these works Geertz (1973) noted:

Most ethnography is in fact to be found in books and articles, rather than in films, records, museum displays or whatever; but even in them there are, of course, photographs, drawings, diagrams, tables and so on. Self-consciousness about modes of representation (not to speak of experiments with them) has been very lacking in Anthropology. (Geertz 1973:19)

Further, Geertz (1973:26) claimed that the work of the anthropologist is more like that of the literary critic than that of the scientist, a claim which is part of what is now called "postmodernism" but then was unidentified by "title" as a shift in practice.

11. This final inversion is actually more relevant to works which follow fieldworker ethnographies in which cultural analysis is accomplished through methods of textual analysis.

PART II

An Interpretation of Fieldworker Ethnography: Crisis in the Field

CHAPTER 4

All in the Family

> What should therefore be the very strength of anthropology—its expe-
> riential, reflexive and critical activity—has been eliminated as a valid area
> of inquiry by an attachment to a positivist view of science, which I find
> radically inappropriate in a field which claims to study humanity.
> (Rabinow 1977:5)

The rejection of a positivist view of science common to fieldworker ethnographies, and the assumption of a wholly interpretive epistemology, were the
underpinning for other significant and similar changes in these works.[1]
These included: (1) the privileging of experience over observation; (2) the
interpretation of field interaction as confrontation suffused with power and
domination, and (3) ethnography seen as resolution and reconstitution. This
chapter sets out the claims and intentions of fieldwork ethnographers. What
did their authors intend to do? What did they claim as new in their practice?
In short: what did these ethnographies say *about* their work, *in* their
work?

KEY TERMS OF FIELDWORKER ETHNOGRAPHIES

Experience over Observation: Objective Observation
Becomes Subjective Experience

> Once one accepts a definition of anthropology as consisting of partici-
> pant observation as I had, then one's course of action is really governed
> by these oxymoronic terms; the tension defines the space of anthropol-
> ogy. (Rabinow 1977:79)

According to their authors, a central aim in fieldworker ethnographies was the production of works which were not framed by and informed by science. Rather than predetermining the form and content of their work through an adherence to "current theoretical concerns" (Dwyer 1982:21) in Anthropology, which they saw as primarily scientific, the intention of fieldwork ethnographers was to produce works which used interpretation as the frame for ethnography, and experience as the base within the frame. In their view, science created a distortion and denial of their own experience and that of the ethnographic other. Dwyer, for example, stated:

I suspected that a clear research project, designed to respond to current theoretical concerns in anthropology, would tend to suppress and severely distort the spontaneity and normal behavior of people I encountered, forcing them to fit into categories, modes and aspects defined by the project. (Dwyer 1982:21)

Fundamentally, the rejection of science was an objection to its premise of the objectivity of the scientist as observer in the research project—the premise they saw as most destructive to an anthropological enterprise. Objectivity, these anthropologists argued, resulted in a series of separations, between and within subjects and objects, between anthropologists and informants. Dwyer (1982:256), for example, argued that anthropology inherited the "contemplative perspective" of science, in which the subject-object split was accepted; that is, the observer (anthropologist as subject) stood apart and "contemplated" the observed (Anthropological subject as object). "The salient effect on anthropology . . . was the discipline's acceptance of the central contemplative premise of the scientific attitude. The object of study—in anthropology's case, the non-western Other—would be 'observed' by the subject, the Western self" (Dwyer 1982:257).

Thus, fieldwork ethnographers asserted that there was an inevitable and inherent dichotomy within participant observation which critically permeated and ultimately divided the anthropological enterprise. For these anthropologists the "oxymoron" of participant observation was the entry point for the subject-object split. The science of participant observation engendered and sustained problematic separations within the subject (anthropologist) himself. This was based on the assumption that within traditional methods (the methods of science), the ethnographer's self could, and should, be objectified, that is, separated from its own experience. The anthropologist became an objective instrument, one consistent with the demands of science.

Further, these anthropologists claimed that the objectification of the anthropologist's own experience was concurrent with the objectification of the informant by the anthropologist. The informant in this process was observed by the anthropologist as an object through which information significant to the anthropologist became available. For example:

The informant became for the anthropologist an instrument to aid in the pursuit of an abstract object. . . . The normal practice of Anthropology runs the risk of silencing the Other's full voice at the outset by abstracting it from its context and closing off its input as a means of critical reflection on the Self by masking the relationship between the inquirer and informant. (Dwyer 1979:71)

Additionally, part of the "masking" of the relationship between the anthropologist and the informant, as argued in fieldworker ethnographies, was the masking of the anthropologist's intervention in the informant's experience. As Rabinow (1977:119) claimed:

Whenever an anthropologist enters a culture he trains people to objectify their life-world for him. Within all cultures, of course, there is already objectification and self-conscious translation into an external medium is rare. The anthropologist creates a doubling of consciousness.

Crapanzano (1980:8, 11) also asserted this "doubling" of the informant's consciousness by the anthropologist. In discussing his construction of Tuhami's life history, he observed:

The life history, like the autobiography presents the subject from his own perspective. It differs from autobiography in that it is an immediate response to a demand posed by an Other and carries within it the expectations of the Other. . . . the specific questions posed by the Other reflect certain generic expectations within his own culture, but the very question of life history itself may be an alien construct for the subject and cause in him an alienating *prise de conscience*. Not only did my presence and my questions prepare him for the text he was to produce, they produced what I read as a change of consciousness in him. (Crapanzano 1980:x)

In the view of fieldworker ethnographers, intervention in the form of questions asked of the informant and the latter's externalization of cultural knowledge created a separation between the informant's self and experience similar to the separation of self experienced by the anthropologist doing participant observation.

In fieldworker ethnographies all forms of objectification (objectification of the anthropologist as subject by the anthropologist, objectification of the anthropologist by the informant, objectification of the informant by the informant through the intervention of the anthropologist) were rejected and replaced by experience. The rejection of objectification was simultaneously then a rejection of science as the epistemological and methodological foundation for separations between self and experience.

In fieldworker ethnographies, objectivity in both anthropological locales away in the field and at home in the process of writing was argued as not only undesirable, but impossible as well. According to Rabinow:

There is no valid way to eliminate consciousness from our activities or those of others. This central fact can be avoided by pretending it does not exist. Both sides can be frozen. We can pretend that we are neutral scientists collecting unambiguous data and that the people we are studying are living amid various unconscious systems of determining forces of which they have no clue and to which only we have the key, but it is only pretense. (1977:151)

The result of this "pretense" was the "freezing" of both sides in the ethnographic encounter, which from their point of view ultimately produced "frozen" accounts of anthropological knowledge in the form of the written account (referred to in Chapter 5 as "standard ethnographies"). Crapanzano claimed:

By eliminating himself from the ethnographic encounter, the anthropologist can deny the essential dynamics of the encounter and end up producing a static picture of the people he has studied and their ways. It is this picture, frozen within the ethnographic text, that becomes the "culture" of the people. (1980:ix)

These anthropologists argued that rather than the "frozen" picture of other lives, the basis for Anthropological practice was to be found in interactions between the "selves" produced by different cultures. Further, the meaning of these encounters was to be culturally constructed and "publicly" negotiated. That is, in fieldworker ethnographies the dialogue and interaction between anthropologist and informant was not understood as personal, rooted in the psychology of its participants, but as phenomenological, that is, "public"—constructed through cultural and historical mediation and accessible in, and through, the interactions of "cultural selves."

The self (of both anthropologist and informant) . . . being discussed is perfectly public, it is neither the purely cerebral cogito of the Cartesians, nor the deep psychological self of the Freudians. Rather it is the culturally mediated and historically situated self which finds itself in a continuously changing world of meaning. . . . Therefore, anthropological analysis must incorporate two facts. First that we ourselves are historically situated through the questions we ask, and the manner in which we seek to understand and experience the world, and second, that what we receive from our informants are interpretations, equally mediated by history and culture. (Rabinow 1977:6, 119)

The cultural and historical mediation of anthropologist and informant meant that both participants brought their "cultural selves" to the ethnographic interaction. In fieldworker ethnographies these interactions were described as "encounters" and experienced by fieldwork ethnographers in a particular way, that is, as confrontations.

An ethnography—and I use the word in its most comprehensive sense to include what might more properly be called ethnology—is a symptom of particular confrontation between two or more individuals—the ethnographer and those others whom he, the ethnographer, refers to impersonally and presumptively as his informants. (Crapanzano 1977:69)

The Experience of Confrontation: Power and Domination

Anthropologists writing fieldworker ethnographies assumed and asserted that the research experience through which anthropological knowledge was significantly and appropriately derived was one of confrontation between anthropologist and informant(s), rather than one of distance through objectification. According to these anthropologists, the field experience consisted of a series of encounters as confrontations created by "breakdowns in communication" (Rabinow 1977:29). These breakdowns between participants in the ethnographic encounter were seen as sought-after and necessary, as they ultimately revealed the fissures in mutual understanding which had to be resolved through dialogic interaction. According to Rabinow (1977: 29–30):

One could construct smooth and seemingly conflict-free modes of interaction with people (during the course of many hours of trivial conversation) which would suddenly break down. One assumes in everyday life, when it goes smoothly, that people share what has been called a life-world—certain primary assumptions about the nature of the social world, about social personae, about how events occur and more or less what they imply. . . . Common sense, everyday interaction always implies more than itself. . . . (my informant) and I were from different cultures, and the implications which we drew in Marrakech about daily life were leagues apart.

Breakdowns were understood to occur when individuals (in this case the anthropologist and informant) who did not ordinarily share a "lifeworld" made different assumptions about the nature of the social world and explanations relevant to events, interactions, and so on, within it. From this perspective, breakdowns in understanding between participants revealed differences in cultural views of reality, and its interpretation in the form of experience.

According to fieldwork ethnographers, these encounters were experienced *in situ* as defined and shaped by culturally meaningful constructions of power and domination. In fieldworker ethnographies, power and domination were assumed as an intrinsic part of the historical and cultural mediation of (cultural) self and Other acted out in ethnographic encounters between two participants. Crapanzano, for example, stated:

Expressed within a pragmatic mode . . . (this presumption) permits a certain disengagement from the reality of the transaction. The disengagement helps to insulate the parties to the encounter from the repercussions of failure. It permits too, a superior stance in the inevitable jockeying for power that occurs within such negotiations. (1980:ix–x)

Dwyer (1982:xviii) asserted power and domination as significant in more explicitly political terms relevant to structures of inequality:

The partners' contributions are certainly complementary, but they are definitively not equal. This particular kind of inequality is not an accident of personal preference but is one aspect of a wider social confrontation between the West and the rest of the world that in recent history has never been symmetrical, the West has systematically intruded upon the non-West and reworked it, sometimes subtly, sometimes violently according to the West's own needs. . . . The personal experience is thus inevitably tied to the interest of the society from which the anthropologist comes and all he says and does—how he gives form to experience, how he shapes and directs his questions, how he interprets and proceeds from the answers he receives—provide a commentary on those interests.

Rabinow (1977:129) articulated this differential confrontation as a form of "symbolic violence" in which the anthropologist knowingly transgressed the integrity of the informant through an intentional failure to respect his resistance to impart certain information.

To those who claim that some form of symbolic violence was not part of their field experience, I reply that I do not believe them. It is inherent in the structure of the situation. This is not to say that every anthropologist is aware of it, for sensibilities differ. The form and intensity no doubt vary greatly, but they are all variations on a common theme. (ibid.:120)

The experience of the anthropologist was thus asserted in fieldworker ethnographies as an asymmetrical confrontation between the anthropologist and informant. But in the conception of fieldworker ethnographers, these confrontations, seen as breakdowns in communication between anthropologist and Other, were the means through which the negotiation of meaning took place. Finally, it provided the means through which the subject—object split was resolved, and anthropological knowledge attained. Fieldworker ethnographers sought to overcome the separation between subject and object through an examination of the interaction between self and Other, through a dialogue with the Other, and by reflection on culturally informed understandings. This dialogic construction of anthropological knowledge was also seen as dialectic. For example, Dumont (1978:5) argued:

A relationship between "I" and "they" is necessarily dialectical and eventuates in three logical, yet overlapping and as it were "progressivo-regressivo stages"—a confrontation, a search for meaning, and optimally a recognition. These three stages correspond roughly to the three dialectical steps: thesis, antithesis and synthesis. The confrontation corresponds to the dialectic process in which an exchange takes place, or in which they figure me out and I figure them out, so to speak. Finally, and optimally (which means that it does not necessarily happen) recognition takes place, at which point the other is recognized in his/her otherness.

In short, in fieldworker ethnographies, fieldwork was understood as a "dialectic between reflection and immediacy" (Rabinow 1977:38), in which neither the subject nor object remained the same. For these anthropologists, interaction, especially in the form of dialogue between participants, was thus placed at the center of their analysis as they concerned themselves with it as a phenomenon on which they reflected.

In the view of fieldwork ethnographers, confrontations between anthropologists and informants were not only an inevitable and universal aspect of research; they were essential to the production of anthropological knowledge. It was in the process of the struggle and recognition of the nature and significance of this confrontation that anthropological knowledge emerged through negotiations of meaning, which while not perfectly representative of either view, were sufficient for both. "The ethnographic encounter, like any encounter between individuals or for that matter, with oneself in moments of self-reflection, is always a complex negotiation in which the parties to the encounter acquiesce to a certain reality. This 'reality' belongs . . . to none of the parties to the encounter" (Crapanzano 1980: ix).

Although fieldwork ethnographers agreed that it was the cultural self which was explored in the process of research, they also held the view that anthropologist and informants were personally changed in the course of their encounter as a biographical experience. For example, Rabinow described a process in which "taken for granted" categories of the cultural self changed: "As I began to question Ali . . . about the curing, my scientific categories were modified" (Rabinow 1977:38). Dwyer (1979, 1982; cf. Lukacs 1971; Goldmann 1964) phrased this aspect as the "staking" of the personal self in the ethnographic encounter, as a wager, and argued that the anthropologist must be willing to take "personal" risks in the engagement.

If Anthropology is to embrace this relationship between Self and Object (or between "self" and "other") it must as it pursues the Other, also become able to pursue the Self, and the Self must therefore be exposed. Yet anthropologists, perhaps sensing that to expose the Self is necessarily to place it in jeopardy, have for the most part been unwilling to take such a gamble. Avoiding this risk with unusual virtuosity, they have refused to admit that the very possibility of dealing squarely with the Other is tied to the capacity to put the Self at stake. (Dwyer 1979:205)

Reconstitution and Resolution

Fieldwork was further understood in fieldworker accounts as, in Rabinow's phrase, a "metaphysical marker" of the profession and the professional anthropologist—the experience through which students of Anthropology became anthropologists. Field research was not just a method of "gathering knowledge" but part of the socialization of the incipient anthropologist, the "rite of passage."

In the graduate anthropology department at the University of Chicago, the world was divided into two categories of people, those who had done fieldwork and those who had not. The latter were not "really" anthropologists, regardless of what they knew about anthropological topics. Professor Mircea Eliade, for example, was a man of great erudition in the field of comparative religion and was respected for his encyclopedic learning, but it was repeatedly stressed that he was not an anthropologist, his intuition had not been altered by the alchemy of fieldwork. I was told that my papers did not really count because once I had done fieldwork, they would be radically different. Knowing smiles greeted acerbic remarks which graduate students made about the lack of theory in certain of the classics we studied. Never mind, we were told, the authors are great fieldworkers. . . . Yet I knew of no book which made a serious intellectual effort to define this essential rite of passage, this metaphysical marker which separated anthropology from the rest. (Rabinow 1977:3–4)

The "away" (in the field) frame of fieldwork was the Anthropological journey (Dwyer 1982:267) and it was this journey that was claimed as the subject of fieldworker ethnographies in a process in which the ethnography then became a vehicle through which the anthropologist returned as a professional.

According to fieldwork ethnographers, their texts were a means to resolve and reconstitute the ethnographic encounter as well as the role of the anthropologist. In the field, anthropologists struggled in confrontations with the Other, which these ethnographers claimed to resolve through dialogic negotiation between cultural selves. But the anthropologist at home, following his return from the field, was still struggling to make sense of the encounter in the field, as well as of himself. In the latter setting, "The act of writing—the evocation of the response of the Other, and the constitution thereby of the self and his meaningful world—is reified, in its product, the written word" (Crapanzano 1977:71). There is a sense then, in fieldworker ethnographies, that the self of the anthropologist, and the risks to which it was exposed, while personally felt in the field, were professionally resolved through ethnography, at home.

The fieldworker ethnography is thus seen by its authors as a vehicle for the reconstitution of the self which had been disrupted and threatened in the field. They were the means by which the anthropologist not only made sense of the Other; they were also a significant means through which the anthropologist made sense of himself in the field experience and its aftermath. According to fieldwork ethnographers, both processes were necessary for the production of anthropological knowledge. As Crapanzano put it: "Whatever the reason for the dissociation, the fact remains that the con-

frontation does not end before the ethnography, but if it can be said to end
at all, it ends *with* the ethnography" (ibid.:70).

From the viewpoint of anthropologists writing fieldworker ethnographies,
the two locales of fieldwork—"away" in the process of research, and "at
home" writing ethnography as the product of research—were thus inextricably and saliently linked as an experience. The end of fieldwork, insofar as
it was understood by these anthropologists to end, was not marked by the
return from the field, but by the construction of ethnography through reconstruction and reflection on the experience while away. "It is only then
that the anthropologist truly returns from the field in a process of self-
dissolution and reconstitution" (Crapanzano 1977:73). Through this focus
on the experience of the ethnographer and the self as present and active in
the process away and at home, a "final" significant aim of the ethnographic
experience and the writing of ethnography was to be accomplished—the
understanding of the fieldworker's (cultural) self.

As articulated by Rabinow, fieldworker ethnographies aimed at "the comprehension of the self by the detour of the comprehension of the other"
(Rabinow 1977:5; cf. Ricoeur 1969:20). The effort was not to present an
objective view of another culture presented in the "monologue" of science,
but a conversation, interaction, or dialogue, for reflection and interpretation.
As Dumont put it: "In this venture, I hope to gain some insight about 'me'
and 'them', otherwise I do not see the point of having gone there" (1978:
ix).

Fieldworker ethnographies were thus claimed as an ethnographic form
which resolved a biographical and personal experience, in professional terms.
According to these authors, ultimately the resolution of the subject-object
split was framed through a focus on the experience of the participant observer and the observed, framed as a text, reflected on and re-interpreted in
the writing of ethnography. This, they argued, was anthropological "praxis"
in which the "enterprise of inquiry" was essentially continuous with its results (Rabinow 1977:5).

The terms of fieldworker ethnographies as described above were derived
from the claims which fieldworker ethnographers made in their work, about
their work. But ethnographies, as referential forms, do not consist wholly
of what their authors say in them or about them. This chapter has focused
on what fieldworker ethnographers said about what they were doing. The
rest of the chapters in Part II use these terms as an entry to examine "what
they did."

NOTE

1. There are, of course, significant differences among these ethnographies as well.
For example, strategies for the presentation of the substance of fieldworker ethnographies are similar in their rejection of standard ethnographies, but have differences

in presentation. Crapanzano and Dwyer make particular use of verbatim interview texts gathered in the field, while Rabinow and Dumont have virtually no such presentations. Further, there are different emphases in theoretical underpinnings. Rabinow, for example, relies more heavily on literary and phenomenological frames, while Crapanzano is strongly influenced by Freudian underpinnings which are almost entirely absent (at least as an explicit frame of reference) from the other works. See the Appendix for a brief summary of these works on their own.

CHAPTER 5

Experience over Observation

I think the moment was right epistemically for this kind of thing to emerge. I think Geertz and Levi-Strauss got up to the edge of it and the next step was there. And someone like Clifford has shown, I think convincingly, that the genre constraints that were in place since the "twenties" were coming to an end and off we went. (Rabinow 1989)

THE INTERPRETATION OF EXPERIENCE

The epistemological shift from science to interpretation created the space and the underpinning for theoretical and methodological changes argued for and claimed in fieldworker ethnographies.

Part of the effect of the rejection of science as the epistemological underpinning for method and analysis in fieldworker ethnographies was the collapsing of all science into scientism (referred to here as Science).[1] Specifically targeted was objective observation as the cornerstone of such practice. In fieldworker ethnographies, scientific objectivity was not only assumed as implausible, and asserted as impossible, it was argued as undesirable. Objective observation was replaced by subjective experience as the salient aspect of fieldwork and as the basis for ethnography. Thus, a break between epistemological paradigms was manifest in the written account.

THE SCIENCE OF STANDARD ETHNOGRAPHIC PRACTICE

In science, objectivity can be taken for granted in part because of the implicit and explicit differences between the phenomena under study. For example, taking physics as the quintessential science, the planets are physical entities and the observers are human. Within these "limits" the subjectivity of the observer is seen to have no effect on that which is observed (the Heisenberg effect notwithstanding), and that which is observed is separated fairly readily, by category, from the observer. The subject of study is thus equally readily taken as an object of study since the investigated phenomena are not understood to have a subjectivity. In part because of these intrinsic separations between the observer and that which is observed, any observer is theoretically replaceable by any other observer with no effect on findings or conclusions.

In general, it was this understanding of the goals and methods of science which informed the presentation of "standard ethnographies" and which, unannounced and unreflected on (in Anthropology) permeated and, in important ways, produced that form, including its narrative voice.[2] This was followed by the turn to interpretation, which formed the context and foundation for a series of linked inversions in the goal and practice of Anthropology. These included the general goals of Anthropology to describe or understand culture as its subject, and the means through which this was presented in written practice, including the conventions of ethnographic presentation.

THIS END UP
The Subjective Participant Replaces the Objective Observer

Both styles seemed to me deficient. The scientific approach, I thought radically distorted the experience because at the very least, it overlooked the role played by the anthropologist in constructing the situation and eliciting the behavior that he or she later reported in ethnographic monographs or professional journals. The personal account, although placing the anthropologist within the experience, usually presented that experience "naively" without questioning the implications of the anthropologist's presence and comportment. Both styles, whatever their differences, were more like escapes from, than solutions to, the problems of conveying the experience to people who had not participated in it. (Dwyer 1982:14)

Related to the privileging of experience over observation in fieldworker ethnographies was the effort to find and sustain a position between the objective and the personal in the project of ethnography. Although the primary energy of these works was focused on the rejection of the process of turning subjects into objects in the written account in earlier experiments with ethnographic form, the subjective presence articulated through personal experience was also rejected. These earlier experiments, which comprised so-called "confessional literature," had been written by professional anthropologists but had not been considered professional works within the discipline, primarily on the basis of their being read as too personal. While standard ethnographies, rooted in Science, were in a sense too epistemological, that is, too rigid and demanding in method and representation, "confessional" works were viewed as written in an epistemological vacuum. As separate ends of a continuum of ethnographic practice, both were to be avoided: "between these two forms of the same monologue, there must be something else" (Dumont 1978:3, 9).

The "something else" sought after in fieldworker ethnographies was an epistemologically more adaptable, interpretive process which "defrosted" the "frozen" participants of the field experience and resolved the subject-object split produced by science. Thus, experientially in the field and intellectually once at home, the subject-object split was to be resolved in fieldworker ethnographies through the "cultural self." In such an endeavor the anthropologist became a "reflective tool" (Dumont 1978:11) through which a negotiated understanding of self and Other would be accomplished. Because the anthropologist did not then objectify his own experience, his experience (including relationships) with Others, as well as the Others' experience, was changed. This change encompassed the claimed and constructed foundations of Anthropological knowledge in the field, and in a continuous process, its presentation in professional form in the written ethnography.

I had already written a book about the Panare . . . it was more about Panare objects than about Panare subjects. More about "their thing" than about them. Now I am about to take a second look at the Panare, I wish to shift the focus of my analysis, reorienting it with the goal of anthropology of the subject. Not only will I continue to direct my gaze at them, in addition, I want to consider how they gaze at me. My effort will be directed toward perceiving, apprehending and interpreting the "and" of the relationship which my fieldwork built between an "I" and "they." (Dumont 1978:5)

CARTESIAN WILLS: THE SPLIT BETWEEN THE MIND AND THE BODY OF THE WORK

The intellectual and intentional shift from objectivity to subjectivity as the presumptive underpinning of experience and practice resulted in structural changes in the body of the written ethnography, which stood the conventions of standard ethnographies "on their heads." In both the presentation and the subject of the work, fieldworker ethnographies represented an *inversion* of standard ethnographic practice. But interestingly, while fieldworker ethnographies included a critique of Science as the foundation for ethnographic practice, there was no substantive discussion of the characteristics of that form, nor any detailing as to how it manifested scientific practice. Similarly absent were detailed analyses or delineations of conventions, including style of practice produced by their own epistemological assumptions.[3] Thus, while the "failure" of standard ethnographies as works produced by Science was fundamental to the project these anthropologists undertook, references to the actual means through which standard works represented and presented subject-object splits were more at the level of comment than analysis. Unexamined in these works was the relationship between Science and written standard ethnographic practice, including the conventions of ethnographic practice they asserted were produced through this paradigm. That there was a relationship between epistemology and written practice was apparently taken for granted in these works. But fieldwork ethnographers were not unique in this respect. Other anthropologists who wrote more specifically about the conventions of written ethnographic practice agreed that standard ethnographies were the product of science but did not make the linkages between them explicit. Edgerton and Langness (1974), as representatives of the more scientific "end" of Anthropology, referred to standard ethnographies as the "scientific style of standard ethnography."

Marcus and Cushman (1982:30), writing from an incipient postmodern perspective, also saw a relationship between science and standard ethnographies, a form they referred to as "ethnographic realism." In Edgerton and Langness's (1974:56) view: "In ethnographic writing, as in any other scientific presentation, the goal of accuracy goes hand in hand with the goal of efficiency." Marcus and Cushman (1982:30), in their description of standard ethnographies as "realist ethnographies" asserted them as: "*the* genre for anthropologists and *the* 'literary institution' serving positivist scientific goals." However, while statements linking such works to science were made, there was little or no discussion as to the specific nature of these links. The links are significant here insofar as, just as the style of standard presentation was grounded in scientific practice, so the style of fieldworker ethnographies inverted that style as it rejected science. Thus, while fieldworker ethnographies did not directly engage the conventions and underpinnings of ethnographies produced through the paradigm of Science, they illuminated their view of other Anthropological work through the claims they made for their own.[4]

If specific changes in presentation were not addressed in these works, what changes *were* explicitly announced? First, as noted, was the shift from objectivity to subjectivity as the basis of ethnographic practice. The inversion in form was part of, and a result of, the general move to interpretation and the related change in method from observation to experience. Thus, the announced intellectual differences produced unannounced shifts in presentation. So, for example, the switch from the objective observer to the subjective participant also incorporated a conversion in which the position (and experience) of the anthropologist became significant as a subject of study and the topic of ethnography.

DERIVED THROUGH EXPERIENCE

Presence of the Ethnographer in the Written Account

Fieldworker ethnographies were primarily presented through the subjective presence, the "voice," of an ethnographer, continually interpolated throughout the work. Through the explicit and active presence of the anthropologist, the experience of the ethnographer was stylistically highlighted by the strategic and intentional presence of the ethnographer as "I."[5] The use of "I" in the description of the intention to present the ethnographer's own point of view as negotiated with that of the native both embodied and made explicit the ethnographer's presence in the field and in the written work. (Emphases are added to underscore the use of "I" and other personal pronouns in the following passage).

I do not try in this book, to give a view of Moroccan culture from within. The attempt to discover what a culture looks like from personal-historical documents has always struck *me* as an act of great naivete. Rather *I* look at the way in which Tuhami makes use of the particular idiom at his disposal to articulate his own experience, including his personal history within *our* [*sic*] negotiations of reality. With less perspective perhaps, certainly with greater resistance *I* look at the use of *my* own idiom within our negotiations. (Crapanzano 1980:xi–xii)

As in standard ethnographies, photographs which confirmed the presence of the ethnographer in the field were included and in these works highlighted the presence of the ethnographer, including the ethnographer as a particular individual. For example, Dumont, Dwyer, and Rabinow included photographs of themselves in the field (sometimes in native garb), not just photographs of others, but photographs with others, thus "doubly" confirming their presence not only through photographs which they took themselves (sending the message "I was there to take this photo") but photographs which had been taken of them on-site. Dwyer [1982] reinforced the impression of personal involvement with handwritten labels for his photographs, similar to those which might be found in a family album. (*Tuhami* is an exception since Crapanzano included no photographs).

Focus on Representation of the Experience of Individuals

While standard ethnographies focused on the group, fieldworker ethnographies focused on a single male, or series of male individuals who acted as informants. Further, while in standard ethnographies viewpoints were ascribed to particular "individuals," these "individuals" were constructions by the anthropologist and often represented many different informants. In standard ethnographies, aspects of individuals such as personality and personal experience were taken out and individuals were reduced to "composite creations" (Edgerton and Langness 1974), or "common denominator people" (Marcus and Cushman 1982:32). When this occurred in fieldworker ethnographies it was presented as a means to provide coherence, rather than one designed to leave out idiosyncrasy or personality; a process of "condensation."[6]

> This book is a studied condensation of a swirl of people, places and feelings. . . . Some informants with whom I worked are not mentioned, some are collapsed into the figures presented here, and others are left out altogether. Anyone who had such a set of progressively coherent encounters while in the field and was fully conscious of it at the time, would not have the kind of experience which I have reconstructed here. (Rabinow 1977:6–7)

Fieldworker ethnographies included a series of encounters with one or several informants presented as specific individuals. Often appearing only on the margins (introductions, footnotes, etc.) of standard ethnographies, these informants as particular and specific individuals were highlighted in fieldworker ethnographies. However, while the group, including "condensed" people, were largely absent from fieldworker accounts, there was a common denominator among the majority of individuals these ethnographers presented in their work—the specific Others with whom ethnographers interacted were often described as marginal within their own cultural context. In *Reflections on Fieldwork in Morocco*, the Moroccan Ali was "like several other people with whom I worked . . . a marginal character in his own social world. He was not the average villager, he was far from the solid citizen stereotype of Sefrou" (Rabinow 1977:43). Tuhami (Crapanzano 1980:5) was "exceptional . . . considered an outsider, an outcast even, by the people around him."[7]

Description of the Particular and Specific

In fieldworker ethnographies, just as individuals were described in terms which included particular physical and personality traits, events and conversations were recorded in specific and particular detail. Conversations presented were often the actual transcripts of interviews (see especially Dwyer 1982; Crapanzano 1980), which were then interpreted in terms of themselves (in the specific terms of the particular exchange) rather than generalized or universalized. Ethnographic encounters, such as attendance at a festival which occurred annually, were presented in their particularity through the details provided by the anthropologist. For example, Dwyer described attending the *Amouggar*, an annual festival in Morocco:

Only I was looking far forward to the annual festival, or *Amouggar*. . . . At 7:00 in the morning, the pickup truck that would take us to the *Amouggar* arrived, and we added our equipment—reed mats, several low, round wooden tables, earthen cookware, teakettle and teapot, tea glasses, some wood for fuel, and two timeworn but not yet threadbare rugs—to what the other passengers had already packed in. All of this was securely tied to the wooden frame of the pickup, and ten adults and twelve children, all male, worked themselves into the remaining crevices.

We drove for almost an hour over dirt roads, and reached the large open field of the *Amouggar* about 8:00. Some of the passengers left us then for different gatherings, but we greeted a few other villagers sitting with Ali, who had found space for all of us under an olive tree. This year, the trees had not been well irrigated, their foliage was scant, and their shade would only partially block the sun. (Dwyer 1982: 90–91)

Details included in fieldworker accounts not only incorporated an emphasis on the ethnographer's attendance, but on the unique circumstances of a particular day (time, weather, foliage, etc.). And further, the listing of specific items brought to the festival was presented with no statement as to how typical these items were from year to year or even group to group within a particular year.

Presentation of Experience in the Ethnographic Encounter

Where standard ethnographies presented data from the field experience sifted through Western analytic categories familiar in the social sciences (e.g., kinship, religion, politics, economics, and the like), fieldworker accounts were presented through a series of encounters between the anthropologist and Other(s). While the content of analytic categories in standard ethnographies was included, it appeared through the experience of the ethnographic encounter. For example, Rabinow's initial contact with his informant Ali was presented as an event.[7] Included were the explicit presence of the ethnographer, and his self-awareness, as well as elements of geography, social interaction, economics, history, and so on. Participants in the extended example below were Rabinow; Ali (his informant); Ali's friend, the shopkeeper Soussi; and various "passers-by."

Ali greeted me warmly, pulled up another rickety chair, and called across the way for two glasses of sweet mint tea. . . . The intersection lay at a juncture of three curving slopes . . . Ali and Soussi seemed to know practically everyone who passed by. Quick and cursory welcomes were exchanged in rapid spit-fire fashion as the voice and its owner disappeared around the bend. As a New Yorker and a devotee of street life, I felt much more at ease here than in the formal and quasi-suburban atmosphere of the Ville Nouvelle. In addition, it was immensely "ethnographic" and fulfilled all of my images of myself as anthropologist sitting in the heart of a thousand-year-old walled city with my turbaned friends, notebook on my lap, drinking tea and being the participant observer.

As the morning passed the tea kept coming. Tea and sugar have a tyrannical and almost obsessive centrality in Morocco. Its preparation and consumption are daily rituals of generosity and exchange, but it is also economically a heavy load to bear. . . . As much as 40 per cent of a poor peasant's cash income can be spent on tea and sugar. . . . Actually, tea was introduced into Morocco by the English in the eighteenth century, and its use did not become widespread until the nineteenth. . . .

A Berber woman . . . with a very small baby strapped on her back. . . . exchanged a few words with Ali and bent over. Ali took the head of the baby . . . firmly in his hands. Putting his mouth to the child's mouth he swiftly and with great assurance made a quick sucking noise. The baby began to howl. With an air of professional pride Ali showed the mother some spittle containing a black speck. She seemed satisfied, gave him a few coins, and left.

The completely casual way in which Ali had performed this act was stunning in its simplicity. The shifting of perspectives, almost without a pause, was eye-opening. The whole scenario was taken for granted by Ali, Soussi and the woman. Only the baby and the anthropologist were disturbed by it. I recovered my composure quickly enough, and noted that I had identified a curing practice.

Fieldwork is a dialectic between reflection and immediacy. Both are cultural constructs. Our scientific categories help us to recognize, describe, and develop areas of inquiry. But one cannot engage in questioning and redefining twenty-four hours a day. The scientific perspective on the world is hard to sustain. In the field there is less to fall back on, the world of everyday life changes more rapidly and dramatically than it would at home. There is an accelerated dialectic between the recognition of new experiences and their normalization. (Rabinow 1977:33–35)

Here diverse cultural material was presented through the experience of the encounter as an event, rather than through categories of analysis found in standard ethnographies. Further, parts of the encounter were highlighted by providing "background" within the description (e.g., tea as socially, economically, and historically meaningful) as well as intellectual reflection on the experience of fieldwork. The "story" and the chronological element absent from standard ethnographies was used as an overall organizing feature of "fieldworker ethnographies," which all began with personal experiences of the ethnographer before his arrival in the field, followed by "episodes" in the field, and ended with a description of the process of leaving the field. Thus, similar to travelers' tales, these ethnographies were intentionally presented with a beginning, a middle, and an end, with encounters described in the chronological sequence of their occurrence.

The book is composed of two parts. Part I: "A Record of Fieldwork" begins with a prologue that provides some background to life in a southern Moroccan village and to my encounter with Faqir Muhammad; it then proceeds, in each succeeding chapter, to present an event that occurred during the fieldwork and a subsequent dialogue between me and the Faqir about it. . . . The events and dialogue are presented in their actual chronological order. (Dwyer 1982:xii)

The encounters in fieldworker ethnographies took many forms, including conversations, dialogues, interviews, and attendance at particular events (i.e., weddings and festivals), and "complete" with their interpretation became the basis of chapter divisions. In a move further "away" from the social sciences, interpretations were often refracted through the lens of the humanities, particularly literary analogs and analysis.

Professional Language

The contrast between standard and fieldworker ethnographies was not a change in the *use* of professional language typified by its general presence or absence, but a change in the *source* of professional language. Terms in standard ethnographies were criticized as scientific "jargon":

Whether using a vocabulary that is evolutionist, cultural, ecological, cultural materialist, or structuralist, it is avowedly scientific and seeks explanations for all crucial differences between human groups in terms of an objective language that transcends these differences, that permits difference to be interpreted as variations on universal themes. (Dwyer 1982:257)

Such criticisms in fieldworker accounts were also intertwined with the rejection of objectivity as part of the written presentation, but were themselves replete with jargon, albeit drawn from different epistemologies, and different specializations. For example, according to Crapanzano (1977:69–70), "Such stylistic devices as the self-conscious avoidance of the 'I' . . . , elimination of polysemic language and the calculated use of scientistic, jargonistic, generally monsemic or stenic language becomes a defensive attempt to isolate the act of writing and its end product from the confrontation itself."

Insofar as professional or technical language becomes a "jargon" to outsiders (Edgerton and Langness 1974:56), the terms used are illustrative of differences in paradigms of practice in which standard and fieldworker forms were rooted. Thus, criticism of the jargon in standard ethnographies simultaneously demonstrated the changes in paradigms of practice, and the ways in which, in professional terms, other anthropologists were "outsiders." The interpretive vocabularies of phenomenology, hermeneutics, literary analysis marked the turn from science. The shifting of categories of "subject" and "object," consistent with science and implicit in standard ethnographies, and its transformation to categories of "self" and "other" consistent with phenomenology and explicit in fieldworker ethnographies, resulted in the transformation of other anthropologists into "outsiders." Further, while "scientistic" language was critiqued or falsely universalized, the dilemma which this epistemological and language shift produced, was that, for "other anthropologists," the shift in which the "self" was overly privileged also shifted the grounds for evaluation. Self-proclaimed as particular, individual and a product of the author's experience, the criteria on which fieldworker ethnographies were themselves criticized were personalized, but ironically perhaps, also effectively reduced.

A SHIFT IN THE PARADIGM OF PRESENTATION

Setting the conventions of standard ethnographies referred to and those of fieldworker ethnographies described above side by side reveals that, in significant respects, conventions of presentation used by fieldwork ethnographers rejected those of standard ethnographies by inverting them. Standard ethnographies focused on the description of the group; fieldworker accounts were "told" by a participant. Standard ethnographies focused on the representation of the native group; fieldworker ethnographies focused on the experience of individuals, including the ethnographer. Standard works presented data through analytic categories; fieldworker accounts presented interactions through fieldwork encounters. Standard ethnographies generalized; fieldworker ethnographies particularized. Standard and fieldworker ethnographies used two different specialized vocabularies, one drawn from science and the other from interpretation.

One way to look at fieldworker ethnographies, then, is as a simple reaction to standard ethnographies. These sorts of reactions are commonly described in Anthropology, at least as analyzed in retrospect. For example, the institution and dominance of science as an epistemological, methodological, and professional standard is itself often understood as a reaction to its "prescientific" period (e.g., see Stocking 1960; Reining 1962; Dwyer 1982; Dumont 1978). In specific theoretical developments, Boas's "historical particularism" is often seen in Anthropology as a reaction to unilineal evolution, which itself is viewed as a response to anecdotal accounts by missionaries and so on. However, while fieldworker accounts are readily construable as a reaction to standard works, the *inversion* of the standard form presented in fieldworker ethnographies was a particular reaction, not an inevitable one. While statements within fieldworker accounts demonstrated that they explicitly rejected and intentionally did not produce standard works, there was no explicitly stated, *intentional* effort to produce an inversion of the style. In fact, there was no evidence in these works that their authors realized that they had done so. Clearly, inversion is not an inevitable outcome of rejection, or for that matter, other kinds of reactions (see for example, "confessional" and other works: Bowen 1954; Miner 1956; Casagrande 1960; Powdermaker 1964; Berreman 1962; Read 1965; Ruby 1982). One place to look as part of making sense of the changed terms of fieldworker accounts is outside the immediacy of the texts themselves, in the broader epistemological "debates" of the time as relevant to Part I and in the still broader political, intellectual, economic—in short, the cultural context of their production, as pursued in Part III. In the next two chapters, the focus shifts from the terms of the presentation of experience to the interpreted terms of experience as presented in the content of these works. Once experience was privileged over observation, questions arise which in some ways bridge the paradigms of science and interpretation. In Chapter 6, the focus is on the "second" question of science: "What is their essence?" that is, "What kind of experience was it?"

NOTES

1. In fieldworker ethnographies, "positivist science," "positivism," and "science," were often used interchangeably, thus collapsing all forms of science into positivist science and ultimately into scientism. As a means to keep in mind that the use of "science" in fieldworker accounts is a particular (though not unique) one, the term "Science" is employed to mark their understanding of science as scientism, and separate it from a more generic usage (science). Definitions of "scientism" used in Anthropology in this time frame were in large part drawn from the Frankfurt School, for instance, Horkheimer's (1937; see Horkheimer, "The Latest Attack on Metaphysics," and "Traditional and Critical Theory," in *Critical Theory: Selected Essays* (New York: Herder and Herder 1972) critique of scientism as a doctrine of unified science, including a universal scientific method common to both the natural and social sciences (particularly as argued by the Vienna Circle). Scientism was not only a particularly rigid application of scientific method, but as argued by the Vienna Circle, science was *the* knowledge and *the* theory—that is, other forms of knowledge were inadequate. Although anthropologists and Anthropology, which were directly antecedent to fieldwork ethnographers, argued against scientism, they included the view that not all American anthropologists were "uniformly naive in their acceptance of a scientific stance" and that other paradigms of science and practice existed (Scholte 1972:450). But as noted above, these distinctions were not made in fieldworker ethnographies.

2. From this point of view, the authority for the account was epistemological, not personal. See Marcus and Cushman (1982), and Clifford and Marcus (1985, 1986) for arguments that the third-person narrative was a personal statement of authority made more powerfully by an absent, seemingly omniscient narrator. My own view is that while these interpretations have some import for Anthropology, they are more relevant to literary than Anthropological practice.

3. Edgerton and Langness, in *Methods and Styles in the Study of Culture* (1974), provide a discussion of the form of standard ethnographic presentation from the standpoint of anthropologists with a significantly scientific set of assumptions, correlated to "standard" ethnographic practice. Marcus and Cushman ("Ethnographies as Texts" 1982) provide a discussion of differences between conventions of presentation in standard and "reflexive ethnographies" (part of a larger group of "experimental ethnographies"). Marcus and Cushman draw from more interpretive, and in important respects then, incipient postmodern viewpoints.

4. The point can be made that there is no specific reason that anthropologists should or would be interested in genre conventions of ethnographic practice as an Anthropological problem. Such interests have fallen at the more literary end of Anthropological work. A word about my methods. The specific conventions of fieldworker ethnographies presented in this chapter were derived through my analysis of these works, then merged with those derived and described by Edgerton and Langness (1974) and Marcus and Cushman (1982). This is not to argue that my analysis is inconsistent with those of others, nor unique. The assimilation of viewpoints was an effort to incorporate different points of view rather than write from a previously articulated viewpoint (although of course, once in place, it represents a particular point of view). The effort was not to take for granted the perspective of the authors of these works, as individuals or as a group.

5. This usage is so systemic that any page or passage in these texts can be used to demonstrate such practice.

6. Note the language here is consistent with Freudian analytic constructs in which "condensation" is a part of dreamwork, and figures, places, and so on, which appear in dreams in condensed form, are multilayered and symbolic.

7. See Chapter 3 for the intellectual framing of "early works," including Geertz's influence and his analysis of the Balinese cockfight (1973:412–453) presented as an event.

CHAPTER 6

Confrontation, Power, and Domination

In fieldworker ethnographies, the content of experience was the conduit through which the cultural self would be revealed. The significance of the fieldwork encounter was less in its singularity than in its interpretation in these works as formed and informed by previous encounters between western anthropologists and non-western cultures. Through this lens, confrontation was articulated as the significant mode of interaction between individuals, mirroring that of encounters between cultures *cum* nation states in which the West held sway. Specifically, fieldworker–Other interactions were taken for granted as informed by, heir to, and expressions of structural, asymmetrical, historical, and contemporary encounters between cultures, played out through relationships of power and domination.

GO WEST, YOUNG MAN

> An anthropological project that stifles the dialectic of Self and Other and refuses to set that dialectic in its particular context leads it seems in the best of cases to personal despair. But there are historical consequences too and they may be pernicious: such a project however modest it may seem when set beside the movement of armies, the missionary enterprise, or the growth of centralized technologies and the dominance of the nation-state, contributes by sheltering the Self and the Self's origins, to disarming and rendering harmless the Other. (Dwyer 1982:33)

In fieldworker ethnographies, even the "personal despair" of ethnographic confrontations was linked to more global (although unspecified) encounters between larger political entities. Power and domination as a directive and foundational aspect of the ethnographic enterprise was taken for granted and explicitly addressed in these works as significant in two linked arenas of Self: cultural (including global interactions) and disciplinary. As set out in fieldworker accounts these arenas merged in the field experience so that the emergence of anthropology itself was understood as part and product of the power and domination of the West in global encounters. From this perspective, Anthropology, as a discipline, embodied and "enacted" through anthropologists the historical, colonialist power of the West.

COLONIAL ARMS

> Modern anthropology owes its development to a particular social system at a critical moment in that system's history. The discipline emerged within a portion of the world whose emissaries—military, religious, economic and cultural systematically intruded upon, plundered and often destroyed outright other human beings. Anthropology, even though it contested specific aspects of this historical process was nonetheless formed by it. (Dwyer 1982:215)

Such aspects informally and significantly permeated the field experience as construed by these anthropologists as they reported themselves to be perceived by Others as embodying and representing the presence and the power of the West. But the intertwined and consequent inequality in the relationship between the ethnographer and Other was itself held as inevitable, albeit impersonal—beyond the control of both partners.

Inequality of partners in dialogue is not an accident of personal preference but is one aspect of a wider social confrontation between the West and the rest of the world that in recent history has never been symmetrical. The West has systematically intruded upon the non-West and reworked it, sometimes subtly, sometimes violently according to the West's own needs. This asymmetry has its counterpart in the anthropologist's project, the self-search for knowledge of the Other's cultural and social territory, to seek a kind of understanding that has been defined by the needs of Western institutions. (Dwyer 1982:xvii)

Notions of Anthropology as enacting global agendas were infused with the power of the anthropologist as compared to that of the Other. The intrinsically powerful Westerner, in global as well as professional terms, granted himself the power to make choices denied to the Other. Rabinow wrote of his interactions with informant ben Mohammed:

That I would journey to Morocco to confront Otherness and myself was typical of my culture (or the parts of it I could accept). That ben Mohammed would enter in this sort of dialogue without self-denigration was impressive. (Rabinow 1977:161)

Here, Rabinow granted himself cultural and personal power in choosing the journey and choosing the confrontation. Further, he granted the ethnographer the power, through self-awareness, to intentionally discard aspects of his own traditions, attending only to those parts "I could accept." The Other's participation without "self-denigration" as "impressive" revealed an unstated assumption (by the ethnographer) that the informant was in some sense at risk in the encounter in a way in which the anthropologist was not. Why otherwise would his participation be "impressive"? The ability of the Other to assuage power aspects of the ethnographic encounter through, for example, the role of host to the anthropologist as "guest," was itself granted by the ethnographer. The roles of anthropologist and Other were played out with these roles and their "boundaries" in mind.

Many of the political dimensions of the informants' relationships were obviated by Dris ben Mohammed's steadfast adherence to the role of host. This eventually establishes the grounds for a dialogue. . . . This absolute difference which separated us was openly acknowledged only at the end of my stay. We had become friends, we had shown each other mutual trust and respect. The limits of the situation were not obscured for either of us. I was for him a rich member of a dominant civilization about which he had the profoundest reservations. (Rabinow 1977:88)

Whether Dris ben Mohammed's "profoundest reservations" were the product of cultural ("dominant civilization"), personal ("a rich member"), or a mixture of both aspects of power, was unaddressed. But overall in these works, these aspects of power were presented as clearly asymmetrical and largely inseparable. The "trust and respect between friends" was understood as mutual, but mutuality was not equality in these relationships.

POWERFUL INTERPRETATIONS

Every interpretive strategy, including those implicit within description itself, involves choice and falls, thereby, into the domain of ethics and politics. (Crapanzano 1980:x–xi)

Political dimensions, both global and individual, were among the aspects of the ethnographic encounter which were most frequently asserted as part of the interaction between ethnographer and Other in fieldworker ethnographies. These works detailed episodes in which encounters with Others were fraught with confrontation and "jockeying" for position in which fieldworkers emerged as powerful through a variety of politically derived and asserted means. Dumont, for instance, articulated a "knowledge is power" version of events allied to the position of the West.

"What do you want?" Asked either in trade-Spanish . . . or in Panare . . . , the question was inescapable, as was the need to formulate an answer. To formulate, perchance to fabricate. Yet, as I scribble now with mixed emotions, some ten years after it really happened, as I am doing my best to recapture the quality of this anthropological experience, I cannot help but perceive the blind power game I was playing. . . . My French, Cartesian, rationalistic self was about to study Panare culture, in other words, the Panare were the objects of my study. They knew something I wanted to know. Since knowledge is power, I had to acquire some sort of power in their eyes in order to accede in turn to their knowledge, which ultimately would be further transformed into my power. . . . Even before making friends, I had to be tolerated, not accepted, and justify my intrusion. . . . Of course, given my threatening introduction by the gendarmes, and the shield that the vast Western world imposed between them and me, the Panare had little, if any political choice in accepting me. (Dumont 1976:43)

Crapanzano articulated control over the Other, in the name of (a previously rejected) science, through metaphors of sexual politics and literary reference:

[Tuhami] . . . was, within his terms, giving, and I with an avariciousness supported by my science, was willing to receive. I wanted to possess everything that Tuhami knew and could tell me and even more. I wanted to know him completely. I have always been fascinated by D'Annunzio's portrayal in *The Triumph of Death* (1900), of hero and heroine's desire to know each other fully. The presumption that such knowledge can be achieved rests either on the belief in total sexual possession—a possession that ends up, as D'Annunzio understood, in total extinction—or on the reduction of the Other to that which is completely graspable: the specimen. The one, the goal of passion, and the other, the product of science, are not in fact so easily separable. (Crapanzano 1980:134)

Anthropologists "possessed" the Other, who was left with "little choice," enacting the "symbolic violence" of ethnography. The confrontation between participants in the ethnographic encounter was interpreted as inevitably structurally and experientially lopsided, with the anthropologist in the position of power. This included the power to accept or reject a particular Other as partner in the dialogue of field experience. So, for example, various natives were "discarded" by anthropologists as unacceptable while others were selected. (The corresponding issue of the unavailability of particular informants, or their refusal to participate in the dialogue went largely unaddressed in these works.)

I had arrived in Morocco as a stranger with a determination to understand at least some small facet of the lives of the people that for whatever reason, I found intriguing and somehow significant. I met many Moroccans whom I found uninteresting and unlikable. I was also fortunate enough to meet a few who were both interesting and likable, and Tuhami was among these. (Crapanzano 1980:133)

The power to shape the experience itself through questions asked and answers pursued included the power to create a subject-object split within the Other through "forcing" him to objectify his own experience. This "doubling of consciousness" was the product of the split engendered when the Other was "forced" to objectify his experience in response to the anthropologist's questions. "As Tuhami's interlocutor I became an active participant in his life history, even though I rarely appeared directly in his recitations. Not only did my presence and my questions prepare him for the text he was to produce but they produced *what I read* as a change of consciousness in him" (emphasis added) (Crapanzano 1980:ix). But this effect on consciousness, or the experience of it as painful, were absent in the voice of the Other. So, for example, despite lengthy direct quotes from Tuhami in Crapanzano's work, the significance of the anthropologist and his questions in the life of the Other were notably absent from remarks by the native, a characteristic shared in other fieldworker accounts. In *Tuhami*, how did Crapanzano "read" the change in Tuhami's consciousness when, by Crapanzano's own account he rarely appeared in Tuhami's recitations? The power of the question and the questioner is asserted, but is otherwise unclear. The relationship between them was asymmetrical but the terms of the imbalance were vague.

Rabinow, in reflection on his interaction with Ali during a wedding he had attended for "professional" reasons, offered some thoughts on a source of disparity in experience and power between ethnographer and informant. According to Rabinow: "This is not an equal relationship . . . the informant has not stopped living his life and has not willingly suspended his fundamental assumptions" (Rabinow 1977:47). This would appear to grant the Other power in the ethnographic encounter, but Rabinow went on to say:

After all the informant has only the foggiest notion of what this strange foreigner is really after. For the rest of the day, the informant returns to his own life, perhaps slightly troubled by the cloud of the anthropologist's questions, of the taunts of his comrades. But as confidence is built up, the informant judges and interacts with the anthropologist in his own habitual style even if the outsider status is never eliminated.

As the explicit self-consciousness of the unnaturalness of the situation declines (it is never altogether absent), the implicit modes of action and judgment of both sides return. The anthropologist is supposed to be aware of this and to control himself. The informant is simply supposed to "be himself." (Rabinow 1977:47)

A curiously ambiguous impression regarding relationships of power in the field encounter remains, as do questions to which there are complex and conflicting answers. What differences did it make that the informant had only the "foggiest notion" of what the anthropologist was after? The informant was "perhaps slightly troubled" or "perhaps taunted." What were the bases of the guesses offered? Had the ethnographer been told that his informant was "troubled" or "taunted" or did he see it as an otherwise unpursued possibility (hence "perhaps")? Who was the "outsider" and who was the insider? From whose point of view? Was the informant the outsider, unaware of the Anthropological enterprise as directed by the anthropologist, or was the anthropologist the outsider, unaware of the meanings in terms of which he "controlled himself"?

DISARMED

> I am certainly not interested in confession and expiation, though both confession and expiation enter inevitably into my enterprise. (Crapanzano 1980:139)

We have seen how in fieldworker accounts the powerful Westerner was assumed to dominate the native and interpreted in broad strokes as having done so. But these works were replete with accounts of specific interactions which provided evidence for a conflicted experience and contradictory conclusions—interactions in which the ethnographer presented himself as continually and sometimes uncomfortably subject to the domination of the Other. This latter relationship inverted that described by the ethnographers as part of global and national sources of political power. Fieldworker ethnographies contained detailed interactions and events in which the ethnographer was "at the mercy" of the Other, and in some instances ways in which the ethnographer was dominated by the process of the field experience, even in the absence of a particular episode. Crapanzano (above) might not have been interested in confession and expiation, by his own account he "inevitably" had to deal with it. But images of "confession" and "expiation" are expressions of a surrender of self. The seeking of forgiveness or freedom from guilt is not a position of power but of vulnerability. Specifically then, what kind of power, domination, and subordination *do* we have evidence for in these works? What were the particular episodes in and through which these relationships were presented? The complicated politics of person and power in the field was demonstrated in a field episode, which I take as an extended example (Rabinow 1977:40–46).

During Rabinow's fieldwork in Morocco, he was invited by his informant Ali to attend a wedding in a village some miles away. Rabinow, who had a car (Ali did not), was to provide the ride to the wedding for Ali and his friend Soussi. On the eve of the wedding, Rabinow fell ill but agreed to go anyway when Ali told him how important his (Rabinow's) attendance was to his research in the area, both because it would provide him with an opportunity to extend his contacts, and because not showing up might be taken as an insult, thus limiting future contacts. Ali, in turn, agreed in advance that he would leave the wedding whenever Rabinow wanted to go home:

[Ali] . . . assured me that we would stay only for a short time. He stressed all the preliminary politicking and arranging he had done; if I didn't show up it would not be good for either of us. So I agreed, but made him promise me that we would only stay an hour or so because I was still weak. He repeated his promise several times saying we would leave whenever I felt like it. (Rabinow 1977:43)

Rabinow and Ali arrived at the wedding and Rabinow described the setting and the welcome he received, noting that he did not understand or fit into the proceedings, and after a while lost interest in them. "Since I did not understand the songs and was not dancing my excitement wore off rapidly" (ibid). On the other hand, Ali was an "enthusiastic dancer," so that when, after three hours, Rabinow again suggested to Ali that they leave, Ali agreed to go in a few minutes, but danced on for an additional hour with no sign of being ready to go. Rabinow became, by his own account, frustrated and upset:

An hour later I tried again and received the same answer. This time, however, I was getting angrier and more frustrated; I was feeling truly ill. . . . I felt entirely at Ali's mercy. I didn't want to antagonize him, but neither did I want to stay. I continued to grumble to myself, but managed to smile at whoever was smiling at me. Finally, at three in the morning, I could stand it no longer. I was feeling terrible. I was furious at Ali and loathe to express it. (1977:44)

Finally, Rabinow decided to leave "regardless of the consequences" and sent Soussi to tell Ali he was leaving immediately. "Soussi went off and returned to the car with a smiling and contented Ali" (1977:44).

In the car on the way home the tensions between Rabinow and Ali surfaced. When Ali used a cultural means to resolve them, by asking "Are you happy?" Rabinow did not provide the appropriate (phatic) cultural response "Yes, I am happy" (ibid).[1] When it was clear that Rabinow would not respond "correctly" (there is no evidence that he actually understood that there was an expected [cultural] response), Ali demanded to be let out of the car and walk the remaining five miles home.

He [Ali] challenged me again asking me if I was happy. I could not bring myself to answer yes. My superego told me I should. But the events of the evening combined with the frustration of not being able to express myself fully to him in Arabic got the better of me. After another exchange and bluff on his part, I stopped the car to let him get out, which he now had to do. (1977:45)

The interaction as Rabinow described it was fraught with "anger" and "challenge"—the vocabulary of confrontation. Rabinow provided no clues to Ali's feelings although we know that he initially returned to the car "smiling and contented," while Rabinow had been "frustrated," "furious," and "loathe to express" these feelings to Ali or to antagonize him—the vocabulary of powerlessness. The ethnographer, who started out as "powerful," as the driver of the car and as an honored guest, ended up feeling victimized. He spent a restless night in which he worried about his future as an anthropologist.

I had probably made a grave professional mistake because the informant is always right. Otherwise, I was unrepentant. It was quite possible that I had ruined my relationship with Ali and that I had done irreparable damage to my chances of working my way into the village. . . . I remembered a story a friend had told me before we took our doctoral exams; he had nightmares for a week before the exams in which he saw himself as a shoe salesman. I mentally tried several occupations on for size as I drifted aimlessly among the villas. I felt calm. If this was anthropology and if I had ruined it for myself, then it simply wasn't for me. (1977:46)

The next day, Rabinow, using Soussi as his mediator, in an image of supplication, offered his "profuse apologies" to Ali. We will return to this episode again, as despite the images of "being at the mercy" of the Other, Rabinow ultimately interpreted the episode as one in which he made a fortuitous breakthrough which gave him culturally apt (in Moroccan terms) power in the field. But Rabinow was not alone—concerns and fears about powerlessness, and personal *cum* professional failure were considered endemic to all field experience in fieldworker ethnographies.

Today, I wonder whether my eagerness to rationalize, validate and justify my presence was not more for my own sake than theirs, whether it was not a defense mechanism against my fear of being rejected. . . . My anxiety about the whole situation was not to be expressed, but repressed and I would appear as self-assured as I possibly could, while I knew damn well the stakes of the game: one goof and I was out of anthropology and the remote glimmering of an academic career. (Dumont 1978:46)

This exposure of professional fears, although personally experienced and articulated, was considered common to all fieldwork experience in Anthropology, and was thus neither unique nor the product of particular individual interactions or personalities. "The reason I am dwelling rather heavily on this embarrassing self-exposure is emphatically *not* a belief that it reflects any kind of uniqueness or originality. Quite to the contrary, I firmly believe these feelings to be fairly common in any fieldwork experience . . . but more importantly, they are part of the experience and a constitutive part at that" (Dumont 1978:5).[2] Anxiety and fears of personal and professional rejection as part of the field encounter were the "other side" of the ethnographic experience of the powerful Westerner. But in fieldworker accounts, personal power did not reflect the asserted experience of global interaction. Breakdowns between their own assertions and their own depictions and others (in this instance other anthropologists) went unreflected and unresolved.

Was there then, evidence that the anthropologist had meaning to the informant at all? Crapanzano described his last encounter with Tuhami:

I told him we were leaving. At first he did not understand. When he did he showed no strong emotion. He accepted my departure with resignation, just as he accepted the innumerable disappointments in his life. At dinner that night—and unlike most of my other friends who came, Tuhami maintained a strong sense of himself, of his independence and his dignity. He kept the conversation gay when the others would have turned it maudlin and sentimental. When I drove him home, I gave him a large steel hunting knife. I told him that I hoped the knife would give him strength and be the key to his liberation. He was at a loss for words and put the gift quickly away. . . . Lhacen kissed him goodbye. He was surprised when I kissed him goodbye too, and he mumbled something about my coming back to Meknes soon. His last words were a promise that he would be strong. Lhacen and I watched him make his way down the narrow path that led to his house. We were both crying. (Crapanzano 1980:172)

Here we have evidence for Crapanzano's and even his interpreter Lhacen's sorrow at parting. What was less clear is how Tuhami experienced and interpreted these events. Tuhami "kept the conversation gay when others would have turned it maudlin." Was this evidence of his strength of character or evidence of his lack of concern? The explicit affirmation of the ethnographer's significance, his power in the life of the Other, variously interpreted, is difficult to find even in the depiction of the Other's experience. Quoted at length, the following is an interchange between Dwyer (D) and the Faqir (F):

D: When I lived in that room in the village, that first time I was here, I spent most of my time in the village. Now I don't go there much at all, I stay at your place for four or five days in a row, without ever leaving.

F: Yes.

D: What effect has that had on your house? For example, when I'm not here, you all eat in the *dar*. Why when I'm here, don't we all eat in the *dar*?

F: What, eat in one small room, with the children making all that noise? Sometimes we don't even spread out the furnishings: we just eat without sitting, and go on our way. And most often, even if the others eat in the *dar*, I still eat here. For dinner, I don't even eat there. They bring my dinner here.

D: You eat alone?

F: Yes. I eat here and then go to sleep.

D: And the rest of them all eat in the *dar*?

F: They eat there. And such noise: the kids go around fighting and yelling. . . . What do we want that noise for? What, would the kids let us talk? Never!

D: So, we're not eating in the *dar* because of your wishes or because of my wishes?

F: Because of all our wishes. And that way, the women don't hear us. There is talk that the women shouldn't hear. What if we wanted to talk and the women would hear it? That should not be.

D: That's no good.

F: No, that should not be. And they want to talk too, and we would hear their talk. That also should not be.

D: What else changes now that I'm here?

F: That's all. Nothing else but that.

D: Think a little. Isn't there something?

F: Nothing. There is nothing that changes—nothing, nothing. That's all.

D: If you and your brother are disputing, do you tone that down when I'm here?

F: We don't decrease anything. What there is, is whether you're here or whether you're not. Wherever the event happens, its the same.

D: Do you speak less in front of the others when I'm here?

F: It's just the same. I always speak a small amount.

D: Always?

F: Hmmmm.

D: Do you speak less to your sons?

F: With them I always speak a small amount, because they don't have thoughts.

D: If you search your mind now, you don't see anything else that changes when I'm here?

F: No. Just the meal moves from there to here, that's all.

D: And even when I'm not here, most of the time you still—eat here.

F: Yes, because in the evenings, I don't go over there at all.

D: The first time I was here, I spent a long time, about a year and a half. What were your thoughts when I left?

F: Well, I thought, "God help me, and God help you." You went off to do your work, and I stayed to do mine. And we parted in good will. I hadn't tried to outsmart you, and you hadn't tried to outsmart me. There was no problem. . . .

D: With all that we've talked about now, is there anything we have left out?

F: If so, we just didn't think of it. We may have forgotten something that happened in my life, but all that we remember we've talked about.

D: And now, what do you think about all that I've been asking you in these days, these months, that have passed.

F: I think that there will be a lot to talk about with those people in your land. As you said to me earlier. "What will I tell the people in my country if? . . ." That's what I imagine. From this they will learn, from this you will tell them what is, in fact. From it they will learn the situation itself, as it is. That's what I think. (1982:231–236)

Toward the end of this, their final interview, Dwyer stopped to formulate a few final questions: "I looked down at my notes for several seconds. When

I turned toward him again, he was asleep" (ibid.). The evidence here, and in other fieldworker ethnographies is often not about intervention in the life or lifeworld of the Other, or the problems of "doubling" the Other's consciousness, but a view of the informant whose life went on much as usual. This sense of the insignificance of the anthropologist in the life of the Other was not totally unremarked in these works, but reflection about it was one-sided. Where was the evidence of the informant's sense of "risk" in the field encounter? Where was the evidence of the violence of the "doubling of consciousness?" While Dwyer heavily pondered final questions, the Faqir dozed off. The Faqir could see the relevance of their talks to Dwyer's world, but we have no evidence that he saw them as significant in his own. Through Saleh, the son of the village mat maker, Dwyer continued to grapple with themes of power and domination he argued as implicit in dialogic interaction:

The encounter with Saleh in the fields provoked for me a number of questions . . . and I began to think about the ties between Morocco and Europe, between Moroccans and Europeans. . . . I also began to see that the questions themselves, although certainly provoked by the event, were tied as well to my own social and cultural situation.

Here . . . I would be posing questions about relations between Europeans and Moroccans. My involvement with the Faqir was clearly one instance of these relationships, and our questions and answers on the broader topic would inevitably comment on our ties with one another. If only indirectly, we would be talking about ourselves throughout this dialogue, and I could no longer claim even had I been so inclined before, that our dialogues were essentially an inquiry into external "objective" events. More specifically, it did not seem accidental that I had singled out for attention an event that cast a very unfavorable light on Europe's role in Morocco. This only betrayed on my part an antagonism to colonialism and imperialism that could not help but influence the kinds of questions asked. Some questions as I formulated them, seemed clearly designed to push the Faqir toward a condemnation of colonialism. (Dwyer 1982:135)

In the above instance, as is typical in fieldworker ethnographies, the interaction is recounted as between individuals, but it is interpreted as supraindividual, in this instance constructed as "Europe versus Morocco." The ethnographer (Dwyer) placed himself as a European in that setting, although he was an American. While Dwyer may have been like a European from his own point of view and that of Moroccans, the reader has no means to know this or why this would be so. It would not be surprising, for example, if Moroccans, once ruled by the French, differentiated between the French and Americans as Westerners.[3] Fieldworker ethnographies claimed to say something about the views of the Other, but in extending the net of "the West and the rest" over mundane interactions, they left out the voice of the Other. No evidence was provided that this was the view of those among whom research was conducted. As part of this extension, a second issue was intensified, since not only was there no differentiation among specific "actors" (countries, histories, habits, in short, cultures) in the confrontation between Western and non-Western selves in fieldworker ethnographies; they were pervaded by the assumption that the West was inevitably construed as playing a powerful and negative role in the cultural life of the Other. Dwyer (above) reflected on the questions he asked and recognized that they represented his own view in which the West was conceived as an imperialist, colonialist power ultimately harmful to Moroccans—a view with which he expected the Faqir to concur. However, the Faqir interpreted Western presence as an opportunity for entrepreneurs such as himself. The written account of the verbal exchange between ethnographer and Other included no dialogue about its meaning. Here was the "cultural self" played out in specific exchanges, but as was common in fieldworker accounts, no evidence of reflection on it *in situ* by either participant was included. Its "public" nature did not secure recognition, dialogue, negotiation, or resolution. Crapanzano took for granted that Tuhami shared Crapanzano's version of the West as powerful and sought to reverse that relationship when interacting with the ethnographer. "There was always something captivating about Tuhami's discourse. It was as though he wanted to entrap me, to enslave me through the power of the word in an inevitable fantasy and reality—to reverse if you will, the colonial relationship that I as a foreigner . . . must have suggested to him" (Crapanzano 1980:140). The ethnographer assumed that Tuhami *must* have understood Crapanzano as dominant in their encounter, but there was no discussion based on the interactions between fieldworker and informant of why this "must" have been so. The Panare were presented by Dumont as left with "little or no political choice" about accepting him when he appeared on the scene.[4] For Rabinow, the Other as "host" could mask the dominance of the anthropologist but the host was ultimately constrained by it. Rabinow also provided a view of himself (as a "friend," although a "rich member" of a "dominant civilization") which he claimed as the view of the Other in his presentation of his relationship with ben Mohammed. But on what basis was Rabinow's view credible as the view of ben Mohammed as an individual, or the Other as a cultural construct?

Questions about the grounds of, or evidence for, views in these accounts raise the question of the ethnographic basis for the claim that Westerners were perceived as powerful or dominant by the Other, beyond the anthropologist's own assertion.[5] The foundation for the view of anthropologists as dominant Westerners, and the basis for the perception of the West as powerful in the field setting, was implicit while the grounds for doing so were explicitly absent.

Thus, despite the call for a dialogic and negotiated construction of the cultural self, in a complicated and conflicted way, fieldworker ethnographies both took for granted and rejected power as part of the ethnographer's position. When Dwyer, concerned with his own impact as a representative of a powerful colonialist, imperialistic, and ultimately negative influence in Moroccan life, "pushed" this view, he did not have it confirmed by the native:

Despite the number of exceptions I have mentioned, the Faqir insists that the overall pattern has been beneficial. My search for a condemnation of this aspect of the colonial experience is thwarted. This happens again and again in the questions and answers that follow. (1982:256)

If the informant as Other felt subordinate to, or was wary of "the West" there was little evidence to confirm it in these accounts. So whose view was it? Dwyer illustrated an aspect of power included in, sometimes worried over, but not reflected on, in fieldworker ethnographies—the power not of the anthropologist but of the ethnographic Other. But fieldwork ethnographers included a means through which their authors emerged as powerful in the ethnographic account in a way in which they were not, as presented in the ethnographies, empowered in the ethnographic encounter itself.

POWER SURGE: WESTERN CLAIMS AS INTERPRETIVE HEGEMONY

By their own account, fieldworker ethnographers were often powerless in the politics of the field encounter, and in this sense their description of individual (and to some extent personal) experience inverted their own view of themselves as powerful. But the writer-ethnographer had the power to select among and reflect on experiences and interpretations of past events. This selection and reflection allowed the anthropologist to dominate the Other—at least on paper. To illustrate, we return to Rabinow's (1977:46ff.) account of his interaction with Ali the day following the wedding.

Although by his own account "unrepentant," Rabinow offered "profuse apologies" to Ali out of a concern that his ability to work successfully in the village might have "irreparably harmed." He also reported a more personal, psychological reaction to what he had begun to experience as a loss of identity. "If the informant was always right, then by implication the anthropologist has to become a sort of non-person, or more accurately a total persona" (1977:46).

Rabinow simultaneously "resolved" this confrontation and reasserted his own sense of identity not through the apology to Ali, itself, but through an interpretation in which he (Rabinow) emerged as powerful. Following the account of his apology, Rabinow, at home, five years later, reflected on the nature of the confrontation:

At the wedding Ali was beginning to test me, much in the way Moroccans test each other to ascertain strengths and weaknesses. He was pushing and probing. I tried to avoid responding in the counter-assertive style of another Moroccan, vainly offering instead the persona of anthropologist, all-accepting. He continued to interpret my behavior in his own terms: he saw me as weak, giving in to each of his testing thrusts. . . . Even on the way back to Sefrou he was testing me, and in what was a backhanded compliment, trying to humiliate me. But Ali was uneasy with his victories, and shifted to defining the situation in terms of a guest-host relationship. My silence in the car clearly signaled the limits of my submission. . . .

The role of the host combines two of the most important of Moroccan values. . . . The truly good host is one whose bounty, the largesse he shows his guests, is truly never-ending. . . .

If the generosity is accepted by the guest, then a very clear relationship of domination is established. The guest, while being fed and taken care of, is by that very token acknowledging the power of the host. Merely entering into such a position represents an acceptance of submission. In this fiercely egalitarian society, the necessity of exchange or reciprocity so as to restore the balance is keenly felt. Moroccans will go to great lengths and endure rather severe personal privation, to reciprocate hospitality. By so doing, they re-establish their claim to independence.

[Following my apology] . . . we had reestablished our relationship. I had in fact acknowledged him. I had, in his own terms, pulled the rug out from under him— first by cutting off communication and then by challenging his gambit in the car. There was a fortuitous congruence between my breaking point and Moroccan cultural style. Perhaps in another situation my behavior might have proved irreparable. Brinkmanship, however, is a fact of everyday life in Morocco, and finesse in its use is a necessity. By finally standing up to Ali I had communicated to him. (Rabinow 1977:45–49)

In this written resolution of the encounter as interpreted by Rabinow, he accorded himself the power to "acknowledge" Ali (a recognition we have no evidence Ali sought) by "pulling the rug out from under him" (by not giving him a culturally appropriate response), which we have no evidence Rabinow understood was available or expected. Rabinow returned from the field, reflected on the encounter, reinterpreted it (saw his own personal style as fortuitously culturally appropriate) and emerged as powerful.

Crapanzano's description of his preparations to leave the field was similarly produced at home years later:

I had to respond to Tuhami in the immediacy of our relationship. I was relieved. . . . Tuhami was relieved too. He yielded to me. He came to speak my language—the language of the "real" rather than the 'imaginary,' however sanctioned it was by his traditional idiom. I was unable at the time to recognize the putative quality of the real; I did not understand that the 'real' as well as the "imaginary" can serve a metaphorical function. The colonial relationship was restored. I was secure and could rationalize my position as protector-therapist. Tuhami accepted this reversal with ease, not simply because it is always easier to return to old ways, especially when dependency is involved, but because he could at last understand our relationship.

Although my ways were mysterious to him, their mystery itself was familiar. The ways of the Moroccan curer, like the ways of all curers, are always mysterious. (Crapanzano 1980:142–143)

Crapanzano thus "turned himself" in his role as "protector-therapist" into a kind of Moroccan curer in the resolution of his relationship with Tuhami. In a footnote he added: "I have spoken here as though only the change in *my* attitude was responsible for the change in our relationship. I have thus preempted the initiative, have declared Tuhami and myself active and free of influence, and have falsified the dynamics of our relationship. Even the most directed relationships involve a negotiation of reality by both parties" (Crapanzano 1980:143). But acknowledging the limits of his own interpretation did nothing to ground it. The negotiation which Crapanzano asserted as present was unavailable to the reader. In earlier dialogues with Tuhami (T), Crapanzano (C) as the interpreter emerged as very powerful indeed, again with no visible negotiation.

C: Were you angry at your mother?

T: No.

C: Why?

T: It was Shitan who wanted my mother to marry. My mother was working. I was working too. There was no point in her marrying. If she wanted sex, all she had to do was go out and get it and come back.

Crapanzano (1980:40) offered the following interpretation:

The displacement of motivation to Shitan, the Muslim Satan, (whom Moroccans hold responsible for sexual misdemeanors), is unsatisfactory. Moroccan sons do not refer to their mothers' sexuality. Tuhami's suggestions that his mother should satisfy her-self with anyone was a mark of extreme contempt. Despite his denial Tuhami was clearly very angry at his mother. It was she who abandoned him. Tuhami's attitude toward his stepfather . . . was more realistic.

Tuhami's view of his own life was thus subject to the re-interpretation of Crapanzano as the ethnographer *cum* psychiatrist who had the "last word" and in the process dominated Tuhami's own sense. The understandings which fieldwork ethnographers reached were negotiated through the mind of the analyst, not the interaction of participants.

UP-FRONT AND PERSONAL

Fieldwork, as described in these ethnographies, was composed of a series of encounters between individuals. Recounted from the viewpoint of the ethnographer, these encounters were inevitably, although not necessarily ex-

clusively, personal, despite ethnographers' claims that interactions were
grounded in the politics of international relationships. Despite the claim of
their significance as part of global histories, and international encounters,
fieldworker accounts were inextricably grounded in the politics of personal
ones. In the immediacy of the interaction, as reconstructed, the power of
the ethnographer over the Other, asserted as part of cultural encounters,
was not confirmed in individual interactions. The interpretation was of
power and domination in the fieldwork setting, but the experience was described as "ego dystonic" (Crapanzano 1977; cf. Devereaux 1967); one in
which the anthropologist had to "repress" rather than "express" his anxiety
about the present situation and future job prospects (Dumont 1978:46).

What sense then, is to be made of the assertion of significance, power and
domination of the ethnographer in the field and in the life of the informant?
Dwyer himself approached this question at the end of *Moroccan Dialogues*
(1982:212) and extended it to the general condition of fieldwork interaction
conceived as a wager and a paradox which "consistent with paradox itself,
we must both accept and refuse it at one and the same time." The anthropologist struggled to resolve the paradox, which (paradoxically), if it were
resolvable, would cease to be a paradox. The power and domination of
ethnographers, explicitly claimed as part of global political relationships between "the West and the Rest" enacted in the field encounter, was turned
"on its head" as the Other became the power broker in day-to-day interactions. Secure in his own surroundings, the native regularly dominated the
interaction while the ethnographer was "at risk." Accounts in fieldworker
ethnographies demonstrated that the informant could be and often was explicitly aware of the anthropologist as a particular kind of visitor—one who
needed something from him. What the ethnographer required was a particular kind of knowledge, and in the field, it was, as noted by Dumont, the
native who had it and the anthropologist who had to get it. Where the
anthropologist had to "control himself," the informant simply had to "be
himself" (Rabinow 1977:47). The fieldworker's vulnerability in these accounts was, like the terms of presentation, available but unaddressed. Here
the issues have salience as both an Anthropological question and an anthropologist's problem. The fieldwork ethnographer sought to resolve the cultural disruption to the self, *in* the ethnography through powerful Western
interpretations and psychological disruption *through* the ethnography produced as a rite of passage. Unprotected by claims of objectivity through
which Science *denied* personal dimensions of interaction between the researcher and the researched, interpretation as practiced in fieldworker accounts raised but sought to submerge personal dimensions through other
intellectual strategies, in the absence of the field encounter itself.

Power in these works was thus not established in the encounter abroad
but in reflection on it at home. Clearly, time is always a factor in the construction of ethnography, as differential forgetting and selected memories

play a substantial role—especially in the reconstruction of events which have not been specifically attended to as part of the research project. But for these purposes, more significantly, the interpretation which these anthropologists offered was not constructed through negotiation in the field as part of an ongoing series of interactions, but through reflection on past interactions. The movement back and forth was an activity of mind, not ethnographic experience. This spatio-temporal gap was critical in the production of these works as they became ethnographies of the fieldworkers' experiences. As such the power and dominance of the anthropologist was founded less in Western hegemony than in familiar but unreflected and unexplored cultural categories, which produced an interpretive hegemony by the fieldworker. It was he who ultimately spoke for both parties in the encounter, a resolution "of sorts." To the empiricist's question "*How* do you know?" can be added perhaps the first question of interpretation: "*Who* knows?" or more specifically, "Whose experience was it?"

NOTES

1. I am grateful to a student from Morocco for explaining to me that this exchange, although largely phatic, includes cultural expectations which are seriously violated when the appropriate response is not provided between friends. Even if the asker knows you are not happy, the response that you are dismisses the subject and accompanying tensions. Failure to provide the correct response results in a breach of expectations and occurs very rarely, despite underlying feelings.

2. Fieldwork as an "ego dystonic" experience (Crapanzano 1977; cf. Devereaux 1967) was a common denominator in fieldworker ethnographies but not one shared by all anthropologists, either for all members of their generation or those of other generations. Berreman (1989), when asked about his own early fieldwork, offered the following reflection:

I did research in the Aleutian Islands where there was a lot of suspicion and dislike of whites. But I was very young and looked even quite a lot younger than I was, and I got very good rapport with the village people there. But its by being doubly careful never to let them down. You know—never to pursue something they don't want you to pursue, never to tell them you won't retell it to someone else and then do so, and things like that. . . . [As for feeling like a non-person]. . . . No, I didn't experience that. . . . One thing that was true in the Aleutians, and it's true in India, is that you quickly get to feel you're like them—much more like them than you actually are. It's genuinely the case that when I see pictures of myself with them it comes as a real jolt to see, for example, how very much shorter my friend . . . the blacksmith is, than I am. I have the feeling he's just about the same height I am, but he's a very much smaller person. And of course I notice how white I look beside them . . . I was never at all integrated in the sense of, from their point of view, being one of them, but I certainly felt that I was with people who I was like, except in language and so forth . . . that we were all just people.

Here Berreman did not recall a sense of disrupted self. In contrast to fieldworker ethnographies he also did not claim a sense of "symbolic violence" as part of the field enterprise; rather, he was careful not to violate their sense of autonomy. Hymes

(1990), a member of the same generation of anthropologists as Berreman (one up from the authors of the works under discussion here), when asked a similar question regarding early field experience, responded that what he was struck by in his first fieldwork experience was "how different life could be for people, living just a hundred miles away . . . just over the mountain." Eleanor Gerber, who did fieldwork in Samoa in the early 1970s, thus a contemporary of authors producing fieldworker accounts, recalled in terms strikingly similar to Berreman's: "I started 'seeing' myself as the same color as Samoans and had a jolt when I looked in the mirror." Up until the time of our conversation she had not reported this "phenomenon" to anyone, thinking it was anomalous, and probably a function of her personality. The accounts by Hymes and Berreman suggest that Gerber's experience, similar to their own, was at least as common as the self-conscious "suffering" of fieldworker ethnographers.

3. An associated issue is the field location of fieldworker ethnographers, where they considered themselves as representative of powerful and dominant cultures in their view and the view of Others. American fieldworker ethnographers had their field experience in Morocco, a former French colony. The French ethnographer (Dumont) went to South America. This was not, of course, mere coincidence but was in part determined by historical and then present political realities in which access to the field for anthropologists of various nationalities was available in some places and not in others. French ethnographers were not welcome in Morocco. Meanwhile, Americans could not go to South America in the relevant time frame, due to U.S. government activities on that continent in which anthropologists in particular had been implicated in insurgency work (see Chapter 7).

4. The confirmation of this sense from a Panare partner was absent. Dumont, however, made less of his own power once living among the Panare. His tone throughout is less insistent on the issue of his personal power as a Westerner than is the case in the other works.

5. The lack of foundational evidence in which analysis is grounded is similar to problems of interpretation in Geertz's work. As Thompson (1990) argues in an assessment of Geertz's "Deep Play: Notes of the Balinese Cockfight" (1973):

Brilliant and imaginative though this interpretation is, Geertz does not provide any convincing defence of the claim that this is what the cockfight means to the Balinese who participate in it. He does not conduct interviews with a representative sample of participants (or if he does, he doesn't tell us) nor does he offer his interpretation to the Balinese to see whether they would regard it as an accurate rendition of their own understanding. (Thompson 1990:133–134)

Crapanzano (1986:74) also critiqued Geertz's work on the Balinese cockfight in related terms:

Despite his phenomenological-hermeneutic pretensions, there is in fact in "Deep Play" no understanding of the native from the native's point of view. There is only the constructed understanding of the constructed native's constructed point of view. Geertz offers no specifiable evidence for his attributions of intention, his assertions of subjectivity, his declarations of experience. His constructions of constructions appear to be little more than projections, or at least blurrings, of his point of view, his subjectivity, with that native, or, more accurately, of the constructed native.

Crapanzano's critique is apt for his own work, *Tuhami*. "Specifiable evidence" in *Tuhami*, as in Geertz's work on the Balinese cockfight, rests on the cogency of the interpretation (or lack of it) for the reader, rather than affirmation from the Other(s). Hermes dilemma is Geertz's and also Crapanzano's. (The phallic nature of the allusions in Geertz's text to which Crapanzano refers in "Hermes Dilemma" as well as those found in "Hermes Dilemma" introduced by Crapanzano himself, I find interesting, but leave for other analysts.)

CHAPTER 7

Come the Resolution

As graduate students we are told that "anthropology equals experience";
you are not an anthropologist until you have the experience of doing it.
But when I return from the field, the opposite immediately applies: anthropology is not the experiences which made you an initiate, but only
the data you have brought back. (Rabinow 1977:4)[1]

I use the phrase "sense of self" here to denote loosely, a reflexive awareness of a centered unity and continuity, an identity, that oscillates between reification and resistance to reification. (Crapanzano 1977:41)

YOU SAY YOU WANT A RESOLUTION

In the field, the ethnographer struggled to keep himself as a "centered
unity" while he was experientially at risk. As Rabinow (1977:154) described
it: "My gestures were wrong, my language was off, my questions were
strange, and interpersonal malaise was all too frequently the dominant
mood, even after many months when some of the grossest difficulties had
been bridged by repetition and habit. . . . The inadequacy of one's comprehension is incessantly brought to the surface and publicly displayed." The
anthropologist took the risk of becoming a "total persona" rather than a
person. He was expected to "completely subordinate one's own code of
ethics, conduct and world view, to suspend disbelief as another colleague
was proud of putting it" (Rabinow 1977:46). In fieldworker ethnographies,
the comprehension of the "requirement" of the "nonperson" failed to separate the interpretation of experience from the experience itself. Once the

anthropologist had physically left the field the process of participant observation became an intellectual process and an intellectualized product.

In these works both personal and professional selves had a stake in the
field. The neophyte anthropologist in the field was struggling with the fear
of failing at the professional task and losing the career, which had not yet
begun. Fieldwork ethnographers understood fieldwork as significant beyond
the experience itself, as a "metaphysical marker" which transcended the activity itself and gave it another level of meaning.

W(RITES) OF PASSAGE

The experience of rites of passage as liminal and anxiety-provoking is well
documented in Anthropology. Consistent with descriptions of such rites,
students of Anthropology, viewed as initiates, are ritually (following completion of certain specific requirements) separated from their everyday life
(as students, and as members of their own "lifeworld" [Schutz 1971]) and
"forced" (a degree requirement) to inhabit a different and separate reality
(the field experience). Crapanzano (1980:137) described this aspect: "The
ethnographer's entry into the field is always a separation from his world of
primary reference—the world through which he obtains and maintains his
sense of self and his sense of reality."

An important element in part of the rites of passage is the symbolic rebirth
of initiates following this separation, as they re-enter society, in this case the
society of anthropologists. Fieldwork ethnographers expected their return
from the field to incorporate the central component of these rites, a change
of status on returning from the field, manifested in professional academic
appointments. But for these anthropologists (with the exception of Crapanzano) this "rebirth" into a secure professional position took years rather
than months. Part of a general and profound change in opportunities for
anthropologists since the end of World War II, these changes were personally experienced. And for these anthropologists, the field experience as personally disruptive remained professionally unresolved in unexpected ways
after they returned home. For example, Dwyer (1982:xv), uncertain of his
aims after completing his dissertation,[2] incorporated in his fieldworker ethnography trips back to the field in 1973 and 1975 as he sought to reconstitute his professional and personal self through his relationship with the
Other. According to Dwyer:

A project that is vulnerable is one that may fail, how, then can anthropologists seriously embrace the possibility of its own failure? . . . if the anthropologist initiates
the project facing the risk of failure, it is a basis of his or her hope that the project
will be successful. Only with this hope would one become willing to stake an important part of one's life on this specific effort. (Dwyer 1982:272)

Dumont described himself as unable to settle down following his return from the field.

> I was not sure where to go. . . . The culture shock was so great that I found myself writing poetry, something I had taken up in the field to maintain my sense of identity, instead of writing my dissertation. . . . I still had the taste of manioc beer on my lips when I was asked to act as a consultant for a British television film on the Panare. . . .
>
> Revisiting the Panare under these conditions was more an escape than anything else. . . . Data collecting had now become epiphenomenal to the reality of my social experience. At the same time, revisiting Turiba Viejo as an old acquaintance rather than as an anthropologist was my way of demystifying my fieldwork. The revisiting soon came to an end. Then and only then could I begin to emerge from the opacity of the anthropological experience, upon which I could now begin to reflect with more serenity. (Dumont 1978:31)

Actual revisiting or revisiting through reflection on fieldwork and the self in that encounter, as well as the writing up of these experiences, was intended, or acted as a means for resolving the disruption of self in the field. In turn this activity was expected to constitute the anthropologist's professional identity, thus in part, reconstituting the self.

I'D BE SO NICE TO COME HOME TO

> *Q*: What about criticisms that *Reflections on Fieldwork in Morocco* is too personal?
>
> *Rabinow*: I don't understand those criticisms. I tried very hard so that it wouldn't be personal and I don't think it is. (Rabinow 1989)

Despite their quasi-autobiographical presentation, the "who" in fieldworker ethnographies was intended to be the "culturally mediated and historically situated self which finds itself in a continuously changing world of meaning" (Rabinow 1977:6). But the "I" as presented in chronologically sequenced episodes was salient for both ethnographer and Other in the specific encounters of fieldwork experience.

MIRROR, MIRROR ON THE WALL. . . .

The disruption between self and Other which fieldwork ethnographers claimed as inevitable in the field, was mirrored at home in the disruption between the intention of their works and the way in which they were read by early reviewers. While their authors intended to produce interpretations of culture negotiated between the cultural selves of anthropologists and Others (dialogic negotiations as the sieve through which the field encounter was sifted), reviews written by other anthropologists often included assessments and sometimes criticisms of these works as too personal.[3] *Moroccan*

Dialogues was described in one review as an "experiment in personalistic anthropology, followed by several chapters of reflections on the nature of ethnography itself" (Hatt 1983:380). Whitten's (1982a) review of *The Headman and I* (1978) praised Dumont's ethnographic content[4] but Whitten (ibid., 259) ended by hoping that his review would "dissuade other writers from emulating Dumont's "mode of production":

To emulate Dumont's implied standards, our mode of work might be to take our products as they now stand . . . cut each chapter into segments and paste the cut-ups together into an interesting mosaic. Then we could reminisce for a decade about our favorite subjects and paste in the reminiscences between the now broken sets of information. (ibid.)

Whitten's objection was to what he saw as a personal view presented through the ethnographer's decisions about what went into the mosaic. A "reminiscence" is, after all, a profoundly personal exercise, and further, one which ordinarily conflates emotion and memory. Henley also considered Dumont's work to give a "very good" account of what sharing daily life with the Panare was like, but went on to say:

On the other hand, I do not think that he has given an effective answer to the question of who (or what) he was for the Panare. . . . Instead he has demonstrated that much of a fieldworker's understanding of the people whom he studies derives from his own interaction with them and not merely from observing how they interact amongst themselves. (Henley 1980:205)

Rosen (1984:598) contended that throughout Dwyer's work, he "exaggerates the extent to which he himself 'constructs' the reality of which his informant speaks." Magnarella (1983:981) argued that even in the dialogic approach Dwyer suggests, "the anthropologist selects the events, poses the questions, and determines when a sufficient answer has been given." These decisions were seen as personal as well as professional ones, thus Toth's review (1983:281), for example, argued that "dwelling on the personal level diverted attention from the equally important place of supra-personal relationships which define groups, national and class inequalities."

Even reviewers uncritical of the effort in fieldworker ethnographies saw them as revealing a particular anthropologist. For instance, Daisy Dwyer (at one time married to Kevin Dwyer and a member of an extended cohort of which these ethnographers were a part) called Rabinow's *Reflections on Fieldwork in Morocco* "a valuable work, which if it has a flaw, it is perhaps that it is too well crafted in the sense that the relationships that Rabinow delineates have been described in terms of a consistency of import that likely reflects its own degree of differential forgetting" (Dwyer 1979:964). Thus, despite the ethnographers' intentions and objections, accounts of field experience as produced by Rabinow, Dumont, Crapanzano, and Dwyer were seen by diverse reviewers as products of personal interest and memory. Such reviews revealed a sense by reviewers that what was produced was a personal rather than a cultural sense-making.

It was likely that part of the reading of fieldworker ethnographies by others as personal works was the presentation of encounters and reflections on them through the "I" of the ethnographer. An unfamiliar presence in standard ethnographies at the time, the first person voice of the ethnographer represented the turn to the subjective framing as part of the effort to bridge the distance between self and Other. For other anthropologists, unused to reading accounts so presented, the presence of the ethnographer in the text was likely to signal a personal account, as had been the case in memoirs by anthropologists as well as "confessional" works. Compared to then current practice, the use of the singular personal pronoun may by itself have been sufficient for these ethnographies to be read as personal. In part, the space between the reviewer's view and the ethnographer's view illuminates a set of tensions as dilemmas which go beyond Anthropology as they reveal that lines demarking personal, cultural, and professional selves are not so easily defined, even as wholly analytic constructs. In the everyday world of practical engagement, interpretations claimed as cultural in fieldworker ethnographies were significantly a matter of professional choice of intellectual strategy through which the "personal expedition" (Dwyer 1982:xvii) was recounted. Such interpretations were in part a means through which the personal self was disclaimed. Crapanzano, for example, simultaneously asserted both the power of the interpreter and his own culturally engendered "impotence" in selecting a particular theoretical structure through which to offer an interpretation. "The reader will recognize too, especially in my questions, a psychoanalytic orientation that I have found impossible to eliminate, so embedded is this orientation in contemporary Western thought" (1980:10). However, while a psychoanalytic orientation may be embedded in contemporary Western thought, it does not inevitably permeate it to the degree or in the way in which Crapanzano used it in *Tuhami*, as its absence from other fieldworker ethnographies confirms. Further, since there was a person making the professional choice, the choice perforce has biographical and, to that extent, personal underpinnings as well. Thus, the choice of intellectual housings through which field experience was interpreted was a conscious and rationalized structure—more a strategy than a self, but one which inevitably had elements of the latter insofar as individuals were drawn to one viewpoint over another.

The term "cultural" in fieldworker ethnographies was often used to refer to various intellectual edifices constructed as means through which the confrontations between self and Other were interpreted and made meaningful. In part these edifices were used as bulwarks against criticisms in Anthropology which had derided or devalued previous experiments with the ethnographic form. In Anthropology, accounts of field experience read as "too personal" had regularly been relegated to categories such as "confessional literature" where, no matter how lucid or elucidating, they were consistently excluded as professional work, despite being produced by professionals. Fieldworker ethnographers themselves accepted this rejection of these earlier efforts, which focused on the experience of the field. Dumont, quoting Rabinow, reflected on this work in an assessment of "fieldwork literature."

> With few exceptions . . . most of this literature is confessional, undoubtedly informative about its authors and the sixties. At the same time, and not unexpectedly, it is very repetitive. The human group that the anthropologist studied became the pretext for his/her lyricism, and by the same token almost disappeared. . . .
>
> Accurately, Rabinow notes that those works which have dealt with the question of participant observation "have varied a great deal in keenness of perception and grace of style, but they all cling to the key assumption that the field experience itself is basically separate from the mainstream of theory in anthropology—that the enterprise of inquiry is essentially discontinuous from its results" (Rabinow 1977:5).
>
> And yet, I would like to take a stance less severe than Rabinow's as a judge of this literature. Indeed, I perceive the self-indulgence. But I also prefer to see in it the begun, yet unfinished movement of a programmatic dialectic, the antithesis foretelling the synthesis to come. (Dumont 1978:9)

This "synthesis" was to be found in the use of theory as a means to present the field experience. The power of the anthropologist as a participant in the field encounter was that of the cultural (*sic* intellectual) investigator. Theory provided the articulated boundary of the Anthropological self:

> Every fieldworker has experiences . . . discovery procedures through which the very articulations of the studied culture and society manifest themselves. Instead of focusing either on objects of study or on the perceiving subjects and in so doing blurring both, it seems to me that we should focus on the happening of anthropology itself, that is, on these inequities through which an authentic understanding can be constituted between the West and the rest. (Dumont 1978:35)

Crapanzano merged literary and psychological theories to frame his approach:

> My conceit is psychological. My aim is to emphasize the degree to which theory itself is a response to the encounter and also serves to formulate the encounter and its burdens or perhaps more acceptably to valorize the idiom through which the encounter and its burdens are formulated. (Crapanzano 1980:xvi)

Dwyer constructed his understanding of the fieldwork encounter as an interaction in which the field experience was a setting of risk for both anthropologist and informant, best understood as a "wager" which included "the possibility of failure and the hope of success" (Dwyer 1982:273).

REFLECTED RESOLUTIONS

In fieldworker accounts, the breakdowns necessary to produce awareness of cultural difference were reported, but there was scant evidence of their on-site examination. While such an effort may have occurred in the field, the evidence for it was missing in these accounts. Once at home, reflection on an old experience is less a process than a product. A particular aspect of the gap between work in the field and the construction of fieldworker ethnographies was that these ethnographies were ultimately the result of a reflective, rather than a reflexive project. The differentiation between "reflexion" and "reflection" suggested by Fabian (1983) in his analysis of *Time and the Other* helps to make this clearer. Fabian's "reflexion" is seen here as "reflection."[5] Fabian argued:

It may be useful to introduce a convention which distinguishes between *reflexion* qua subjective activity carried out by and revealing, the ethnographer, and *reflection* as a sort of objective reflex (like the image in a mirror) which hides the observer by axiomatically eliminating subjectivity. . . . Reflexivity asks that we "look back" and thereby let our experiences "come back" to us. Reflexivity is based on memory, i.e., on the fact that the location of experience in our past is not irreversible. We have the ability to present (make present) our past experiences to ourselves. More than that, this reflexive ability enables us to be in the presence of others precisely inasmuch as the Other has become content of our experience [*sic*]. This brings us to the conditions of possibility of intersubjective knowledge. *Somehow we must be able to share in each other's past in order to be knowingly in each other's present.* If our experience of Time were nonreflexive, unidirectional, we would not have anything but tangential knowledge of each other, on the level of interpersonal communication as well as on the collective level of social and political interaction. (Fabian 1982:90–91; emphasis in original)

Note that Fabian's notion of reflexion produces the unidirectional experience found in fieldworker accounts. The difference at this level between reflection and reflexion is analogous to the difference between looking at an image in the mirror and someone holding up a picture of him/herself and looking at the reflection of the picture in the mirror. While both are reflections, the face in the mirror is mobile, while the pictures produce multiple, but still static images. While neither of them is "the thing" itself, the reflected face is a better representation than the pictures, but both of these processes are static and, as applied to Fabian's ideas and fieldworker ethnographies, "routinely and axiomatically" eliminate the subjectivity of the Other in the present.[6] Recalling the presence of Others does not constitute the present. From this point of view, the intended aim, to produce a "re-

flexive, experiential and humanistic" (Rabinow 1977:5) account was in part
out of reach once fieldworker ethnographers had left the field.

More specifically, to be reflexive in the dialogical and dialectical sense,
which these ethnographers claimed to be, they would have had to (1) reflect
on an interaction (breakdown in communication), (2) dialogically negotiate
its meaning with the Other, (3) assimilate the jointly constructed "reality"
and then move on to the next encounter, and repeat the process from the
shifted ground of their newly constructed understanding. The continual
movement back and forth from interaction to negotiation about that interaction, to understanding that interaction, using that understanding in another interaction, and so forth, is a reflexive project. While this may have
been what happened in the actual field experience, there is little evidence of
it in these ethnographies. Instead, the geographic and temporal gap, which
separated the field experience from the analysis of it, as presented in these
works, took on an enormous significance in their production as the movement back and forth between text and context was one-dimensional. The
movement back and forth was quintessentially a look back. Just as these
ethnographers held standard ethnographies as "lifeless" as an account of a
one-sided display of data, fieldworker ethnographies "froze" the Other in
a one-sided interpretation of experience. Crapanzano, for example, critical
of the "frozen" (1980:ix) accounts in standard ethnographies created by
the subject-object split, gave evidence in the description of his encounter
with Tuhami that this gap can be created by other methods as well:

As I look back over my notes, and as I attempt to recall my meetings with Tuhami
some ten years ago, I am immediately struck by the impoverished quality of my
emotional response. My questions seem frequently cold, unemotional, and detached.
Was I frozen before Tuhami? In part, the question must be answered in the affir-
mative. There were times when my relations with Tuhami specifically or with Morocco and the 'Hamadsha more generally—the two cannot easily be distinguished—
were such that I could not permit myself any response but the most distant. It was
at such times that I took refuge in my difficulties with Arabic and exploited I suppose
the presence of Lhacen [Crapanzano's interpreter]. It was at such times, too, that I
made use of "ethnographic distance" and various theoretical positions, most notably
the psychoanalytic but others as well, to distance myself and to defend myself from
an onslaught of presumably intolerable emotions. (I should add here that Tuhami
took refuge at times in Lhacen's presence, in "ethnographic distance" as he understood it, and undoubtedly, in his own theoretical understanding of what was tran-
spiring.) (1980:139)

Crapanzano "presumes" about his own ("intolerable") emotions as well
as those of Tuhami. Where was the negotiation or affirmation of what Crapanzano saw as "undoubtedly" the case for Tuhami? Is "world view" the
same as "theoretical understanding?" There is, here and elsewhere, scant
evidence of any negotiation between self (variously defined) and Other as

asserted by fieldwork ethnographers. The movement back and forth was framed and constrained as a look back. The reflection in the ethnographer's mirror was, in central respects, his own.

Thus, while fieldwork ethnographers claimed that their works were about cultural selves, the submerged subject within the subject of participation observation was not the Other but the anthropologist reflecting on his own activity in the setting of his own cultural milieu. Dumont wrote in his opening sentence: "This book is about the Panare and me, the investigating anthropologist . . . not only will I want to discover how they gaze at me. My effort will be directed toward perceiving, apprehending and interpreting the 'and' of the relationship which my fieldwork built between an 'I' and a 'they' " (Dumont 1978:3). Crapanzano (1980:138–139) asserted (cf. Rabinow 1977:5):

Fieldwork must be understood in its temporal dimension as a process of continual discovery and self-discovery. There is considerable truth in Paul Ricoeur's involuted definition—quoted by Rabinow (1977)—of the hermeneutic as the "comprehension of self by the detour of the comprehension of the Other."

Dwyer (1982:255) revealed another aspect of the effort to "comprehend the self." "In an honest effort to appreciate and understand . . . the Other, we must as we do this, pursue the Self and try to expose it. . . . The practice of anthropology is therefore rooted in a vulnerability of the most fundamental sort." Here Dwyer referred to an analytically separable but interwoven aspect of fieldwork in which the vulnerability of the anthropologist as both a personal and professional self was revealed and was significant in the field. In fieldworker ethnographies, the objective observer of standard ethnography became the subject and objectified the Other by talking about him in his absence while claiming to take his presence into account.[7]

COME THE DEVOLUTION

Assumptions about reflection, resolution, and reconstitution in fieldworker ethnographies overturned the traditional use of participant observation as the method to produce a description of cultures, and ultimately a theory of culture. In these accounts, fieldwork as the traditional method used to produce the data of standard ethnography was inverted and became the subject of ethnography. But further, reflection, as the method used to construct fieldworker ethnographies, produced a work which was about the experience of the anthropologist rather than about the Other. The unit of analysis shifted from "the group" described by an (absent) narrator to the individual who offered an account through the voice of his own experience. Fieldworker ethnographies turned over the Anthropological enterprise as they addressed not a theory of culture, but a "theory" of fieldwork, constructed through the re-interpreted experience of the fieldworker. The cultural self, as fieldworker ethnographers claimed or intended to reveal it through their own analysis, was largely undelivered in these ethnographies. But the unexamined terms of their constructs for analysis, including the assumption of breakdowns in communication, power and domination as permeating interaction, and experience as the foundation for practice are taken here as themselves culturally constructed and salient for understanding the cultural self as revealed and linked in and through these works. In reflection, the power of the ethnographer, not in the field, but in the text. But what did these texts reflect?

NOTES

1. Rabinow demonstrates fieldwork conceived as a "rite of passage" in the beginning of *Reflections on Fieldwork in Morocco*:

I arrived in Paris in June of 1968, several days after police had cleared the last students from the faculty of medicine. . . . I met a girl. . . . As we wandered by the Seine, the war-like atmosphere and uncertain future made me feel like a character in one of Sartre's novels, very existential. Two days later I had my hair cut . . . and left for Morocco.

Rabinow mentioned this preparation for going to the field, but did not examine it. I note that in having his hair cut he participated in a common initiation into a rite of passage as described by anthropologists.

2. Dwyer did fulfill the academic requirement in the form of his dissertation on entrepreneurial activity in Morocco (1974). He did not, as the others did, produce a first, more standard ethnographic work. I do not know whether this was by choice or by design, considering his articulated reservations (Dwyer 1977, 1979) about Anthropology. While the other fieldwork ethnographers took part-time, then full-time academic positions, Dwyer went to work for Amnesty International.

3. Fieldworker ethnographies were often reviewed by other fieldwork ethnographers. Comments from these reviews are not included in the following discussion.

4. Dumont's was the only fieldworker ethnography cited by reviewers for its "cultural" content.

5. Alexander (1995) describes Sartre's conception of the actor in which has relevance to this discussion in content, as well as Sartre's identification by fieldwork ethnographers as significant in their work. In contrast to fieldwork ethnographers, "Sartre's conception of the actor insists on role distance, self-consciousness, and a projective orientation to the future."

6. Further, while the past can be recalled in the present, it does not constitute the present, and its "recall," as indicated by contemporary memory research, is more properly understood as a "rehearsal" since memories are never recalled the same way twice because they are always sifted through present context and content.

7. This inverted Fabian's critique of traditional ethnography. Fabian argued:

On the one hand we dogmatically insist that anthropology rests on ethnographic research involving personal, prolonged interaction with the Other. But then we pronounce upon the knowledge gained from such research a discourse which construes the Other in terms of distance, spatial and temporal. The Other's empirical presence turns into his theoretical absence, a conjuring trick which is worked with the help of an array of devices that have the common intent and function to keep the Other outside the Time of anthropology. (Fabian 1983:xi)

In fieldworker ethnography, the use of reflection occurs only in the Other's theoretical presence and is fundamentally produced in his empirical absence.

PART III

An Interpretation of Culture: Crisis at Home

CHAPTER 8

We Hold These Truths
to Be Self-Evident

This chapter traces some of the interactions between American anthropologists and the public realm[1] through the activity of the American Anthropological Association as a professional organization and the activities of anthropologists as citizens and scientists, particularly in the 1960s and 1970s. In Anthropology, the struggle with disciplinary identity, and specifically the terms of objectivity, was neither unique to fieldwork ethnographers nor limited to theoretical argument. It was in the broad American political arena that the struggle of anthropologists to engage the terms of objectivity in the field was brought home. Juxtaposition of American political events with the politics and politicization of the Association of American anthropologists reveals some of the American content of American anthropology.

I OBJECT

Part of the struggle of American anthropologists in both professional and public realms has been the product of the objectivity, which Anthropology claimed for itself as a science. In theory, strict definitions of science defined the boundaries of objectivity and required it in two venues: (1) the context of research and (2) the context in which research is applied (the public realm). In both these venues neutrality was a required "by-product" of objectivity. But, examination of events and discussion in the professional realm from the end of World War II through the early 1970s reveals anthropologists struggling to make sense of and address the public realm, and exposes shifting boundaries of science in the complex relationship between disciplinary, professional, and public realms. In this context, the turn to subjectivity as part of fieldworker ethnographies was part of a continuous chain of Anthropological definition and re-definition. Despite the differences in practice experienced in the field and manifest in ethnography, the "past is present" as intellectual dogma and human activity come face to face.

In significant ways, when objectivity was abandoned in fieldworker ethnographies, it was consistent with an ongoing Anthropological project; a project which, despite the claims and demands of positivists as purists, was often linked to the public realm. While these links were powerful in their own right, the power of these realms to affect each other has been differential and often lopsided.

Although anthropologists, including fieldwork ethnographers, often claimed and accused each other (and occasionally themselves) of manifesting power in public settings, there is little evidence that Anthropology has overall been taken very seriously as a policy science. (This is not to say that its findings have not been used to carry out policies.) Alternatively, the power of the public realm has both practical implications (i.e., in barriers and opportunities for anthropologists, both geographic and financial) and implications for practice (what are the boundaries of the anthropologist as scientist and as citizen?). The issues of the public realm impinged on practice as anthropologists struggled to reset the boundaries of their practice as scientists.

ANTHROPOLOGISTS AND THE SCIENTIFIC BASIS OF CITIZENSHIP

The post–World War II effort by anthropologists to attain and/or maintain separations between scientist and citizen in the professional and public realm was linked to issues of objectivity and neutrality, and sheds light on the ways in which public events frayed and tangled these boundaries. On the one hand, science demanded objectivity, but objectivity, as linked to neutrality, had been largely forfeited during the war, as well-known anthropologists, including Margaret Mead, Ruth Benedict, Geoffrey Gorer, and Gregory Bateson, went to work for the U.S. government to help in the war effort. The separation of the scientist and citizen, always a potentially troubled one, was compounded by the concomitant role asserted within the American Anthropological Association that confined its activities to those of a "purely scientific organization."

THE BATTLE OVER SCIENCE

Following World War II, the American Anthropological Association, at the request of the United Nations, prepared a Statement on Human Rights (AAA 1947:539–543) which was presented as scientific, despite the fact that there were no scientific grounds or findings on which it could be, or was, based. Human rights claimed as part of the Statement (for example, to equality, liberty, and the "pursuit of happiness") were philosophically established in the Enlightenment, set out in American founding documents, and (by implication) valued in the United States, but were neither objectively researched nor empirically demonstrable. In scientific terms, there were no objective research and no empirical findings to validate the claims that humans had any rights whatsoever, let alone the specific ones included in the American Declaration of Independence and repeated in the AAA Statement on Human Rights. In the nation, laws protected these rights, and in the discipline, cultural relativism, used since Boas as a means to claim objectivity sought to protect them, but no claim could be made for their basis in science. (This was especially true in the case of the Statement since specific, negative references to Nazi Germany were sprinkled throughout.)

Reaction to the Statement by a large number of members of the Association was primarily directed to the impossibility and inadvisability of producing any document under the terms required by science. Here the quarrel was not with the terms of science, but with the issuance of a statement, which had no basis in science. It was considered appropriate for scientific findings to be used as the basis for the Statement. The problem was that there were no such findings. Thus, it was argued that scientific positions could not be taken on human rights because that would entail an evaluation of human relationships in terms of some absolute, universal set of values. The absence of scientific methods adequate to establish such a set of values made claims and documents based on them impossible.

Anthropologists thus sought to re-define their practice. As scientists, some anthropologists argued they could not base statements on values, which they held as citizens and as Americans, including those reflected in particular forms of justice and governance. For example, rights to equality, freedom, and democratically elected representatives were clearly set out in the statement. Other anthropologists argued that objections raised were intellectually and theoretically cogent, but in practice, neutrality in the face of recent world events (i.e., the Holocaust) was not acceptable. While at this point anthropologists did not make their own values explicit by directly stating them, they had, during the war years, publicly excoriated German scientists who stayed neutral in Germany. Even anthropologists holding positivist and "pure science" views argued that during World War II neutrality had to be abandoned (there is no evidence that this was extended to all wars). But they also argued that its abandonment had been an abandonment of science itself. Now that the crisis was over, anthropologists as scientists were, in the view of these anthropologists, obligated to return to objective and neutral positions. For instance, Julian Steward, the first president of the Society for Applied Anthropology, argued against the publication of the Statement by the AAA:

The Board was asked to do the impossible when asked to keep political stands and
value judgments out of the Statement. . . . We have gotten out of our scientific mode
and are struggling with contradictions. During the war, we gladly used our professional techniques and knowledge to advance a cause but I hope that no one believes
that we had a scientific justification for doing so. As individual citizens, members of
the Association have every right to pass value judgments and there are some pretty
obvious things that we would all agree on. As a scientific organization, the Association has no business dealing with the rights of man. I am sure that we shall serve
science better and I daresay that we shall eventually service humanity better if we
stick to our purposes. (AAA 1947:352)

Homer Barnett (AAA 1947:352–355), who in his professional work was
a proponent of a strictly enacted version of science (positivist), articulated a
variant of Steward's position. In common with Steward, Barnett held objectivity as modeled on the natural sciences as appropriate for Anthropology
as a discipline and the role of the Association. However, he took a step that
Steward did not by subscribing to the view that it was not always possible
to sustain such a position. But in those instances, it was the obligation of
the Association to make its reasons and its reasoning explicit.

(There will be) times when the Association must support proposals and movements.
. . . Then let us admit, either tacitly or explicitly that we have an axe to grind and
dispense with the camouflage. Above all, let us not delude ourselves that in defining
the right, the true and the just we are building upon the "firm foundation of the
present day scientific knowledge of Man". . . . In light of the failure of the Statement
submitted on behalf of the Association to meet scientific standards, we must conclude
that the performance of anthropologists as professed scientists, was not very promising. We can do an excellent job of reporting and analyzing, but beyond that we
are badly confused. And as long as we cannot ourselves divorce our opinions from
our facts we cannot expect others to take us at face value as scientists. (ibid.:354)

Barnett here alluded to the values embedded in the statements such as
the "right to justice" as insufficient for scientific statements about human
rights. As argued by Steward and Barnett, the dilemma that faced those
authoring the Statement had two possible resolutions: (1) to make no scientific claims for the assertions in such a Statement or (2) to produce no
Statement at all. Since the former position meant that there would be nothing in the Statement that had a valid claim as knowledge, the latter was the
better option. Both of these views were consistent with the increasingly
positivist versions of science that took center stage in the 1950s. But John
Bennett, who in 1948 analyzed the "Redfield-Lewis debate" (an earlier
version of the Mead-Freeman debate in Anthropology) as the product of
observer focus, critiqued the Statement not on the basis that it was not
scientific, but on the basis that science was so rigidly defined and applied.
Bennett (AA 1948:329–333) argued that Steward's view was incomplete

because it assumed that science can escape from the dilemmas presented by world events by selectively withdrawing from them, using adherence to its own practice as a justification. Barnett's view assumed that scientific behavior was readily separable and distinguishable from other systems of behavior and that such separation could be achieved by pronouncement.

Bennett argued that withdrawal from the world of social interaction was only theoretically possible. Even if it were to be accomplished it meant that anthropologists would abandon data to others who wished to use it, but would have no certainty about their motives. In the "contemporary period" (the period immediately following World War II) Bennett saw this as especially significant "where all actions have come to hold political significance and most especially the case in the social sciences, where the nature of much of the data precludes any simple distinction between "fact" and "value" (ibid.).[2] Bennett went on to argue that the views of both Steward and Barnett although different in some respects, reached the same conclusions, that "any science which accepts values as guides to research is therefore not science" (1948:329). This view, he went on to argue, was "too rigid and logistic" (note here similarities with postmodern arguments that modern social science is too "logocentric"—see Rosenau 1992), since all social science accepted values and valuationally determined premises to some extent, and these issues had been addressed by other social sciences, but not by Anthropology.

According to Bennett, in practice anthropologists had been compromising scientific logic for years,[3] but this was to be expected since "Scientific behavior and knowledge are part of social life. On the whole it is healthy that American anthropologists have at long last been forced to thresh out among themselves these ancient and respected problems. Withdrawn from the world of social debate and ideology for so many generations, American anthropology is now out in the open" (ibid.:333).

The issues may have been out in the open, but the rise of positivism in the 1950s as part of the press of the public realm, especially as the growth of technology was linked to the success of the sciences, marginalized potential problems of science. In the view of many Americans, science "worked" in practical and visible ways. In those terms, the social sciences and humanities suffered by comparison. Further, while the Statement on Human Rights engendered discussion on the relationship between fact and value, objectivity, neutrality, and science, the debate and the Statement were largely academic and in some respects, empty exercises. First, there was no context in which the Statement was used as a legitimating document. For example, there was (and is) no evidence that it provided, or was intended to provide, authority for actions of the United Nations. Second, although one argument claimed that value positions were not an appropriate (proven) foundation and must be removed from practice, and the other position claimed that such positions could be (should be) taken as given "truths," and could not be removed from practice, there was no elucidation of the values themselves. Directed to the "outside" world, the arguments in Anthropology remained removed from it, but these arguments are significant for what they say about its American imprint. Specifically, the significance of this document and AAA resolutions discussed below are relevant here for (1) their effects in the discipline and definitions of the profession and the professional self; and (2) their display of the American cultural self through the positions which American anthropologists regularly took for granted. In the sections which follow, debates in the Association regarding dilemmas of science and practice are used to reveal *a priori* American positions through which American anthropologists made sense of ongoing events in the public realm which formed and informed disciplinary practice.

"ENLIGHTENED" RESOLUTIONS

In 1960, when the American civil rights movement was part of the national agenda of social activists, the Association passed the Resolution on Race (AAA 1961[2]:2) which stated in part: "There is no scientific evidence for the biological inferiority of Negroes. . . . All races possess the abilities needed to participate fully in a democratic way of life and in modern technological civilizations." The AAA's view that this resolution was directed beyond the Association to the public realm was clear, as following the passage of the resolution its text was immediately distributed to national newspapers.

The Resolution on Race claimed scientific evidence (which was more specifically at the time a lack of negative evidence) to state the right and ability of Negroes to participate as equals in American society. Science ostensibly provided the authority for passage, making such a resolution tenable for a self-proclaimed scientific organization. But rather than embodying scientific findings, it clearly embodied value positions submerged under the aegis of science. Sherwood Washburn, physical anthropologist and president of the Association, spoke out in support of the resolution, using Enlightenment values as expressed in American documents as the authority for scientific findings. According to Washburn:

The Founding fathers were wise to join life, liberty and the pursuit of happiness, because these are intimately linked in the social and cultural system just as the restriction of social and economic opportunities reduces intelligence, so it reduces length of life. . . . Human biology finds its realization in a culturally determined way of life, and the infinite variety of genetic combination can only express themselves efficiently in a free and open society (Newsletter 1961:522).

Claims for equality were linked to "liberty" and "happiness" and in turn to human biology which, in order to "express" itself "efficiently," required a "free and open society." Thus Washburn specifically linked equality and freedom as causally related, "required," to human biological functioning, stating it as a finding of science. However, there were "findings" of science which, contrary to those logically constructed by Washburn (based on *a priori* cultural and Anthropological premises in which "liberty," "happiness," and "freedom" were taken as truths), lent support to difference rather than likeness between and among races. In fact, much of the data amassed by anthropologists on race before the 1960s were from projects that claimed to establish rather than deny physical differences between and among the races, including size of cranial case, morphology, facial features, and so on. As Lowie (1949) had argued in an earlier discussion on race in the Association, anthropologists and others had proved that there *were* differences between the races. When Washburn (Newsletter 1961:523) spoke on behalf of the Resolution on Race he dismissed earlier findings by anthropologists which detailed differences between and among races as the product of observer focus (cf. Bennett 1946) an argument which (at least implicitly) cast the objectivity (therefore scientific integrity) of earlier generations of anthropologists into doubt.[4] According to Washburn (ibid.), in past research: "Anthropologists were so concerned with the subdivisions within our species and with minor detailed differences between small parts of the species that the physical anthropologist forgot that mankind is a species, and that the important thing is the evolution of this whole group, not the minor differences between its parts." Despite the clear social and political implications of this resolution and its even clearer underpinnings in Enlightenment views "masquerading" as science, the resolution passed without debate. Here, American "cultural logic" (which in central respects coincided with professional "Anthropological logic"), grounded by constructions of social equality, was implicit but not specifically addressed or argued. Questions that might have been raised concerning observer focus (i.e., were there cultural "presses" that made differences more interesting than similarities, that sought such differences for social and political purposes etc.?) or scientific findings (if there were differences, what difference did such differences make?) went unraised and unaddressed. The criticisms that might have been leveled at "careless" physical anthropologists who "forgot" that "mankind is a single species" were swept aside. The rhetoric of the resolution and supporting statements revealed that equality of the races, and associated social goals, were held to be appropriate and shared by American anthropologists.

Similarly, resolutions "memorializing others" (Goldschmidt 1984), for example, those passed after the assassinations of President Kennedy and Martin Luther King, also made explicit value statements, yet went undebated. In these resolutions the Association's membership pledged to work toward the ends valued by these men in their lifetimes, including particular social goals which again revealed values placed on equality and other presupposed human rights (e.g., to the "pursuit of happiness" attained through fair housing practices and the end of poverty, discrimination, and racism). Equality, particularly of opportunity, was supported without discussion in the resolution following President Kennedy's assassination. The AAA annual meeting was being held at the time of Kennedy's death, and within a few hours the following resolution reflecting American beliefs regarding freedom and equality passed unanimously without further comment.

We as members of the AAA and as individuals pledge to President Johnson to continue to press toward the larger goals for which President Kennedy lived, worked and died. The promotion of the welfare of every region of our country with special concern for the depressed such as the culturally deprived and the poor. The protection of the freedom and dignity of every American of every race, creed and color. The advancement of freer communication among the peoples of the world so that the safety and well-being of all mankind may be realized.

Here anthropologists crossed boundaries established in previous Association practice,[5] by coalescing categories of citizen and scientist ("as members of the AAA and as individuals"). This resolution as well as the one which condemned the assassination of Martin Luther King as a racist act were worked out from cultural logics which claimed "truth" in political positions, based on moral (value) grounds. The King resolution was claimed as appropriate for professional consideration (the claim itself evidencing an unspoken concern with crossing the "line" into events of concern to citizens) when King's assassination was stated as "symptomatic of the kind of tendencies against which anthropologists have traditionally fought" (Newsletter 1968[7]:2). To be against racism was accepted as consistent with the findings of science (see also the Resolution on Race), as well as firmly and explicitly rooted in the authority of past professional (taken for granted as scientific) practice. Justification for the resolution was rooted in "truth" and no discussion of why anthropologists "traditionally fought" against these kinds of "tendencies," or even whether there was clear evidence that they had done so, was held.

As part of the King resolution, there was also a request that the AAA "establish a special committee to see how anthropological material can be used to combat racism and its asocial effects" (ibid.). Such activity was seen as consistent with other educational projects directed to the public realm undertaken by the Association. Supporters contended: "If it was appropriate for the Association to support educational projects such as curriculum studies . . . it is equally appropriate for it to sponsor some particular activities related to combating racism" (ibid.). The specifics through which these activities were held as analogously appropriate were unaddressed. AAA involvement in the subject of racism, including calls for equality, was claimed (and accepted insofar as no dissenting views appear in the Newsletter which at the time had a policy of printing all letters) as a reasonable scientific and educational issue rather than addressed as a political or moral position based in particular values. Efforts to combat racism were validated as a matter of education, and value positions were submerged under the cloak of reasonable curriculum (see also the "Teaching Anthropology" column, Chapter 10).

While the Resolution on Race and "memorial resolutions" embodying American values passed without discussion, there were other resolutions proposed and passed in the same time frame which provoked serious discussion and in some cases divisive debate. These debates demonstrated what happened when the terms of proposed resolutions were not so easily agreed to for political, logical, or professional reasons—when the constructs with which Americans approached the social world conflicted with each other, as their contents and contexts were viewed as more complex. In such cases, there were no pre-eminent, presumptive common grounds, leaving room for difference and division. These resolutions and their underpinnings were not taken for granted but were argued by those opposed to them (but not those supporting them) as explicitly invoking value positions. Both sides turned to the appropriate (professional) grounds of resolutions, that is, their foundation in science; supporters agreed that resolutions must be rooted in science, and argued that they were. Opponents disagreed.

DISARMING THE DISARMAMENT RESOLUTION

The Disarmament Resolution, proposed by outgoing president Margaret Mead and biologist and social activist Barry Commoner, was introduced as a "response to groups of younger men from both sides of the continent . . . eager to do something significant in the present world crisis" (Newsletter 1961[7]:4). This introduction itself casts doubt on later claims by Mead and others that it was introduced for scientific reasons. The "crisis" in this case was the Cold War. "Younger men" in this instance was a reference to the growing number of anthropologists entering the profession after World War II.[6] Passed in the same year as the Resolution on Race had passed undebated, the Disarmament Resolution passed, but its passage was followed by two years of debate. The Disarmament Resolution began:

Whereas as anthropologists, we recognize that mankind, a single interconnected biological species is now threatened with the possibility of extinction through methods and preparations of modern warfare, nuclear, biological and chemical; be it therefore resolved (1) . . . in cooperation with other scientific groups and associations here and abroad (2) to call upon governmental bodies, federal, state and local, to make fuller use of anthropology and other human sciences in pursuit of our stated policy of the search for disarmament and the search for peace and; (3) that individual anthropologists seek appropriate opportunities within their professional competencies to develop with colleagues in other disciplines, ways and means to ensure the survival and well-being of our species.

In the opening sentence of their proposed resolution, Mead and Commoner asserted a common ground with the Resolution on Race, and based their own statement in the "unity of the species of mankind." The Resolution on Race argued as based in the "biological unity of mankind" was taken as a standard, since (1) it had passed and (2) as part of its passage its claimed scientific basis had been "established," *ergo* its passage could be used as a precedent. Further, since Anthropology along with other sciences, social and otherwise, was *for* the survival of the species (a position not rooted in science), the proposers also suggested that the "search for peace" should be undertaken "in cooperation with scientific organizations and associations here and abroad" to "ensure the survival and well-being of the species" ("well-being" was similarly undefined, but is consistent with classical and Enlightenment underpinnings expressed as valued aspects of definitions of the "good society"[7]). The resolution was thus situated by its authors as consistent with: (1) scientific practice, (2) Anthropology as a discipline (a focus on the human species, crossing national boundaries, etc.), (3) Association past practice, and (4) the aims of other scientific organizations. (There was no evidence presented that other scientific organizations agreed with or were pursuing such an effort.) Submerged in the phrase "a single connected biological species" were asserted positions in American documents which in the 1960s were being "newly" re-interpreted as part of legitimating American documents, regarding the equality of "men" interpreted as others, including women, races, ethnicities.

Objection to the Disarmament Resolution was primarily centered on its "fundamentally unscientific" position as it trespassed on boundaries of scientific objectivity and neutrality. Rather than arguing against value-laden and contextually relevant assumptions (the same resolution would not have been likely in 1945) that peace was better than conflict, the argument was against disarmament as a means for peace. That is, in the absence of research demonstrating that disarmament was a necessary or even useful condition for peace, such a resolution could not claim to represent scientific findings. Further, not only was the resolution seen as endorsing a course of action (disarmament) unacceptable to science due to the lack of study showing that it would work; it was argued that serious problems of scientific ethics, the role of Anthropology as a discipline, and the relationship of individual anthropologists to the group as a whole were raised by its passage (Newsletter 1961[9]:2). Specifically cited in this debate was the stated position of the AAA that as a professional organization it did not endorse scientific pressure groups or take political stands. This position had been repeatedly challenged and solidified through the 1950s when McCarthy's House Un-American Activities Committee nearly annihilated free speech in the United

States.[8] Taking political stands was argued as inappropriate because it meant that a position was not taken on the basis of science but on the basis of some subjective judgment which had no place in the activity of a professional organization. Opponents concluded that the Disarmament Resolution was unscientific because it placed Anthropology "in the field of politics as much as if we had contributed as a group to support of a major political party" (Herskovits, Newsletter 1961[9]:2). The dilemmas argued by anthropologists over the Statement of Human Rights a decade earlier had not gone away, they had shifted. The claim to survival and "well-being" of the species went unchallenged as lacking in science. Instead, the challenge by those arguing insufficient science focused on disarmament as a proposed solution for which there was no empirical evidence, and other arguments were characterized as partisan and political rather than scientific.

In response to arguments against it, supporters of the Disarmament Resolution stated that critics had misunderstood—the resolution was not a program for peace (which had clear political implications) but a search for peace. The resolution, they contended, was not political but scientific, since it called for empirical study. All solutions were to be objectively studied and given equal consideration (Newsletter 1962[9]:4) (itself consistent with American constructs regarding equality, insofar as science does not demand equal consideration except when alternatives are empirically established as equally valid). From this position, supporters asserted their objectivity (necessary for science), but their position on neutrality was unclear. If doing "something significant" in the present "world crisis" meant only doing empirical studies on avenues that might lead to peace (which also included the assumption of peace as a good), then there was a less serious problem for those who demanded "pure science" than if having done the studies, anthropologists worked to implement the results. (Even when results could be validated, scientists were not seen as policy makers.) Practice, in this sense, was unacceptable. Objectivity as well as neutrality were argued as requirements of science, and further, all alternatives must be held as theoretically equal unless method or empirical evidence proved them unequal.

The exchange regarding the terms of the resolution and whether such resolutions could ever be appropriate went on for two years, evidence that the significance of the issues transcended the particular resolution. When placed side by side with the Resolution on Race, it is clear that underlying value positions and the ways in which they were construed in interaction with the public realm were at stake. The Resolution on Race was at this time no more firmly rooted in science than the Disarmament Resolution. Undebated, it represented a value position regarding equality and rights that was consistent with tenets of American Anthropology (and anthropologists, at least as evidenced by its passage), which were in accord with typically American conceptions. The Disarmament Resolution did not have any such "protection" despite the efforts by its authors to similarly ground it.

But also of significance here was a third position which entered the fray at the end of the debate (whether the debate had simply run its course, or the third position changed its course is unclear), but which received no written response from either of the sides previously engaged. The third "voice" charged those involved in the debate thus far with having mistaken its terms. Speaking from a third perspective, a "younger" (albeit female, cf. Mead 1961) (Newsletter 1961[7]:4) anthropologist, Muriel Hammer (Newsletter 1963[9]:6), reflected neither the position of supporters nor opponents. Hammer's view broke with familiar disagreements about objectivity and neutrality. She argued instead that objectivity in anthropological practice was impossible and further, that it was undesirable insofar as it was (inappropriately) enacted as neutrality. (This is consistent with revisionist positions to be discussed, and is evidence that such thinking was already percolating among [especially] younger anthropologists.) Despite the differences in how they made sense of the specific content of the resolution, both opponents and supporters claimed that Anthropology as a science was appropriately objective. Their disagreement was over whether (1) what was being proposed was an empirical study or an assertion of a viewpoint, and (2) whether anthropologists had a role in the public realm. In Hammer's view, these elements could not be separated. An empirical study was inevitably the product of a viewpoint, and was formed and informed by contexts outside the discipline:

Science, is produced by scientists, i.e. people, and is affected by what these people are interested in. . . . The purist definition which ignores the complex of extra-scientific variants necessarily involved in any scientific account may be comforting to some scientists but they are inadequate and misleading as guides in the practice of science. The question is not *whether* science affects the world—it does. The scientist can consider *how* it affects the world . . . or he can blindly contribute to the world's damnation (as he is often paid to do). (Newsletter 1963[9]:3) (emphasis in original)

After two years the debate disappeared from the pages of the Newsletter at a time when the policy was to publish all letters. More abandoned than resolved, it arose with new intensity later in the decade.

THE BATTLE BEGINS: THE UNSCIENTIFIC BASIS OF CITIZENSHIP

The assassination of Kennedy and the escalation of the evil fiasco in Viet Nam changed anthropology, as it did the nation. I would date the beginning of this effect on our profession with the Denver meeting of the AAA in 1965, when the anthropological involvement in Chile in the proposed counter-insurgency research of the U.S. Department of Defense . . . became public knowledge and we became aware that anthropology had become a "policy science." (Goldschmidt 1984:167)

As anthropologists habitually crossed into non-Western countries for the very substance of their work, they and Anthropology were involved in events and activities outside the United States, sometimes peripherally sometimes substantially. In the 1960s, this involvement was powerfully brought to public attention in (negative) press coverage of anthropologists doing research in Chile as part of Project Camelot, in which anthropologists were accused of participating in U.S. counter-insurgency in that country (see Horowitz 1967a). This marked the beginning of a series of events in the 1960s and 1970s identified as crises by anthropologists active in the American Anthropological Association; crises which "began" in the public realm, pushed on the professional realm, and pressed on anthropologists and the definitions and boundaries of American anthropological practice.

CRISIS IN THE FIELD: FROM CAMELOT TO THAILAND

As part of their complaint against Americans working in Chile on a U.S.-sponsored research grant, Project Camelot, the Chilean Chamber of Deputies charged that American troops had been stationed in the Dominican Republic to intervene in any Chilean uprising. Of most concern to American Anthropology was the Chilean government's charge that the placement of these troops was the direct result of information supplied by anthropologists (and others) through Project Camelot. This charge led to the closing of doors to American social science research as foreign governments and scholars increasingly saw American research overseas as a tool of specific American policies, thereby serving political, not scientific, ends. American scientists were claimed as a threat to those among whom research was carried out—a crisis of faith in American credibility and the credibility of American researchers, which led to a perceived crisis in the discipline. As executive director of the AAA, Stephen Boggs stated: "No issue in the past several years has led to so much concern" (Newsletter 1965[1]:1).

Despite denials of political purpose by those involved in Project Camelot, its sponsorship by agencies of the U.S. government heightened suspicions that anthropological research was being used to further American foreign policy abroad. Charges that American universities regularly served as cover for intelligence operations were strengthened following press reports involving a U.S. Central Intelligence Agency (CIA) training project undertaken by Michigan State University in Vietnam. There were immediate international repercussions which impacted on American social science following the report of this new project. For example, a new research foundation in India proposed by President Johnson, with American scholars as part of its staff, was rejected by indigenous scholars on the grounds that it might be a cover for espionage. The Venezuelan government began to question ongoing projects in Venezuela set up by the Massachusetts Institute of

Technology, which had, as it turned out, previously unrevealed direct support from the CIA. The AAA Newsletter headlined a report ("Defense Department to Invade University" [Newsletter 1965[3]:3]; see also "Science" [February 3, 1967]) that the U.S. Defense Department was planning to establish up to fifty new interdisciplinary centers involving more than 400 universities in the United States.

These charges and their implications were considered serious enough to involve President Lyndon Johnson. (The specific aspects of these events Johnson and his advisors saw as most serious were not part of the Newsletter discussion). In response to the charges regarding American researchers and government funding and activities, Johnson directed the study of government-subsidized research projects in the social sciences. The State Department's Foreign Affairs Research Council was formed to meet the presidential directive to "assure the propriety of government sponsored social science research in the area of foreign policy" (Newsletter 1966[1]:11). Additionally, the Office of Science and Technology empaneled by President Johnson in January 1966 was charged with examining "privacy and behavioral research," and proposing appropriate guidelines. In the meantime, one of the consequences of the ties among U.S. government agencies, American universities, and individual researchers was a growing lack of access by anthropologists to other countries for whatever the stated purpose of research. As noted earlier, American anthropologists, including fieldwork ethnographers, were largely barred from doing research in South America, in part because of the strong feelings created by Project Camelot and MIT research in Venezuela. (Meanwhile, Dumont, born in France, worked in South America, rather than in Morocco where France had been a colonial presence.) Problems for American researchers were compounded because governments and universities outside the United States usually made no distinction between privately sponsored and government-sponsored research (AAA 1965[8]:2). Even if anthropologists refused government funding there were countries unwilling to allow them entry as anthropologists, specifically as American anthropologists.

As part of the discussion of problems of access and government-sponsored research, standards of ethics set up by the profession arose as a specific and powerful subject of discussion. A clear statement of acceptable practice was argued as necessary to the survival of the profession. Whatever guidelines came from the government, the profession itself had to make a statement on its own behalf. The pattern of secrecy in which foreign countries were unaware of funding sources and in which even anthropologists were often unaware of the "bottom line" source of funding or those to whom information was to be made available, cast a serious shadow over statements by the American government, American universities, and American researchers. It was argued that if anthropologists could not be trusted by foreign governments, not only their ability as individual researchers to carry out research was in jeopardy, but the future of Anthropology itself was threatened. Widespread and often argumentative concern was voiced at the AAA annual meeting in 1965 as professional ethics became identified as the primary issue in what was now clearly labeled a "crisis . . . more serious than any since the reorganization of the Association in 1946" (Newsletter 1966[3]:1). The Association sought to deal with this crisis in part by issuing a Statement of the Relation of Anthropology to Government Problems of Foreign Area Research. The statement cited problems since the end of World War II concerning the integrity of social sciences and American universities, and asserted that it would support all efforts to prevent intelligence agencies from using academic research to carry out their operations (Newsletter 1966[6]:7).

As a result of the obvious disquiet at the Denver meeting of the AAA in 1965 (see Goldschmidt 1984), Boggs undertook a survey of anthropologists concerning collaboration with colleagues abroad, including an estimate of future impediments to research in their geographic areas. Ralph Beals was appointed voluntary chair of a new AAA Committee on Research and Ethics formed to study appropriate boundaries of government involvement in Anthropological research (Newsletter 1966[3]:1).

The AAA executive board specifically responded to Project Camelot in a statement sent to the *Washington Post* (July 8, 1966) in which they asserted that universities should not undertake activities unrelated to normal teaching, research, and public functions. Further, full disclosure of funding sources and purposes of research were to be made, along with public reporting of the results subject to protection of personal privacy of those studied or assisting in research.

As lines of professional and national interest crossed, Anthropology was increasingly in the public eye. The U.S. Senate Committee on Government Research requested testimony from representatives of the AAA. As those representatives, Boggs and Beals testified on the appropriate relationship between the government and social science. Boggs, having just completed his survey of anthropologists returning from fieldwork, testified that there was a widespread impression overseas that most U.S. social researchers exploit people to a degree by gaining information which they take home and use for their own purposes without any return to the host country, or any concern with advancing the study of similar problems by professionals in the host country. According to Boggs:

This . . . charge is almost unknown outside the profession and not widely known even by my colleagues. It has not yet appeared in the press. But it constitutes another example of what the term "neo-colonialism" means in the developing areas of the world. It means to put it briefly, treating the world as if it were your oyster; exploiting the world on your own terms rather than with an eye to the needs of the people, though they are supposed to be alert to these needs; to look no further than their own needs when they go abroad to do research. (Newsletter 1966[9]:1)

Both Boggs and Beals saw these charges against American social scientists as serious and widespread. In their view gathering information and data which could never be made available to the public did not constitute scientific research and should not be so represented (ibid.). This position was consistent with the one set forth several years later in the Principles of Professional Responsibility (1971). These anthropologists added the *use* of research and its availability to all audiences to the criteria of what constituted acceptable science. This position was reiterated by the Ethics Committee of the AAA several years later and was part of the viewpoint represented by Berreman in his 1970 run for the presidency of the AAA (as well as in the professional ethics statement which Berreman helped to write).[9] Boundaries between the professional and public realm, never comfortably defined, were increasingly subject to re-interpretation. What was clear in conception was muddled in context. Was science defined by responsibilities as well as methods? What were the boundaries of Anthropology as a profession and for professional anthropologists? What did being an American and an anthropologist mean in this context? When doing funded research, what were the rights of those who studied and those for whom the study was done? Who had the rights to use research? American anthropologists had made careers of looking at different cultures, but had not looked at the difference that being a member of their own culture made in their professional work. Even when being an *American* anthropologist had become a central issue, American anthropologists grappled with its implications for research elsewhere, but not what it meant for their own practice as "cultural baggage." As we will see, repeated calls for "self-study" defined the "self" as a professional one, argued through citizen-scientist splits, rather than through ideological or cultural awareness.

In an effort to clarify some of these issues, in 1968, Charles Frantz (Stephen Boggs's successor as executive secretary of the Association and editor of the AAA Newsletter) produced a special statement in the AAA Newsletter ("The Cultural Milieu of the Immediate Future of Anthropology") which situated Anthropology in its political roots. This interest had slightly earlier been pursued as general (and "ancient") disciplinary history (i.e., Rowe 1965) and was now simultaneously being pursued as an intellectual one (see, for instance, Chapter 9, and the discussion of *Reinventing Anthropology*). Frantz wrote:

Anthropology is not the result of centered systematic development, but . . . always . . . shaped by historical expansion westward across the continent; influenced and in some cases constrained by opportunities and financial support . . . it is no accident that the aborigines of the U.S. and its possessions, the Philippines and neighboring areas were the first populations to be studied in depth. (1968[5]:2)

Frantz further asserted that his own research indicated that up until the last two decades, U.S. anthropologists had relatively easy access to other countries "because U.S. interests abroad were ostensibly more economic than political," but that as the United States assumed an increasingly active political role in world affairs, opportunities and support for research changed significantly. This reflected a prevalent view at the time that did not in these accounts include economic presence as exploitation or part of a colonialist agenda. Expansionist activities were still primarily understood as politically motivated.

In the meantime, new Foreign Area Research Guidelines issued by the government acknowledged responsibility for avoiding actions that would interfere with the integrity of American academic institutions. But in Frantz's view, government guidelines that "where possible" research "should" (1) advance knowledge; (2) not be secret; and (3) be made available to the host country and support local scholars, were not strong enough. Frantz asserted that if anthropologists in particular and American research in general were to be trusted, sponsorship must always be publicly stated by the sponsor, the university, and the researcher involved. Further, anything that could not be made available to host country scholars and governments should not be undertaken. This view stressing the significance of Anthropology's own surroundings for Anthropological work became a subject for discussion and research and Association resolutions (see, e.g., the Anti-Warfare Resolution discussed below). These views were explored in the early 1960s, and by 1970 were asserted as part of professional statements (including the formal statement on ethics passed by the AAA ("Principles of Professional Responsibility," 1971).

The press of events outside the Association impacted on internal discussion and events in the Association and was then reframed as part of Anthropology's public professional position. In particular, issues central to the perception of the United States and American researchers as "neo-colonialist" pressed the Association to make Anthropology's professional boundaries public and similarly pressured anthropologists to define their professional boundaries in the public sphere. However, as Boggs's study in the mid-1960s had already made clear, American anthropologists had been described as neo-colonialist *before* issues of funding and government influence on and use of research emerged as a significant issue for discussion. As identified in Boggs's study, American anthropologists were perceived by others as having a "neo-colonialist attitude" propelled by their own (professional wrapped up with personal) interests, in which they often abrogated or ignored those of indigenous scholars, peoples, and governments. "Neo-colonialism," as a term interpreted by Boggs as a result of his study, was not directed toward the American government or culture, but was more personally directed to American researchers, as those among whom research was conducted detected an individual rather than national agenda.

Boggs's report was the first time in the Association Newsletter (first published in 1947) that the term "neo-colonialism" was used in reference to

Anthropological practice. Further, its use in 1965 was not the same as its use later in the decade. In the interim there had been significant and critical changes in the surrounding milieu through which use and understanding of the term were derived. Events in Chile were "small change" compared to events later in the decade in Southeast Asia, in which an overt national agenda was being carried out.

In 1965, "neo-colonialist" referred to "treating the world as your oyster, exploiting the world on your own terms rather than with an eye to the needs of the people." Further, according to Boggs, the "accusation" that American anthropologists were abusing their position in the world as Americans was "not well-known," even among anthropologists (Newsletter 1965[9]: 1). But definitions and public knowledge were shifting in 1965. The uncovering of previously covert relationships between governments, researchers, agencies, and universities, plus the escalation of the war in Vietnam and public reaction to it abroad and at home, impacted on American and Anthropological self-definition and boundaries of practice. By 1968, Frantz's description of cultural milieu and the development of Anthropology revealed and embodied this shift, as Anthropology was described as the result of "westward expansion," "opportunity," and economics ("financial support")—the language of political, not personal neo-colonialism. No longer a personal exploitation of others as a resource, neo-colonialism was now understood as the political and economic exploitation of the resources of others. Although we have no evidence that Frantz interpreted his own language in this way, nor intended to situate American Anthropology as colonialist (a specific rather than inevitable interpretation), this view of Anthropology as exploitive was accepted by many anthropologists (generally those who had received degrees after the Second World War) as applying to both public and professional realms. Anthropology funded by and responsible to government agencies was argued as carrying forward political agendas. But the agenda was markedly different from that taken for granted as a "good" during World War II. Now the United States, as an entity viewed from abroad, was charged with carrying out a program of exploitive political domination. The government of the United States was perceived by many Americans as doing the same thing at home. Massive public protests, student demonstrations, the clamor of myriad disenfranchised and newly enfranchised voices were raised against government activities at home and abroad. The anthropologist as citizen "returned." But the terms of the debate shifted again. Anthropologists struggling to define boundaries between citizen and scientist, had largely accepted that there was such a separation. What was argued were its terms and where they were to be appropriately applied. The new argument challenged the existence of any separation. Like Hammer years earlier, those holding this view did not argue "scientists as citizens," they argued "scientists were citizens," as public and professional realms were merged in civic action.

NOTES

1. In this chapter, discussion of the public realm is limited to those events and activities which have broad relevance to members of American society but were specifically raised as relevant to Anthropology in discussion and debate within the community of American anthropologists, as made public in documents of the profession. Insofar as anthropologists engaged (as documented) in issues in the public realm, I refer to their activities as "civic."

2. This is not far removed in some respects from Crapanzano's articulation of the view in fieldworker ethnographies that all human interaction is in some way political. The difference here as I see it is that Bennett's concerns were global and primarily directed to international politics; fieldworker ethnographers' primary interests were individual and directed to personal politics.

3. Bennett noted that this compromise was especially evident in applied Anthropology and the Anthropological discussion of race. Although Bennett did not elaborate, he was probably referring to arguments among the first generation of American anthropologists that applied Anthropology compromised the logic of objectivity through involvement in policy matters and the like. In the case of race, although the Association had long been on record as supporting the equality of the races, there was, at the time, no conclusive "scientific" evidence that established that they were in fact "the same" (see Lowie 1949:664, and the issue as relevant again in the 1960 Resolution on Race, later in this chapter).

4. The argument of observer intervention could of course be referred to in the relatively narrower frame in which it had been raised through Heisenberg (1927) in physics. I say narrower here since the interest of the observer as intervening in the results of observation did not in that formulation include the emotions and subjectivity of the observer.

5. Briefly, in the 1950s the American Anthropological Association was asked to come to the assistance of Richard Morgan, an anthropologist employed by the Ohio State Museum but fired for alleged membership in the Communist Party. After appointing a special committee to look into the appropriate response to the request for help by a member of the Association, the AAA decided it could, as a scientific organization, write a letter on behalf of Morgan attesting to his professional credentials. It was not considered appropriate to issue a statement regarding any personal qualities or activities of Dr. Morgan, nor to take any position regarding his dismissal. His professional record was to speak for itself in the realm of professional employment.

6. This group included the generation of anthropologists who made up part of the group that "hissed at Margaret Mead from the floor" (Helm 1984a) of the meetings a decade later, when she announced the results of the Committee on Thailand's investigations (see Chapter 9). At this time Mead did not see a generational or ideological gap with these anthropologists.

7. Montesquieu, for instance, did not refer to the species but argued that the basis for common welfare was the identification of the individual good with the common good. The reference by Mead and Commoner to the "species," presented their resolution as rooted in biological (and scientific) rather than philosophical foundations. There was, however, no scientific evidence to support their claim.

8. There is a "gap" between the end of World War II and the beginning of the

1960s, in discussion and correspondence directed to the public realm appearing in AAA materials. While some of this discussion might have seemed less relevant in the Association due to the power of positivist versions of science, including associated disengagement from the public realm, it was also the case that anthropologists who held this viewpoint had become more powerful in the Association, serving as officers and so on. There had been a "battle" in the late 1940s, when Clyde Kluckhohn, serving as president of the AAA, worried about the "centrifugal forces" tearing the Association apart. At that time, the Association went through a re-organization which gave more power to the "young Turks" (Goldschmidt 1984). The "young Turks" included, for example, Julian Steward, noted earlier as a critic of the Statement on Human Rights, based on its unscientific basis. As president of the Association for Applied Anthropology in 1947, Steward threatened to set up a rival organization, a threat which acted as catalyst for the re-organization of the AAA in that year. In the reorganized AAA, Steward and like-minded anthropologists emerged with considerably more power in the profession. Positivist views which demanded objectivity and neutrality were especially "rewarded" in the 1950s as consistent with "good" professional practice. But such views also kept the Association largely out of entanglements in the McCarthy "witch hunts" of the time (see note 5 above).

9. In 1970, Berreman (age 40) was the youngest candidate to ever run for president of the AAA and the first to be nominated in accordance with by-law provisions, which allowed nomination by five Fellows of the Association. Berreman's nomination was largely understood as a move by the "younger generation" of anthropologists (including students) to gain equality and power within the Association. Berreman's nomination was moved and seconded by many of the anthropologists regarded as "revisionists," including Hymes, Wolf, David Aberle, Kathleen Gough Aberle, Joseph Jorgenson, along with others, such as David Schneider and Jack Potter, who are not so identified. Before Berreman's nomination, three other candidates (Spaulding, Spuhler, and A. F. C. Wallace) had been nominated by the usual process of selection by the Nominations Committee and names sent on to the Executive Committee. Spaulding and Spuhler withdrew their names from consideration shortly before the election and Wallace won the office. Berreman (1980:143) reported that one of the candidates who withdrew from the race later informed him that he had done so at the urgent request of the president of the Association in order to "pit the strongest candidate against Berreman and avoid the possibility that the 'responsible' vote would be split three ways leaving the anti-war 'radical' vote as the electing plurality." Writing of these events a decade later, Berreman tied the war in Vietnam, activities of the Association, and his own involvement, specifically on the Committee on Ethics of the AAA, to the outcome of the election.

In 1970 at the peak of controversy over the war in Vietnam and American anthropologists' complicity therein, the author was nominated to run for the presidency of the American Anthropological Association. The nomination was made by some of those members most opposed to the involvement of anthropologists in research and consultation useful to prosecution of that war, and it reflected their approval of the critical position taken by the Committee on Ethics of the association of which the author was an outspoken member. (Berreman 1980:142)

Berreman's nomination (and subsequent loss) was enmeshed in, and the product of, events in the public realm as they spilled over into professional politics and practice. Candidates prior to this time generally ran on the basis of personal networks, university affiliation (both where educated and where employed), and the assessment of their scholarly work. While personal networks were still active in the election of the 1970s, political views, particularly as they were linked to events outside the Association which had impact on policies inside the AAA, took on a new significance.

CHAPTER 9

Anthropologists Go to War . . . with Themselves

Between 1967 and 1980, anthropologists passed more than 100 resolutions in the AAA. In retrospect, American anthropologist Walter Goldschmidt (1984:169), a witness to the proceedings of Anthropology since the 1930s, assessed this activity within the Association as "a sudden burst of concern with public issues which involved both memorializing others and bringing our own house into conformity with a consistent voice favoring equality and opposing discrimination and prejudice." While in 1946 a major reorganization of the AAA cleared the way for the passage of resolutions by the membership, only eleven resolutions had been passed prior to 1966. Thirty-five of these resolutions were passed between 1968 and 1969, evidence of the heightened concerns and activity of the time.

The overwhelming majority of the resolutions proposed and passed by the Association from the late 1960s through the early 1970s (more than 140) "favored equality" by demanding full rights and privileges for various groups within American society. These groups (identified by gender, race, ethnicity, age, and sexual preference, for example) were seen as powerless or relatively less powerful. There was no identification within this discussion of who the powerful group(s) were (i.e., those that the less powerful groups were relatively less powerful than). However, the majority of the membership of the Association in the early 1960s were "older" (anthropologists trained prior to World War II), white, and male. Until 1968, full membership in the Association was restricted to Fellows (anthropologists working in the discipline who were nominated by other anthropologists working in the discipline and voted on by members, that is, other Fellows). It was this group that "granted" equality to others, through full membership rights which were extended to students, without nomination by others.[1]

Some of the resolutions passed were specifically directed toward giving
recognition to the rights of others as participants in the Association, others
toward encouraging full recognition of these groups within American society
at large. Goldschmidt's (1984:169) summary of these resolutions demonstrates the overall effort to redress perceived imbalances, which in turn reveals the significance of equality in American and American Anthropological
conceptions.

Of the approximately 140 resolutions and motions (other than ceremonial) passed,
51 dealt with matters of discrimination. Of these, 20 were concerned with gender,
directly or indirectly (e.g., refusing to meet in states that had not passed the Equal
Rights Amendment), 12 with ethnic or racial discrimination, another 12 with academic freedom, and some with other civil rights issues. All were firmly against discrimination or warfare (against, of course) [*sic*]. None of these resolutions related to
Communist Bloc countries. Twelve were what might be called intellectual statements—as, for instance, supporting the UNESCO statement on race. . . . Eight involved the ethics of anthropologists, mostly passed during the period when the
statement on ethics was being formulated.

THE WAR IN VIETNAM COMES HOME

In the Anti-Warfare Resolution, introduced in 1966, claimed as appropriate for scientific practice on the basis of the passage of the Disarmament
Resolution, the view articulated by Hammer provided the basis for the debate rather than a "footnote" to it. In contrast to the exchange over the
Disarmament Resolution, which maintained the terms of a polite discussion,
the debate over the "Anti-Warfare Resolution" took on the tone of a dispute (an "early" manifestation of the "loss of civility" common in the
1990s; see, for example, Tannen 1997). Some critical differences between
these resolutions were important at the outset.

First, the Disarmament Resolution was phrased in very general terms, not
only in title but in content. There was no mention of specific potential
combatants in the Cold War era. In contrast, while the title "Anti-Warfare
Resolution" was general, the resolution itself used specific language about
particular practices by the United States in Vietnam. Members of the Association consistently referred to this resolution as the "Vietnam Resolution" following its introduction, leaving no doubt that it was understood
as making a policy statement about particular circumstances, not suggesting
a theoretical study or making a general pacifist statement. The exchange of
views in this instance quickly took on the aspects of a dispute whose terms
were part of the fragmentation of the paradigm of science within the discipline. Fragmentation within the Association was also linked to political
events and differing interpretations of them, often arising from similar terms
of science which were themselves linked to similar *a priori* constructions.

The discussion over "programs" versus "proposals" which characterized the Disarmament Resolution became passé as supporters of the Anti-Warfare Resolution intentionally threw themselves into the political realm, which they included as part of the scientific and professional one. Supporters argued that scientists were citizens and as American citizens (and scientists) it was their duty to speak out against American activity that violated American values. An interesting aspect of these discussions was the extent to which the underlying values regarding self-determination, freedom, and individual rights were taken for granted, thus submerged in the exchange. The dispute was not over different values, but over the interpretation of them as related to various contexts of activity.

THE ANTI-WARFARE RESOLUTION (A.K.A. THE VIETNAM RESOLUTION)

Decrying the use of methods of warfare employed in Vietnam and calling for an end to the war there, the 1966 Anti-Warfare Resolution read in part:

Reaffirming our 1961 Resolution, we condemn the use of napalm, chemical defoliants, harmful gasses, bombing, the torture and killing of prisoners of war and political prisoners and the intentional or deliberate policies of genocide or forced transportation of populations for the purpose of terminating their culture and/or ethnic heritages by anyone, anywhere. These methods of warfare deeply offend human nature. We ask that all governments put an end to their use at once and proceed as rapidly as possible to a peaceful settlement of the war in Vietnam.

As in the case of the Disarmament Resolution, the Vietnam Resolution raised issues directed to assumptions about the nature of science and its relationship to the public realm through research and responsibility. However, a fundamental change in the terms of the debate marked generational and epistemological differences. In the debate over the Vietnam resolution, anthropologists proposing and supporting it argued that Anthropology was a science, but dismissed the view that Anthropology was or ever could be apolitical.

The contrasting views of representatives of those holding more positivist views of science argued that whether or not the substance of the Anti-Warfare Resolution was reasonable was not at issue. What was at issue was that such a resolution had no place in a professional association because "Anthropology is a strictly empirical science. The question of what offends human nature is not an anthropological problem but a metaphysical one" (Newsletter 1967[7]:7). In a position similar to that taken by opponents of the Disarmament Resolution (and the Statement on Human Rights in the 1940s), it was argued that Anthropology had no place in politics (except through scientifically grounded statements), but a "twist" to the argument

was the re-raising of the role of anthropologists in two settings, as opponents
objected to its passage on the grounds that it reflected a "confusion of roles
of anthropologists and citizens" (ibid.). Naroll (Newsletter 1967[4]:2) argued "We have separate roles as citizens and anthropologists." Collins
(Newsletter 1967[12]:12) demonstrated just how strict the separation was
held to be arguing against the resolution on the grounds that not only was
it political, but that it should be dismissed because those proposing it were
"not even Southeast Asianists." Presumably, from this standpoint, if individual scientists studying southeast Asians were able to identify scientific
reasons not to use certain weapons, the resolution would have been acceptable. But arguing any of these positions on the grounds of some "universal human rights" was, as it had been in 1947, decried as unscientific and
inappropriate for a professional organization.

The distinction of anthropologists as citizens and scientists that had been
part of the discussion over the Statement on Human Rights, but missing
from the exchange over the Disarmament Resolution, re-surfaced. During
the 1950s, positivist versions of science had gained ascendance and this was
reflected in the terms of the 1960 discussion. Anthropologists against the
Disarmament Resolution were focused on what they saw as "good science"
rather than good scientists, and argued accordingly. "Good science" required objectivity; discussion of scientists (acknowledging science as the
work of individuals) simply muddied the water. But, precipitated by events
in the political realm, the argument in 1966 was less over science than the
responsibilities of citizens as scientists—that is, what constituted "good scientists."

The struggle by some anthropologists to hold to strict categories of separation was evidenced by the unanimity of articulated views about the Vietnam War. While the American public argued "for" and "against" the war,
anthropologists, at least publicly, exhibited unanimity in their position
against. The disagreements between and among anthropologists were not
caused by their position *on* the war, but by their position on the propriety
of a resolution *about* the war. Clearly, in the view of some anthropologists
there was no role for the Association in such activity because the terms of
the profession as a science demanded neutrality as well as objectivity. From
this point of view, an individual was one or the other (citizen or scientist,
depending on the venue), while others argued that anthropologists were
inextricably both. Added to the particular nuances of the debate was a challenge to cultural relativism. Just as in the Statement on Human Rights, when
anthropologists struggled under the blanket of cultural relativism, which left
them unable to speak out explicitly against atrocities committed during
World War II, anthropologists sought to cope in context with cultural relativism as the "covering term" of Anthropology.

Cultural relativism can itself be seen as, if not a direct product of Enlightenment ideology, at least consistent with it. Used as a barrier to ethnocen-

trism and a means to create objectivity in intellectual terms, cultural relativism as an "American" contribution to Anthropology has been consistent with American ideas of equality—a kind of "all cultures are created equal." For instance, cultural relativism employed as a means to understand cultures in their own terms was used by Boas as a means to eschew ethnocentrism and thereby become more objective when studying other cultures. All cultures were equal from the standpoint that cultural relativism denied the possibility of using external standards by which cultures could be assessed or judged. Conflict between and among American values, science, and cultural relativism can obviously occur, as it did, for example, at the end of World War II. But the use of cultural relativism as a sub-strata for objectivity and extended to equality raises dilemmas, that is, valuing equal rights includes equal rights not to value equality, which Americans often view as an "inalienable" right. Further, although used by Boas as a bulwark against ethnocentrism, consistent with his "historical particularism," cultural relativism was extended by others (see Benedict's *Patterns of Culture*). In the extension, if all cultures were to be studied in terms of themselves, then cultures and their practices could not be compared and must be, in some sense, construed as equal. In such an understanding, radical cultural relativity produced (and produces) moral and ethical immobilization. In the debate over the Vietnam Resolution, cultural relativism was claimed as the basis for neutrality as well as objectivity. But even cultural relativism was no longer sacrosanct as events in the public realm challenged its terms and its boundaries.

Opponents of the resolution argued that the doctrine of cultural relativism demanded neutrality and that the resolution was "grossly ethnocentric" because it claimed certain methods of warfare as unacceptable (Newsletter 1967[4]:10, 11; Clark 1967[4]:11). The resolution was thus seen as a violation of the "doctrine" of cultural relativity, which set aside personal standards and judgments. From this point of view, no matter how much in sympathy the anthropologist, as a citizen, might be, the resolution (which was argued as clearly value-engaged) was inappropriate as a professional scientific statement. Niehoff's letter (Newsletter 1967[9]:11) advocating this view set off the most heated and sustained comment during the controversy. In his letter, Niehoff exposed the conflict inherent in the use of cultural relativism as the basis for both objectivity and neutrality in which the anthropologist has either to deny his cultural self or his professional self. Niehoff wrote:

I am no happier about Vietnam and American involvement than any other anthropologist and I suppose most Americans, but I object to, e.g., "methods of warfare that deeply offend human nature" on the basis of cultural relativism. As professional "culture-free selves" anthropologists cannot condemn the practices listed in the Resolution, although we might do so as individuals. (Newsletter 1967[9]:11)

That is, since "human nature" was itself undefined, means to "offend it"
were not scientifically specifiable. Here, all weapons are created equal, unless
it can be proved that they offend human nature (as opposed to, for instance,
ending human life). Niehoff suggested that "professional culture-free
selves" exist apart from anthropologists as individuals, leaving the "Self" as
posed, an entirely abstracted entity. In response, anthropologists defending
the resolution strongly objected to cultural relativism as the basis for the
citizen-scientist split in activities in which one's own country was involved.
Such a split, they argued, did not exist. Using the terms of a value-engaged[2]
social science, which denied objectivity as a basis for scientific practice, they
argued that cultural relativity as the basis for such a separation was completely untenable. In their view, cultural relativism was appropriately used
to guard against loss of perspective and judgments when studying other
cultures (e.g., to situate themselves as objective) in the field "away." However, they argued, it was neither necessary nor appropriate to use it to guard
against judgments regarding one's own culture. For example, Barclay
(Newsletter 1967[9]:12) argued that the weapons and strategies of the Vietnam War "are clearly in defiance of values traditionally held and honored
by United States Americans. As anthropologists would it be unreasonable
to suggest that these methods are inconsistent with United States Americans' self-image and conflict at least with the values they seek to perpetu-
ate?" Dunn (Newsletter 1967[9]:14) also argued that "Americans by their
actions in Vietnam have violated their own standards and ideals." These
remarks, representative of other, similar comments, are also significant because, consistent with most of the correspondence on this subject, while
anthropologists declared themselves as explicitly value-engaged they did not
explicitly identify the values or related ideals to which they subscribed. Similarly, those arguing against value-engaged practice did not seek to have the
values identified. Thus, both sides provide evidence that these values were
commonly held (though differently interpreted), and taken for granted. Asserted, but not identified, values regarding human rights, including equality,
human rights, freedom, and self-determination, were presupposed. Thus,
from the perspective of those arguing that cultural relativism did not apply
to American anthropologists in American settings, Niehoff's use of cultural
relativism was a "crude" (ibid.) application of the principle which could not
be legitimately used to justify political neutrality. Part of the arguments
against Niehoff's use of cultural relativity was the separation of "away" and
"at home" where different standards were seen to apply. In the field,
"away" cultural relativism could be used to attain objectivity, but could not
conversely be used to maintain neutrality "at home." Rather than cultural
relativism, it was argued that the basis for the decision as to what constituted
the proper relationship between roles of "scholars and citizens" was a realization of the dangers of claiming a value-free (objective) social science

(for instance, as had been done in Germany in the 1930s and 1940s) where no grounds were available to object to cultural practices.

The Vietnam Resolution was one of the few that sought authority for its passage through scholarly sources, outside of Anthropology (this was also the case for the Disarmament Resolution). Sources from the natural sciences, as well as Aristotle and John Stuart Mills in philosophy, Gouldner in sociology, were drawn on to support their case. Gough-Aberle combined the authority of physics, philosophy, and Anthropology, citing Kluckhohn and Firth, who, following Einstein[3] and Russell on the subject of science and action, held the view that "scientists hold special obligations as *scientists* because of their special knowledge and the power it confers" (Newsletter 1967[10]:8). Again, past examples of scientists who had not spoken out were recalled, and World War II Germany taken as the quintessential case. Binford expressed the view that advocacy of the position not to speak out on public issues was "reminiscent of 'good German scientists' in the 1930s who had hoped to keep their professions distinct from social and political events" (Newsletter 1967[8]:4).

Other anthropologists, rather than calling on scholarly sources, used the authority of (taken for granted and unspecified) American values. Previous experience in World War II was again called upon. It was argued that what separated the Second World War from the war in Vietnam was that the former had been seen as a "legitimate" war, which preserved American values, while in the case of Vietnam, it was, as articulated by Frucht and others, "our own standards that are being violated" (Newsletter 1967[8]:6). But what remained beneath the level of overt discussion in the exchanges of supporters and opponents of the Resolution were the underlying American "standards" to which the discussion referred. Taken for granted by both sides, these terms remained implicit. In part these terms appear consistent with those taken for granted in the Resolution on Race and those memorializing Kennedy and King, in which assertions regarding human rights were promulgated.

What anthropologists disagreed over in these exchanges was not the "standards" (in this case, values) of Americans, but whether or not they could be or should be appropriately applied in Anthropology. The questions were primarily those regarding action. Was the responsible (good) scientist neutral or active? Are venues in which scientists are active or neutral "equal?" Are there means to differentiate between venues? Ralph Beals, in his role as head of the first ethics committee appointed by the AAA, claimed that we have learned from history that "to remain silent was to deny the value of science in the solution of human problems." David Aberle, a sponsor of the resolution, argued (as Hammer had done in 1960 at the end of debate on the Disarmament Resolution), "the question is not whether Anthropology should be made political, the question is what kind of political position it should adopt" (Newsletter 1967[9]:11). The question of on what basis political positions could be or should be "adopted" was never explicitly discussed. Methods of warfare were cited as "offending human nature"; what they offended were ideals and standards regarding human rights and humanity embedded in American conceptions of human nature.

Ultimately, again, dilemmas raised in the public realm for anthropologists in the professional realm were discussed, debated, and argued, but unresolved. Dissenting viewpoints were silenced by the majority, but the "party" in charge shifted by issue and over time. The upheaval of the latter half of the 1960s in American life seeped into the professional and private lives of American anthropologists, creating questions of identity and engendering division. Just as 1960 marked the "beginning" of discussion of Anthropology's place in the public sphere, 1970 marked the beginning of the end of the involvement of anthropologists as professionals in that sphere. The "Thai Controversy" marked the receding of the activist tide.

ANTHROPOLOGISTS GO HOME: THE "THAI CONTROVERSY"

In March of 1970, the Student Mobilization Committee (SMC), a self-proclaimed national radical student group begun in the late 1960s, sent papers documenting the activities of five anthropologists in Thailand to Ethics Committee Chairman Eric Wolf and Ethics Committee member Joseph Jorgenson. In April, the "Student Mobilizer" (newspaper of the SMC) featured an article with extracts from these papers, including accusations by the editors of the paper that American anthropologists (some of them mentioned by name) were involved in clandestine research in Thailand (Newsletter 1970[4]:1). These reports were picked up by local news stations and widely broadcast across the United States.

The day following the public airing of these accusations, Wolf, in his role as chair of the Ethics Committee, sent private letters to four of the anthropologists named, informing them that documents regarding their alleged involvement in secret research had been received. Wolf invited these anthropologists to make a statement to the Ethics Committee if they so wished, "especially in view of the past resolutions of our Association on the subject of clandestine research and restricted, non-public publication of research results" (Newsletter 1970[7]:2). (Wolf here referred to positions taken by the AAA following Project Camelot in 1965.)

In early May the entire Ethics Committee met and after examining the SMC documents, drafted a statement supporting the actions of Wolf and Jorgenson and sent it to the Executive Board of the AAA (Newsletter 1970[11]:7). Two weeks later, the Executive Board issued a statement abstaining from any position on the activities of anthropologists working in Thailand (due, they said to insufficient information), and publicly rebuked Wolf and Jorgenson in particular, and the Ethics Committee in general for going beyond the mandate the AAA had given them to formulate ethical guidelines.

The divisions over this issue went beyond the individuals directly involved in these events and correspondence in the Newsletter, evidenced by then familiar debates over appropriate activity for anthropologists, fragmented along generational, political, and professional lines. Gerald Berreman, at 40, the youngest anthropologist to be nominated for the presidency of the AAA and the first to be nominated according to by-laws that by-passed the Nominations Committee, was defeated when two of the three "mainstream" candidates running for the position withdrew. Berreman's defeat was announced at the same Annual Meeting (1970) where outside the hotel copies of the "Student Mobilizer" from the preceding April were being sold.

Before the meetings had even begun, the discontent of some of the members of the Association (primarily those who had supported Berreman) over the handling of the election and the Ethics Committee rebukes threatened to persist, and thus disrupt the Association as well as the current meetings. The Executive Board asked Berreman to speak at the convention (according to Berreman 1980:170) as a means to help heal the breaches that the election and its processes had engendered, revealed, and inflamed. Borrowing from a work by Charles Reich (author of *The Greening of America*, 1970; an unashamedly "liberal" tract), Berreman entitled his talk "The Greening of the American Anthropological Association," and said in part:

Reich . . . sees a revolution underway in this country: not a violent one, but a revolution in conscience, spreading quickly and pervasively so that laws, institutions and social structure are already changing. . . .

The change to which I refer in our profession is part of that broader change identified by Reich. It represents not just a change in opinion and values but a basic change in the definition of what we are, what we are doing, and where we are going.

Meanwhile, outside the hotel, demonstrations by students (some of them budding anthropologists) against American anthropologists working in Thailand threatened to disrupt the meetings entirely. As a result of the increasingly profound and public divisions this issue represented, the Board announced at the meetings that an Ad Hoc Committee would be appointed to look into the "Thailand issue."

Formal appointments to the Committee (Margaret Mead, chair and members William H. Davenport and David L. Olmsted) were made the following March. Once in place the Committee asked that all materials in the hands of the Ethics Committee, plus all pertinent correspondence, including that which had been sent to the Newsletter, and any which was forthcoming, be sent to them. The immediate practical results of these requests was that no further information regarding this subject was made public.

The "Report of the Ad Hoc Committee to Evaluate the Controversy

Concerning Anthropological Activities in Relation to Thailand" was released to the Association (and the public through the *Washington Post* and the *New York Times*) two weeks before the annual meeting in November of 1971. However, when the membership, as represented at the annual meeting, were asked to vote on formal acceptance of the report, they vehemently rejected it by a wide margin (Newsletter 12[1]:1, 9). When Mead as Committee chair read the report to the membership, their anger was clear, as she was "hissed at as she spoke from the floor" (Helm 1984a:1). As described by Committee member William Davenport (1984:68) years later:

The Ad Hoc Committee's response to the rejection was to destroy all the documentation . . . (7000 pages) . . . that it had collected. This was not done in a fit of pique. The action was taken in order to prevent the materials from being used, in the manner that the SMC had treated the original six documents, to revive the issue. Of course, some zealots accused the Ad Hoc Committee of destroying the evidence of its "failed attempt" to cover up the actions of anthropologists in Southeast Asia. But those were the politics of the time.

Despite the division and uproar created by the Thailand Controversy, dissenters from the Association's formal position were powerless on all sides. Re-raising the issue within the Association was useless since all documentation had been destroyed. Raising the issue outside the Association would have been an impotent gesture, since not only had the report of the Committee already been publicly announced, but Margaret Mead, a well-known and credible figure in the public realm, was its principal author.[4] Further, destruction of these materials also meant that anthropologists accused by the SMC, and embattled by conflicts in the Association, were similarly powerless insofar as they could not use the record on their own behalf, to explain or offer a different interpretation of their activities or the activities of others. Two days after the rejection of the report at the annual meeting, the Executive Board formally ended discussion of the issue, stating, "specific problems posed by the events referred to as the 'Thailand Controversy' stand essentially unresolved" (Newsletter 1972[2]:6).

Fragmentation within the public realm thus contributed to and mirrored those in the profession as challenges to meaning and experience rose in a series of political crises which, despite "ending" remained essentially unresolved. The political experience in the profession of the cohort of anthropologists arguing for change and involvement ended on a whimper, not a bang. Venues of engagement and confrontation between anthropologists in political and Association contexts were analogous to later descriptions by fieldwork ethnographers in which they experienced themselves as setting an agenda that was revealed as significantly in the control of others. By the time fieldwork ethnographers produced their works, Anthropology as exploitation was taken for granted by them, and yet they had, by their own

accounts, been willing participants in it. Fieldwork ethnographers interpreted themselves as often irrevocably involved in a process beyond their
control as Westerners, and hopeful professionals, but in many ways their
accounts revealed interaction consistent with the interpretation offered by
Boggs in 1965 that American anthropologists "viewed the world as their
oyster" and gave nothing back to those among whom they did research.
While Boggs's report represented the view of American anthropologists put
forward by those among whom research was conducted, in fieldworker ethnographies, interactions that led to such views were exposed and in some
respects put forward by the anthropologists themselves. (For instance, fieldwork ethnographers' view of an inevitable neo-colonialist role for anthropologists and the "symbolic violence" through which they "forced" the
Other to serve the interests of the anthropologist.) In these terms, fieldwork
ethnographers linked themselves as individual Americans to the political behavior of the United States in South America and later in Southeast Asia.
They defined themselves as powerful and dominant in fieldwork settings just
as the United States had been in political ones. As these anthropologists
tried to make sense of their activities in relation to public politics and policies, they claimed themselves as powerful through association with dominant colonialist political forces, a power they simultaneously claimed to
reject. They thus decried their own participation in what they asserted as an
inevitably colonialist relationship with the Other. But ironically, fieldwork
ethnographers enacted a role more in keeping with earlier definitions of neo-
colonialism in activities which served their own professional and personal
interests rather than those of the U.S. government.

The changes which Berreman and others had applauded and envisioned
as a new means for defining the discipline and the profession through political positions and activities—Anthropology's "self" never took hold. The
"change" in the public and professional realms was largely rhetorical. The
inability to come to any meaningful resolution as a group through clarifi-
cation of the identity of anthropologists as scientists, citizens, or both, the
failure in American experience to cope with the issues presented by events
in Southeast Asia, was part of a sense experienced and diagnosed by anthropologists, along with other Americans, as a state of "malaise." In an
essay first read at a session on "Rethinking Anthropology" in 1971, Berreman wrote:

We are having this session on "Rethinking Anthropology" because many of us are
. . . (sick to shit) [*sic*] of anthropology as it is exemplified in most of our journals,
books, and courses—even those we have ourselves perpetrated. . . . I felt moved to
say something about the malaise that is affecting our discipline.

When fieldworker ethnographers returned from the field, the American
"landscape" to which they returned had altered dramatically for both those

who had been away and those who had been at home. Rabinow described his sense of displacement upon his return from Morocco:

The "revolution" had occurred during my absence (1968–1969). My friends from Chicago, many of them now living in New York, were fervently and unabashedly "political" when I returned. New York, where I had grown up, looked the same as when I had left it. But the city and my friends were now more impenetrable to me than ben Mohammed. The whole revery of future *communitas* which had sustained me through months of loneliness refused to actualize itself upon my return. I adopted a stance of passivity waiting for it to appear. . . . The maze of slight blurred nuance, that feeling of barely grasped meanings which had been my constant companion in Morocco overtook me once again. But now I was home. (Rabinow 1977:148)

The difference in the experiences described above was in part, one of scale. Activist anthropologists at home had argued the terms of global politics in personal terms; fieldwork ethnographers eventually argued the terms of personal politics in global ones. But before that, the attention of the nation and its citizens, the Association and anthropologists, was already shifting from global to domestic and from national and political to individual and economic concerns.

NOTES

1. I have omitted material related to students and their activities in the Association during this time. I have chosen not to focus on this (somewhat voluminous) material for two reasons. First, although students had become significant in the Association (as evidenced in the decision to include them as members in 1968), their significance was largely through their association and alliance with already established anthropologists who were active in Association affairs (i.e., Hymes, Berreman, Wolf, etc.); or through problems created and discussions of how they could be resolved, brought about by the sheer increase in new members that these students represented. Second, fieldwork ethnographers belonged to the generation of students who established a presence and position for themselves inside the Association, but they themselves did not engage in such activities, as evidenced in Association records.

2. On this issue, Habermas (1968), from whom, along with other critical theorists, revisionist anthropologists drew their own argument, argued that contrary to positivism, social scientific theories developed through "noncommunicative" methods which may themselves be inherently biased. As other social theorists and scientists have pointed out, establishing the difference between value-free and value-laden theories is not a simple project, in part due to the complexity of the relationship between the "context of discovery" and the "context of justification." See Norma Haan et al., eds., *Social Science as Moral Inquiry*. (New York: Columbia University Press, 1983); H. Garfinkel, *Forms of Explanation* (New Haven: Yale University Press, 1981).

The use of the term "value-engaged" in the argument by revisionists is part of the insistence that social scientists must appropriately use the standards of their own society (in this case, their view of American standards) in their critique of, and activity in, the American public and professional Anthropological realm.

3. For much of his career, Einstein had espoused the views of the pure scientist who left the decision about the use of research to others. However, during World War II, when he feared that German scientists had developed a nuclear weapon, he wrote to President Roosevelt, supporting the development of such a weapon by the United States—thus eschewing the role of the apolitical, "pure" scientist.

4. By this time, Mead was less credible among younger members of the Association. Her own work during World War II raised issues regarding the boundaries she argued as appropriate or inappropriate. More immediately, according to Berreman, in the months during which Mead claimed to have read thousands of pages of documents on this issue, she was often out of the country, and without access to these papers. This led many interested and concerned observers, at the time, to conclude that she had not read much of the "evidence" when she issued the Committee opinion. In a 1984 session at the AAA meetings, Berreman concluded: "If I had a dollar for every lie Margaret Mead told in that report, I'd be a rich man."

CHAPTER 10

Power Brokers Go Broke

Sol Tax, . . . where are you? Margaret Mead . . . where are you? Walter
Goldschmidt . . . where are you? To recommend that the American Anthropological Association commission investigations of socially significant problems, and publish them in its journal, becomes a lonely trip.
(Schlesier, Newsletter 1976[3]:2)

There is one last turning point to the present—the shift away from academic opulence to the period of austerity that brought about the de-
mise of the counter-culture movement and that suddenly found students
turning away from the Arcadian promise that anthropology offered and
to the practicalities of the service professions. (Goldschmidt 1984:171)

By the middle of the 1970s, it was clear that a newly perceived crisis was
shaping American life and Anthropology. Already split along generational
and political lines, shifts in the American economy exacerbated old divisions
in Anthropology between academic and non-academic anthropologists, and
created new barriers between employed and unemployed anthropologists.

One of the most telling articles of the 1970s (D'Andrade et al. 1975),
marked institutional recognition of the difficulty in finding academic employment. D'Andrade et al. predicted that there would be long-term short-
ages for anthropologists seeking academic employment. But for many recent
graduates, D'Andrade et al.'s article merely affirmed trends which they had
already been struggling with for several years. The generation to which fieldwork ethnographers belonged was the first to be caught in the downward
spiral in employment since the 1940s, a spiral which D'Andrade et al. argued
would get worse.[1] Within the Association there was an abrupt turn from

political encounters to economic concerns, a shift which reflected a more general American turn which had already affected employment for anthropologists. As sociologist Daniel Yankelovich described it in his study of Americans in the 1970s: "In a matter of a few years we . . . moved from an uptight culture set in a dynamic economy to a dynamic culture set in an uptight economy. The world we live in has been turned upside down" (Yankelovich 1981:34).

By the time fieldwork ethnographers returned from the field, signs of an economic recession, including a shrinking professional job market, were there, but largely unseen and unheeded by the community of anthropologists. By the beginning of the 1970s, when this generation of ethnographers completed their dissertations, they found themselves in a job market in which actualities reversed reasonable expectations of a short time before. Economic shifts were linked to political ones and pressed on an increasingly beleaguered professional and disciplinary sense of self.

OVERPOPULATION, OVERLOAD, AND UNEMPLOYMENT

Following World War II there had been steady growth in all of the social sciences, including Anthropology. Such growth included increases in the number of positions available as well as in the number of anthropologists to fill them, with job opportunities running at a slightly faster rate through the middle of the 1960s. Ironically, however, in the same year (1964) that the demand for anthropologists was at an "unprecedented level" (Newsletter 1964[9]:1), research by American social scientists abroad came under close and eventually damaging scrutiny in Project Camelot. These circumstances as well as others in Anthropology not only coincided, they eventually collided. For example, at the same time that the number of new anthropologists was overwhelming the AAA, the Association had programs in place to increase the number of new anthropologists. At the same time that new jobs were opening for anthropologists and more funding was becoming available for academic anthropology through government and university alliances, suspicion was being cast on those alliances. The activities of anthropologists involved in such alliances as well as Anthropology in general came under serious scrutiny, not only within the profession but outside it as well. At the same time that anthropologists were graduating and looking for jobs in record numbers, demand fell abruptly.

ORGANIZATIONAL OVERLOAD

In the years between 1947 and 1962, the number of professional anthropologists tripled. According to Goldschmidt (1984:166):

The general growth and democratization of higher learning in the U.S. that had been spurred by the G.I. bill was particularly reflected in the growth of anthropology, which became a recognized discipline in almost every American college and university, with dozens of departments initiating Ph.D. degrees. Many of us new teachers were talking about peoples our students had seen but we had only read about.

The sheer increase in numbers was problematic in the beginning of the 1960s. But starting in the mid-1960s the steady growth became an avalanche of new members, peaking in the late 1960s. In only one year (1967 to 1968), 700 new members joined the AAA, most of them students and new Ph.D.s. (This was in part due to the change in membership rules in the Association in response to student demands in the late 1960s). The Association's organizational problems, as created by this new population, were manifested in disarray at annual meetings. As the Executive Board explained to the membership early in the 1960s: "Since 1936, the sheer quantity of cellular growth, unaccompanied by any change in basic pattern, has turned the highly successful small organism into a dinosaur" (Newsletter 1963[10]:4).

In 1961, the AAA was already overwhelmed by the demands that record attendance and involvement had placed on the organization. The number of sessions, papers, program participants, and so on, had risen so quickly that the Executive Board seriously considered a suggestion that some contributors read their papers by title only (Newsletter 1961[9]:2).

In 1963, one thousand students registered to attend the annual meeting, prompting officers of the Association and organizers of the meeting to send a plea to the membership for suggestions on how to meet the new needs. Association officers published a call for help in the Newsletter which ended: "this is too much, we don't know how to handle it" (Newsletter 1964[4]: 9).

Responses to the Executive Board's call for suggestions on how to reorient the annual meeting reflected both Anthropological and American experience. The response to a suggestion from Robert Adams (Newsletter 1964[9]:4) that the Association hold three regional meetings rather than a single national one, was generally unfavorable, but it drew particular attention as it gave other anthropologists the opportunity to reflect and comment on what they considered to be the central purpose of annual meetings. Other anthropologists argued that Adams had not considered the significance of reaffirming the unity of the group as the reason for the annual meeting. The benefit of this ritual, enacted on a tribal scale, was seen to override the benefits of smaller meetings. Goldschmidt, for example (Newsletter 1964[11]:7), argued that although regional meetings might solve organizational problems created by growth in the short term, in the long term such a solution would further fragment the organization by further disrupting group unity. In his view, anthropologists still had an intellectual orientation to some "minimal lineage," thus the primary function of the meeting was to "select clan leaders, and inculcate and evaluate the neophyte in the fraternity" (ibid.). Goldschmidt further argued that proliferation of specializations meant that anthropologists no longer shared a common body of knowledge. Although intellectual discussion could proceed more easily in smaller groups, the sharing of knowledge had become only a secondary function of the meetings.[2]

Sorenson too argued that the essence of the annual meeting was group unity. Using successful American teamwork and experience as the model, Sorenson (Newsletter 1964[1]:4) urged "Let's not break up the Yankees." Rather than separate meetings, Sorenson suggested that anthropologists use their skills to study their Association as a first step to making reasonable adjustments. However, referring to what he perceived as a long-standing bias against work done by anthropologists in their own society, Sorenson considered it unlikely that his suggestions would be implemented. He commented, "my own experience suggests that the response of anthropologists to studying their own sub-society is one of three: (1) suspicious resistance, (2) unawareness that anything might be done; and chiefly among very junior members of the profession, (3) a recognition that we need to know ourselves, but with little hope of carrying out the needed work" (ibid.:5).

Both Goldschmidt and Sorenson were followed by other calls for anthropologists to use their own skills to study "themselves" to seek solutions for problems of professional identity. For example, in 1969, the Planning and Development Committee (part of the Committee on Organization, itself a response to overpopulation, especially increased student membership) recommended that the Association embark on a serious "self-study." Everett Hughes, a Fellow of the AAA and an authority on the study of professions (e.g., Hughes's "Survey of Interests and Attitudes" 1968), was asked to undertake a "study of us," since much discussion by the Committee had centered on the need for "fuller information about ourselves in a period of growth and change" (Newsletter 1969[10]:9; see also DeLaguna 1967).

Despite implementation of some of the changes recommended by the Committee on Development, the AAA remained threatened by growth, which by the mid-1970s was characterized as "overgrowth." A comparison of the Mexico meetings of 1959, at which 250 papers were presented, to the annual meeting of 1975 where there were approximately 1,812 papers presented, led the AAA staff to extrapolate to the year 2000. The staff concluded that at the present rate of growth, in the year 2000 there would be 24,684 papers presented at the annual meeting (which by their estimate would require 48 hotels to house) (Newsletter 1975[3]:4).

PARADOX IN PRAGMATICS

Ironically, in the early 1960s problems associated with growth in the Association were accompanied by expressed concerns over the need for more

anthropologists to fill an array of new positions. The Association itself encouraged an increase in numbers of anthropologists through involvement in
programs designed to increase the demand for them. Major programs supported by the Association, for instance, the "Visiting Lecture Program" and
the "Curriculum Study Project," were designed to serve and heighten interest in Anthropology. The Visiting Lecture Program, begun in 1959 with
help from the National Science Foundation, provided travel and time sti-
pends to anthropologists willing to lecture at universities without Anthropology departments. Within two years (1961) this program was described
in the AAA Newsletter as "too successful" as one of its effects was to create
jobs "which is now a serious problem because there are not enough fully
trained anthropologists willing to take these positions and smaller departments go unfilled" (Newsletter 1961[3]:8). Graduate departments were simultaneously struggling to meet the needs of faculty staffing and reorganize
existing curricula to meet new needs. This process was described as a "major
revolution" in graduate school, and was discussed in terms consistent with
those in neo-evolutionary work current at the time: "We are slowly moving
from a hunting-gathering general anthropology-graduate-type, to the more
advanced level of get-your-own specialization and produce-graduate type"
(Newsletter 1962[1]:2)

The Curriculum Study Project, with funding assistance from the U.S.
Office of Education, was introduced to design appropriate anthropology
curricula for elementary through secondary school age audiences. The expansion of programs directed to disciplinary outreach also included the development of new, as well as separation of extant, Anthropology
departments in universities. As a result a record number of new teaching
positions were created. A new section in the Fellow Newsletter, "Educational Affairs," was introduced to provide a forum for discussion of problems
of continuing concern in the education of anthropologists. Some senior
anthropologists proposed that the Ph.D. be considered a research degree,
and the M.A. a teaching degree, in order to supply qualified anthropologists
more quickly. Goldschmidt (1984:167) recalled:

Indeed the growth of the student population required such an increase in faculty
that it was impossible to keep up with the teaching demand, and faculty were re-
cruited from among students fresh back from the field, before their dissertations were
completed.

The tide of expansion in the early 1960s swept through the field, encouraged and nurtured by developments in the surrounding economic and
political environments. Anthropologists affiliated with universities were being hired in increasing numbers by various government agencies or supported through quasi-governmental monies. For example, the newly
reorganized Agency for International Development (AID) announced two
major studies to assess the progress of scientific development in Latin Amer-

ica. Expanded job opportunities at AID included the hiring of anthropologists as staff advisors at their headquarters in Washington, and in the Commercial Development Division. Concern with the ability to fill these positions was voiced: "When AID calls upon us, as it is certain to do eventually, and asks for anthropologists competent to carry out tasks such as these, where are these anthropologists to be found?" (Newsletter 1963[5]: 6). The Social Affairs Department of the Pan American Union expanded its programs in Mexico, Argentina, and Uruguay. The Ford Foundation moved its Foreign Area Training Program to the Social Science Research Council (SSRC), thus expanding funding for anthropologists (Newsletter 1962[1]: 7). The Smithsonian Institution established a new Office for Anthropology. The Peace Corps was sending appeals to the Association asking anthropology students to join in their training programs, which already employed a number of anthropologists. Moreover, Anthropology, along with other social sciences and humanities, had begun lobbying for federal funding on a level more comparable to that available for the natural sciences. In 1964 (Newsletter 5[8]:1–2) President Johnson established a presidential advisory committee to study funding inequities between natural sciences, social sciences, and humanities. This resulted in an entirely new funding source when Congress established the National Endowment for the Humanities in 1965 (the same year in which Project Camelot became public).

Through the first years of the 1960s, myriad new opportunities were created for anthropologists as part of expanded funding to government agencies. The diversity of these opportunities and the lack of anthropologists to fill them was itself studied by the National Institutes for Mental Health (NIMH). NIMH, which already supported anthropologists in significant numbers at this time, funded a study to determine the unmet need for anthropologists, and at the same time increased funding for graduate support. Like many other Anthropology students of their generation, both Rabinow and Crapanzano received grants from NIMH to pursue their graduate degrees. As Rabinow (1989) remarked in my interview with him: "Those were the good old days when there was money for everybody. I had an NIMH fellowship so when I got back from Morocco I got myself an . . . apartment and wrote the thesis . . . between 1969 and 1970."

Through the middle of the 1960s, the expanding demand for anthropologists showed no visible signs of slowing down. A survey in 1964 (Newsletter 1965[1]:8) confirmed that while the demand for anthropologists working full time overseas for the government was slight, all other demands were at an all-time high. It was in this expanding market for anthropologists that fieldwork ethnographers undertook their undergraduate and graduate work. But in the last years of the 1960s and into the 1970s, the employment picture underwent dramatic changes. The market of the early to mid-1960s shrank so rapidly that when fieldwork ethnographers returned from the field, the social and political changes which had disoriented Rabinow upon his return from the field shifted again, this time as part of the upheaval in the American economy. But while social and political changes were more immediately apparent to those returning, early economic shifts were more subtle, as were their effects.

In actuality, as early as the late 1960s the economic picture of the early 1960s had been turned upside-down, including the employment expectations of new anthropologists.

OVERPOPULATION IN THE PROFESSION

At a time when we are living in what is obviously an economic crisis poorly hidden under the term "recession," it is sheer nonsense to continue to produce anthropologists as if we were in the middle of an economic bonanza.

In business, where the amount of production is measured by the level of profit, the amount of stocked product and the sales level determine the amount of production of any article at a given moment. We have to realize that, whether we want it or not, academia *is not* beyond the elementary laws of economics, at least in this part of the world. (Newsletter 1975[5]:2)

In 1965, the number of anthropologists continued to grow at a record rate, but funding and employment began a downward trend which within five years was a precipitous slide. These changes were part of general trends in the U.S. economy, which in turn were associated in part with U.S. political activities and allocation of government funds. But this turnaround was also significant and specific to Anthropology as part of the fall-out over Project Camelot and similar issues. During the next several years increasing concern over political imbroglios involving social scientists, and the reluctance of other countries to allow American researchers entry, contributed to reduced funding and employment opportunities. In the latter half of the 1960s the symbiotic relationship in which growth in the number of anthropologists and the number of new positions for anthropologists "fed off each other" fell apart.

By the end of the 1960s, when the Foreign Affairs Research Council (appointed by President Johnson in 1965) issued its first report (1969), the decline in governmental support was already visible, although there was no evidence in the activities of the AAA that anthropologists were paying attention to this decline. In fiscal 1969, funding from the government (in particular the National Science Foundation, National Institutes of Health, and Health Education and Welfare), which accounted for between 30 and 40 percent of all university research funds, began to decline. For the first time in almost twenty years, federal support failed to grow with university costs, and in some areas fell below support levels for the previous year. For example, between 1968 and 1969 (when as noted above, 700 new members joined the AAA), the National Science Foundation (NSF), the largest single federal supplier of funds for university research, cut its support to the social sciences by 10 percent. The only exception to the overall decline in funding availability through federal agencies was Department of Defense funding, which increased by 4 percent for academic and other research and development needs (Newsletter 19[1]:11). This correlated with a study done by the NSF warning about the "overproduction" of Ph.D.s. The only groups reported not likely to produce an oversupply of new doctorates were science and engineering (Newsletter 1969[1]:11).

A summary of the 1969 annual meeting written for the Newsletter contrasted sharply with those from recent years as "a more somber mood than usual marked the event." Attendance had fallen by almost 800 members from the previous year. The shift in attendance and mood was attributed to several factors, including "a general atmosphere of belt-tightening" (Newsletter 1970[1]:1).[3]

Even without the decline in available monies from the government and related sources, there were serious indicators of potential problems in employment for anthropologists. Sorenson, who had earlier suggested the "study of us" took his own advice and published "The Mobility of Academic Anthropologists 1962–1969" (1970). In his study Sorenson showed that while the number of positions in Anthropology expanded in those years, professors tended to stay where they were. This was coupled with a tendency for the best-known schools to hire anthropologists who had been granted degrees from their own programs. While the tendency of elite departments to reproduce themselves was part of ordinary hiring practices, the effects of such practice were more pronounced as fewer new openings occurred in all departments. Anthropologists looking for academic employment had to rely almost exclusively on a small increase in new positions—positions for which they were unlikely to be considered unless they had previous institutional ties.[4] (This was also later cited as a factor in the article by D'Andrade et al. 1975.) Overall, these trends and practices left fewer positions available, less mobility, and less opportunity for general employment (Sorenson 1970:4).

It was at this time (late 1960s through the mid-1970s) that fieldwork ethnographers and their cohort of University of Chicago graduates were living in New York, teaching in marginal positions and looking for permanent work. Unlike recent previous generations of graduates who quickly got jobs at their own universities or others of similar status, these anthropologists experienced a kind of limbo in employment.[5]

Fieldwork ethnographers were caught in an overall spiral of growing inflation and economic uncertainty which caused operating deficits for private schools while legislative cuts (both federal and state) had done the same for public ones. For years following their return from the field they struggled to situate themselves professionally, but job opportunities were few and far between for all members of their generation. These struggles were general in the academic community but the group of Chicago anthropologists living in New York took on an increasingly embattled mentality. In the interview I conducted with Paul Rabinow, I asked him about comments I had heard, from other anthropologists in the course of my fieldwork in the discipline, that the Chicago anthropologists living in New York formed a closed and "elitist" group. Rabinow responded:

Let me say that's too bad and that's unfortunate. . . . We felt—first of all we were friends, secondly this group had no official standing whatsoever. It had no power. . . . And we felt tremendously under attack professionally for which there was lots of good evidence and we were just trying to stay alive. . . . I think at the time we weren't very good at . . . [networking] . . . and that was also part of the problem at that time.[6]

The sense that fieldwork ethnographers had of being unwelcome in New York was personally experienced, but the lack of jobs was not necessarily personal. It had long been the practice, especially in elite universities, to hire or find jobs for their own students. "Immigrant anthropologists" (defined by institution of "birth" as an anthropologist, such as those graduating from the University of Chicago looking for work at universities in the New York area) might always have been less likely to be selected over applicants from "native" populations, but in a reduced job market this was even more problematic. Crapanzano, the only fieldwork ethnographer who was not a member of the group meeting regularly in New York, graduated from a New York university (Columbia). He was also the only one of the four who found a permanent job in New York, albeit not in the department or university from which he graduated.

To make sense of the experience of fieldwork ethnographers in the 1970s requires taking into account the circumstances of the time in which not even tenured faculty had job security. The financial crisis at the City University of New York is a specific example of the changes in academic opportunity created by the general decline of the American economy. Rabinow, Dumont, and Crapanzano had been, or were then, employed at various campuses of this university. In my interviews with Rabinow and Dumont they discussed their difficulty in obtaining permanent positions in highly ranked universities as part of their individual experience, which they saw as linked to their intellectual leanings and networks, but their experience was a common one for many anthropologists as a product of the job shortage; they personalized what had become a problem for Anthropology (as well as the other social sciences) as a profession. Further, they attributed power to senior anthropologists who in "ordinary" times were positioned to make hiring decisions. But the power which younger anthropologists attributed to senior New York anthropologists was a relative power. In the recession years of the 1970s there were funding problems at most univer-

sities, which, as discussed below, in the particular case of the City University
of New York, was identified as a crisis. Senior "powerful" anthropologists
observed their own powerlessness to do anything substantive to keep funding and positions. In 1978, Young (Newsletter 1978[1]:1) described the
position of senior faculty in Anthropology in general (in response to a suggestion by Paul Kay at Berkeley that senior faculty members take a more
active role in creating faculty positions for anthropologists within their universities).

Kay implies that tenured anthropologists are somehow analogous to powerful capi-
talists. Tenured faculty are in fact (just as graduate students are) in large measure
victims of circumstances beyond their control. Tenured members of departments are
allocated some gate keeping chores, they do not sit in the board room . . . (and are)
relatively powerless not only in terms of their own institutions but in terms of wider
society. Anthropologists have studied poor and colonized people for several decades,
commonly thinking of themselves as advocates of the people they study, and yet
colonization continues and the poor exist in even larger numbers. In fact it is likely
that all anthropologists past and present have had much less influence on government
policy than the South Korean C.I.A.

THE RETURN TO PRAGMATICS

The budget crisis at the City University of New York became front-page
news in the summer of 1975 when the City of New York, faced with growing general financial problems, delayed approval of the university's 1975–
1976 budget. A plan presented by the chancellor to forestall financial dis-
aster reduced the amount of money available to each college, and included
a plan to consolidate programs in the liberal arts. Anthropology was hard
hit, and although introductory Anthropology classes were still offered, programs for Anthropology majors were to remain only at a few of the senior
colleges. All other Anthropology classes were to be offered through other
departments.

Sydel Silverman, executive director of the doctoral program at the graduate center of CUNY, fought the potential elimination of entire departments
in which all faculty, including those with tenure, could be fired.[7] By Silverman's account, while the university continued to function, it did so in an
atmosphere of crisis, uncertainty, and pessimism. In practical terms, the faculty workload was increased and adjunct and part-time faculty were not
hired for the following semester (Newsletter 1975[1]:5).

Silverman contacted the American Anthropological Association and other
allied societies and foundations with whom the Association had connections,
to garner support and lobby for more funds. The president of the AAA
(Walter Goldschmidt), and the presidents of the American Historical Association and the American Sociological Association were among those who

wrote to the chancellor of CUNY. Well-known anthropologists in New York (e.g., Morton Fried, Rhoda Metraux, Eric Wolf, and Marvin Harris) appeared at a news conference to publicly announce their support for City University faculty and departments.[8]

Ultimately, no decisions were made on the chancellor's proposals and CUNY was forced to close down for two weeks for lack of sufficient funds. The state legislature subsequently approved a reduced budget for the next year with cuts of up to 20 percent assigned to the discretion of each college president. CUNY graduate students were hired as part-time adjuncts to make up for faculty on leave or retired, none of whom was permanently replaced.

The financial situation at CUNY was a public example of the mid-1970s version of crisis in Anthropology, this time economic. Within a short span of time the field went from a period of tremendous growth accompanied by a similar expansion in opportunity to a sharp and severe downturn. The ever larger supply of new professionals continued to arrive as the demand for them disappeared. In the mid-1960s the expectations of Anthropology students returning from fieldwork included finding employment in academic institutions even before their dissertations were completed. By the early 1970s, fieldwork ethnographers and other credentialed anthropologists (e.g., complete with dissertations, degrees, and first ethnographies based on those dissertations and other published articles)[9] struggled to find employment along with other members of their professional generation.

"In-house" suggestions to deal with this crisis in "overpopulation" of the short term were consistent with cultural materialist ideas prevalent in Anthropology at the time. A "zero-growth" proposal by Rosen (Newsletter 1975[3]:8), which would have drastically cut the number of graduate students accepted into anthropology programs, was both applauded and denounced (Newsletter 1975[10]:1).

Rosen's proposal indicated continuing divisions among anthropologists by referring to the "ineffectiveness" of politically engaged anthropologists. Despite the almost complete lack of political and social activism within the Association since 1970, Rosen argued, "Just as radical anthropology does not offer a solution to the ills of the real world, the real world does not offer a solution to the ills of anthropology" (Newsletter 1975[3]:8).

Factors involved in the post–World War II boom in Anthropology were complex; factors involved in overpopulation (also experienced as underemployment) in the field were similarly complicated, tied as they were to overlapping economic and political scenarios. The result in the AAA was a shift in its central focus. For the remainder of the 1970s the AAA directed most of its executive energies as well as its Newsletter space to material supporting anthropologists seeking positions. The Association took various steps to increase jobs and the scope of jobs for which anthropologists applied, as anthropologists were encouraged to seek positions "outside the academy"

(Newsletter 1974[10]:4). A new column, "Research and Commentary," was introduced in the Newsletter to give applied anthropologists a chance to describe their professional biographies and the types of work in which they engaged. A full-time legislative "watchdog" was hired to report any legislation and funding changes in Congress that might impact on Anthropology. The Job Placement Service of the AAA became much more active and expanded as new staff was hired to assist unemployed anthropologists.

This "return to pragmatism" (Goldschmidt 1984:171) was a shift in focus on the kinds of dilemmas which anthropologists saw themselves facing. Rather than dilemmas of privacy, trust, and human rights engaging global events, the focus shifted to the pragmatics of professional survival. A new column, "Ethics and the Anthropologist," appeared in the Newsletter (1975[2]:26). Ethics Committee chairman James Spradley announced the column:

This column is intended by the Committee on Ethics (COE) to increase awareness by anthropologists of the ethical implications of their professional activities, and at the same time, to encourage anthropologists to develop familiarity with the Principles of Professional Responsibility adopted by the AAA. The cases presented here are purely hypothetical and are not drawn from cases brought in the past or pending before the COE (Committee on Ethics). Any resemblance between these hypothetical cases and real ones that may exist is coincidental.

Hypothetical cases were presented which readers were encouraged to engage in by sending possible resolutions for the dilemmas described. The kinds of situations included in this column are evidence of the return to a narrowed conception of professional practice, rather than one which included political activity.[10] Confined to strict boundaries of professional practice, limited to work settings, (academic and applied), these cases focused on professional identity. For instance, anthropologists who had planned to work in academics and now worked outside the academy, complained that they had "trouble preserving and continuing an anthropological identity" (Newsletter 1978[5]:3). The Association once again turned to a study of itself as a means of coping with, if not managing, change. New efforts were made to identify sources of disintegration. The "Committee on Anthropology as a Profession" was appointed to address the problem of reunifying the field (Newsletter 1979[8]:21). At the forefront of "solutions" offered by this Committee were (1) a focus on fieldwork as the central and common experience of anthropologists, and (2) self-study of Anthropology by anthropologists as a means of reconstituting the Association and professional identity.[11]

PROBLEMS OF PROFESSIONAL DEFINITION

Like every other discipline that is active, searching and hence changing, anthropology is pulled in many directions. . . . As long ago as 1904

Georg Simmel pointed out . . . that greater "social differentiation" must be accompanied by greater organizational cohesion. We are obviously in a phase of growth in which the forces toward intellectual and organizational cohesion are lagging as specialization speeds up.

But today anthropological unity is a new key: nobody can keep up even with the names of the new journals, let alone their content. The organizational cohesion that Simmel promised must be earned—without it, we lost both our disciplinary center and our public voice. . . . We are all being asked to do something for the unity and future of anthropological organization. (Bohannan, Newsletter 1978[8]:21)

Criss-crossing lines of division in the Association resulted in smaller and smaller groups of anthropologists sharing the same perspective, agenda, interests, and even vocabulary. While long-term divisions between anthropologists working in and out of academia re-emerged as especially significant, divisions between employed and unemployed anthropologists, which had not been important since the Depression, also grew in importance. The 1978 Annual Report made clear the scope of the disaffection among anthropologists.

Of about 15,000 professional and student anthropologists in the United States, only slightly more than half of applied and academic anthropologists were members of the AAA. By 1978, the growth that had so worried the AAA was turned on its head as the membership of the AAA actually started to decline. Longtime members of the Association were encouraged (by the editor of the Newsletter) to reminisce about earlier smaller, more cohesive, annual meetings.[12] For instance, Spoehr (Newsletter 1978[4]:2) spoke about his first annual meeting in 1936 where, he said, he knew everyone by name. Hsu recalled attending his first annual meeting in 1946, organized in seven plenary sessions for the 150 members in attendance. As Hsu put it: "We were all learning the same thing and speaking the same language" (Newsletter 1975[3]:2). But in the 1960s and 1970s anthropologists did not all speak the same language nor were they interested in learning about the same things, using the same methods, or depending on the same paradigm for practice.

THE SEARCH FOR RESOLUTION AT HOME

An anthropologist, by definition, is a person who has had first-hand experience with the empirical basis of our generalizations in the fieldwork context . . . the unity of anthropology derives from the observation of the interactions of individuals with one another and the uniformities that such observations reveal . . . whatever aspects of anthropology become of primary interest to any one of us, the unifying theme of inquiry is how the specialties we recognize within anthropology contribute to this understanding of the relations of individuals to one another . . . the saving grace for anthropology is, and should be the request that observations of human beings interacting are the primary subject matter . . . this means being able to achieve acceptance as a viewer and a listener. (Newsletter 1979[8]:21–22)

The Committee on Anthropology as a Profession was appointed to address concerns about "the recent proliferation of specializations in anthropology and the resulting loss of common direction among anthropologists" (Newsletter 1979[8]:21). The Committee sought to re-establish the connections between anthropologists by reminding anthropologists of their common experience as fieldworkers. The Committee's definition of an anthropologist as a "product" of the field experience was also articulated in fieldworker ethnographies.

General terms of the fieldwork experience were described and institutionalized within professional publications, but even as these terms were generalized they were particularized, that is, features of fieldwork experience, expounded as common to the group, were described as individually experienced. The focus was often on the cost to the anthropologist as an individual in ways similar to the depiction of fieldwork offered in fieldworker ethnographies. For example, *Human Organization* (which published a long-running exchange on the subject of fieldwork) featured an editorial which was reprinted in the Newsletter (1979[10]:3–4) which read in part:

He . . . (the fieldworker) does not have the aura of a medical degree and a need on the part of the person to whom he is talking to be helped. He is an interloper, he has no place or function in the community. He is intensely vulnerable to the emotional current about which at first, he can have little knowledge.

During the process of developing an effective adjustment to the community, both initially and later, he goes through extreme periods in which he feels himself emotionally insecure and in which the people whom he hopes to use as informants or aids are themselves reacting to him and on him in ways that are in their concentrated form, quite unlike anything he has experienced before. Even after a period of time spent in the same place, he will find that he still has the same problems in different form. He will realize that he should develop new relations, rather than seek refuge in the old, he will have to deal with all kinds of cliques and factionalism directed toward him; and too often, he will find that the people who are the hardest for him to approach or get along with are those whom he must win over if his field work is to succeed.

During this time, the field anthropologist goes through a tremendous emotional experience. He feels himself vulnerable, he projects his own emotional problems on the people with whom he is working. Only gradually at long last, does he achieve a reorganization of his emotional attitudes and acquire an objectivity and a competence in his adjustments to people in the community in which he lives.

But the effort to reconstitute the discipline using this "common denominator" experience as a ritual image for the profession's straits was unsuccessful, just as it was for fieldwork ethnographers. In a time of reduced funding and opportunity for foreign research, some anthropologists presented themselves as cynical and sometimes bitter about the terms of the experience demanded of them by those who had already passed through the rite (even if they had yet to be reincorporated). According to some initiates the purpose and substance of fieldwork was less significant than its locale and hardships. Further, they argued that ethnographies which resulted from fieldwork were judged less on their depiction of culture than on their vocabulary and ability to convolute sentences. In 1970, Nichols wrote to the audience of anthropologists reading the Newsletter,

(1) The value of anthropological fieldwork increases in direct proportion to the distance traveled. If it is possible to do your fieldwork close at home, its value is greatly diminished . . . (2) the value of anthropological reports increases in direct proportion to the length of words and sentences used and complexity of sentences. One should never use ten words when 200 will do. (3) the value of anthropological work increases in direct proportion to the length of time spent in the field. Work should never be completed in a month when it could be stretched to six months. (4) the value of anthropological work increases in direct proportion to the hardships endured. . . . In view of the above it is evident that those of us who have not mastered the art of grantsmanship and are associated with institutions which have few or no funds for fieldwork are at a great disadvantage especially in regard to Rules 1 and 3. It is therefore Rules 2 and 4 which we must strive to use to their fullest if we are to obtain the greatest possible value out of our fieldwork. We must write in the most complex, wordy and abstract manner possible and we must endure the maximum of hardships. (Newsletter 1970[4]:2)

Not only was the identity of Anthropology built on fieldwork but in order to be really anthropological, fieldwork was to be done outside of the United States—the study of someone else, somewhere else. Fieldwork done too close to "home" (in the United States), for less than six months, and without extensive "suffering" was not *real* fieldwork. Replete with double-entendre, the mystique of the field, was part of the mystique of the Field. But just as fieldwork failed to establish a common identity for anthropologists, the field experience failed to establish an anticipated identity for fieldwork ethnographers. The field experience as a model rite of passage had fallen to the vagaries of economics. Completion of fieldwork and dissertations left a well-educated work force out of their chosen work. The marginality, liminality, and efforts at constitution of a professional self which faced fieldworker ethnographers was a general, not a special, condition. The self disrupted in the field found itself in an unpredicted professional and American crisis. According to Crapanzano (1980:137), the "world through which he (the fieldworker) obtains and maintains his sense of self and his sense of reality"—that is, his American "world," was itself struggling with change, division, fragmentation, and unmet expectations.

NOTES

1. D'Andrade et al.'s study predicted that after 1982, two-thirds of all anthropologists with Ph.D. degrees would have to find nonacademic employment. While it had been predicted in an earlier study by Friedl (Newsletter 1974[1]:5) that the downward birth curve which began in the 1950s, and the end of the military draft (which "encouraged" students to begin or stay in school as a deferment) would eventually decrease the number of students who went to undergraduate and graduate school; it was clear that the shift in numbers was not going to occur fast enough to prevent the employment shortfall. Both D'Andrade (et al.) and Friedl identified the causes of the job crisis as the "rapid growth of Ph.D. and M.A. programs, along with a historic downward shift in birth rates" (D'Andrade et al. 1975:753).

2. Writing twenty years later, Goldschmidt (1984:170) commented:

There grew up in this period a proliferation of special interest groups, of hyphenated anthropologists—medical—psychological—educational—economic anthropologists—with their own societies and journals. As of April 1984 the Association office has compiled a list of 86 organizations formed by anthropologists in America to deal with Anthropological subjects, including itself and four of the five "quadrant" societies (the Linguistic Society is not included). Fifty-one of the remainder are either general or specifically cultural and 23 of these in turn, are focused on specialized subject matter. What is particularly interesting about this array of organization is its disarray.

3. This new austerity was one of several factors noted by the Association. Other reasons given for a fall in attendance were "campus unrest, continuing involvement in Vietnam and the advent of a new national administration . . . (the Nixon Presidency) . . . viewed uneasily by many intellectuals, and the growing pains of the Association itself" (Newsletter 1970[1]:1).

4. For example, of the four largest schools in terms of their staffs in Anthropology, Berkeley, Chicago, Columbia, and Harvard, 62 of the original 76 listed as Anthropology faculty and staff were still there six years later, including *all* of Columbia's full- and part-time faculty.

5. A brief review of the professional histories of these ethnographers demonstrates this point, as well as illustrates networks of social and professional connections which, as peers, they had in common; for example, Crapanzano, listed as an assistant professor at Princeton from 1970 to 1974 (although he was actually out of the country doing postdoctoral studies [funded by Princeton] for part of that time). After leaving Princeton, Crapanzano was hired as an associate professor in the department of Comparative Literature at Queens College of the City University of New York. Crapanzano became a professor in that department in 1977 and was accorded equal status in the department of Anthropology a year later.

In Dumont's case, hired as an instructor at Fordham University in New York (1970–1971), he was then hired as an assistant professor in 1972, a position which abruptly disappeared through lack of funding. Dumont returned to France as a visiting assistant professor at the universities of Paris, Nantes, and Tours in 1972, then returned to the United States when academic opportunities in France proved to be no better than in the United States. In my interview with him (1989), Dumont said that when he went to see Levi-Strauss, who had been his professor during his undergraduate years, he was told that jobs were hard to find, and that Dumont himself was at a disadvantage because he had been out of France while others had continued to establish networks there. In a time of scarcity such networks were even more important than usual, which was also true of experience in the United States (see discussion of events at CUNY).

Dumont spent another year as a visiting assistant professor at Queens College of the City University of New York, and a year as a visiting lecturer at Princeton University (1974–1975), before becoming assistant professor of anthropology at the University of Washington, and an associate professor there in 1979.

Rabinow was hired as an assistant professor of Anthropology (1970–1972) at Richmond College of the City University of New York, where he became an associate professor in 1973 (to 1978). However, he too spent time at Princeton (1972–1973), at the Institute for Advanced Studies (where Clifford Geertz had gone after leaving the University of Chicago), writing *Symbolic Domination*. Although employed as an anthropologist, the position at CUNY was hardly a sinecure for reasons to be explored in the next section. Thus, in 1976, Rabinow went to Berkeley to do postdoctoral research sponsored by NEH (Dumont was also there at the time doing postdoctoral work in language). In 1978, Rabinow was hired as an associate professor at Berkeley and became a professor of anthropology there in 1983).

Between the group of anthropologists meeting in New York, and the network extension to Princeton, not only through Geertz, but through others (Steve Barnett), the links among them were considerable as was the degree of discontinuity in professional employment.

6. Rabinow's remarks here were unspecific but given other material in the interview and the connections among this particular group of ethnographers, it appears likely that Rabinow was referring to networks outside the "Chicago group" broadly defined; for instance, networks with New York senior anthropologists with the ability to hire.

7. According to Silverman (Newsletter 1975[1]:1) this was particularly disturbing because an actual accounting of costs for liberal arts programs compared to programs in the sciences which the chancellor had not cut, showed that these liberal arts courses provided a "profit." That is, courses in the liberal arts were less expensive to provide, plus many students were served by them. This was less true of many of the courses in the hard sciences. In broader terms this is another element of the evidence that natural sciences were seen as more significant than social sciences in broader American (including academic) conceptions.

Silverman also described her concern that when she went to the chairs of other liberal arts programs, which had experienced fewer cuts, she received little support. In fact, many of the sociologists and historians she spoke with said that they felt that their departments were well able to take on the responsibility of offering courses in Anthropology since the field seemed to them to be a conglomeration of other disciplinary interests (ibid.).

8. Thus, when Schleiser (1976), in the quote used to open this chapter, was publicly asking where the leaders of Anthropology formerly involved in political venues were, part of the answer was that they too had turned their attention to economic concerns.

9. Part of the lack of "power" that the number of published works had at the time was that in the 1950s the Association announced an "information crisis" (Newsletter 1959[4]:3) caused by a lack of new published material. They traced this short-

age to the demand for anthropologists which was such that students returning from fieldwork were quickly employed without writing their dissertations, and did not have time to write up their notes. Within four years, the information crisis experienced by the Association was the reverse of that in the 1950s. What had been too little was now too much as more trained anthropologists produced more written work, and subjects included over the years as the occasional article in general journals now had their own journals (Newsletter 1963[1]:1). The editors of the various journals published by the AAA announced that they were trying to cope with increases in submissions which had risen 15 percent in the last year (during which time the rejection rate had risen to 65 percent). A Publications Policy review announced (Newsletter 1964[10]:2) a new increase in the size of the journals. However, this was not seen as a long-term solution to the problems of the vast quantity of material being generated. For new anthropologists seeking academic employment, writing books based on dissertations quickly became a standard of practice, and such works began to flood the academic marketplace. The number of new books being published created at least a two-year backlog in book reviews in major journals. Publications became a necessary but not a sufficient basis for hiring.

10. The first case presented to the membership through the Newsletter stands as an example for the kinds of ethical issues to which anthropologists were encouraged to direct their attention.

In "The Case of Disputed Authorship" Professor Big from Cupcake University (who had no direct part in student research project) had included his name as co-author when the paper was published. Big's reasoning included that he had obtained the financial support, which enabled the work to be done. Additionally, he had suggested to the students that his co-authorship was an effort to help them publish their first research (Newsletter 1975[2]:26).

11. These efforts were not so much new as renewed. Colson (Newsletter 1976[1]: 10), describes very similar circumstances and efforts at amelioration in the 1930s.

Along with my contemporaries, I have been here before. Anthropology and the world were in crisis when I entered the discipline toward the end of the 1930's. The economy was in a terrible mess. We had very little faith in the ability of political leaders to pull us out of economic depression or to prevent a disastrous war. We could not expect to find employment as anthropologists. There were no jobs. There was little fellowship or research money. American anthropologists were also face-to-face with the disappearance of what had been the primary focus of the ethnographic field research. When graduate students in the late 1960's and early 1970's began to demand: "Why can't we study ourselves?" they seemed to have lost touch with anthropological tradition and with current work being carried out by those who not only assumed they could but did.

12. This is consistent with Bellah's (1985) research in which, in the face of social and economic uncertainty, Americans idealize and describe a wished for return to life in small towns, as well as research by Yankelovich (1981) in which Americans yearn for a sense of community.

CHAPTER 11

Intellectuals Shift

Since the inception of Anthropology as an academic discipline in the United States, there have been debates about its identity as a science, social science, or a humanity. On a broader scale these concerns are, as noted, part of epistemology and method and the narrowness or scope of their definitions. Specifically, they have significance as part of the content and structure of fieldworker ethnographies.

Fieldwork ethnographers were educated in an intellectual and academic world in which science and interpretation were already seen as conflicting, even competing, paradigms of practice. This chapter focuses on the shifting and overlapping intellectual frames of Anthropology, especially as they permeated the intellectual milieu in which fieldwork ethnographers began their undergraduate education and to which they returned following their fieldwork experience. Discussions already in place in the 1950s regarding rules and roles of science and scientists (e.g., Barzun 1961; Toulmin 1961) were engaged with new intensity as politics, population, specialization, and fragmentation in a shifting and disrupted political, social, and economic setting pressed on viewpoints and perspectives. While fieldwork ethnographers were away in the field in the late 1960s, exchanges between anthropologists holding differing views of paradigms of practice and their constituent elements changed from discussion to argument. By the 1970s the fragmentation of the discipline's intellectual underpinnings was claimed by anthropologists with divergent viewpoints in terms familiar in other realms, as a crisis, this time, intellectual.

AN INTERPRETATION OF INTELLECTUAL CRISIS

Despite Geertz's attempt at rapprochement between science and interpretation in his "theory toward" Anthropology as an "interpretive science,"
the program he propounded offered no successful resolution. Still, Geertz's
work, and that of other anthropologists proposing new programs for the
study of culture at the same time (e.g., Goodenough 1957, 1961; Schneider
1968),[1] were significant in their own terms and influential in works produced by others. All of these works had antecedents and were themselves
influenced and produced within the "interpretive turn" in the social sciences
(e.g., Dallmayr and McCarthy 1977; Bernstein 1978; Ryan 1978).

In general, the "interpretive turn" in American social science was defined
by and included the introduction and discussion of intellectual approaches
from outside the paradigm of science, especially as introduced in European
philosophy and theory (e.g., critical theory, phenomenology, hermeneutics,
symbolism, and literary theory), and which sought "understanding" rather
than "explanation." In Anthropology, anthropologists of diverse specialties
and training questioned the intellectual assumptions in which their own
practice was embedded. Increased and intense interest in self-study and dialectical processes thrived, foregrounding and surrounding the interests of
fieldwork ethnographers in the 1970s. Anthropological work reflected these
interests as anthropologists examined some of the cultural and historical
foundations of Anthropology as a discipline (e.g., Reining 1962; Rowe
1965; Bennett 1966; Hymes 1972a; Hoffman 1973), and reflected on the
position of the anthropologist as observer and participant. Casagrande
(1960) had already edited profiles of twenty anthropologists, which attempted to give access and insight to the experience of the anthropologist
in the field; Berreman (1962) used sociologist Erving Goffman's work to
reinterpret his fieldwork experience and suggest an intellectual framework
for managing parts of the field experience;[2] a slew of "confessional works"
were published as reflections on and descriptions of the fieldwork experience. These works incorporated interpretation, including issues of observer
subjectivity, and represented a turn away from science, albeit still in "marginal" kinds of works. While these works and others like them represented
a shift in emphasis and an alternative perspective on analysis, these anthropologists defined themselves as scientists and Anthropology as a science,
albeit one of a different sort than the natural sciences and without the constraints of positivism.

In the early 1960s, when fieldwork ethnographers began their undergraduate and graduate training, the scrutiny of science and the rumblings
of change were already apparent in the intellectual climate in which they
were generally educated and specifically trained as anthropologists. Rabinow
(1977:2), for example, reflected on his undergraduate experience:

In the early 1960's the great Hutchins experiment in general education was in its last stages at the University of Chicago. . . . The college had offered me the profound and liberating experience of discovering what thinking is really about, but it had also left me with a sense of crisis about the older sciences and disciplines.

The "sense of crisis" and change in intellectual foundations in older disciplines noted by Rabinow in the early 1960s soon pervaded Anthropology as well, rising in volume and broadening in scope. Fundamental assumptions about Anthropological methods, goals, and knowledge were questioned and increasingly attacked, spurred by events outside the discipline and impacting on it. Issues of "fact and value" became especially relevant in political contexts, but they were of central significance to Anthropological practice insofar as they represented a threat to objectivity and a turn toward subjectivity.

Throughout the 1960s well-known anthropologists from diverse backgrounds differed as to its cause and definition but all identified and reified a sense of intellectual crisis in various works. For example, in 1967, Levi-Strauss (1967:4) (whose work *Tristes Tropiques* had engaged the interest of fieldworker ethnographers),[3] wrote of a discipline already in crisis: "Anthropology will survive in a changing world by allowing itself to perish in order to be born again under a new guise." Hymes (1972a:3), editor of an "anti-text" *Reinventing Anthropology*, asked: "If Anthropology did not exist, would it have to be invented? If it were reinvented would it be the anthropology we have now? To both questions the answer I think is no." Jarvie (1975:253–266) argued the "crisis" as a solely intellectual one resulting from an inability to formulate new theories—a "stagnation" of the theoretical process. Diamond (1972:401) saw "crisis" as a pervasive part of the anthropological enterprise and described the discipline as the "study of men in crisis by men in crisis."

A pervasive strand in the sense of crisis as interpreted by anthropologists can be identified through challenges (particularly epistemological ones) to particular theories prominent in the 1950s. These challenges included not only attacks on specific theories but a general assault on science as the framing paradigm for the majority of those theories. For example, structural functionalism and the neo-evolutionary theories of White (1949, 1959) and Steward (1955), prominent in Anthropology in the 1950s, incorporated key methods and terms of science, including generalization, (efforts at) prediction, and the formulation of nomological statements. These theories not only included the goals of science but used analogies based in that frame of reference to discuss their subject. Through structural functionalism, cultures were viewed as analogous to biological organisms seeking homeostasis. Neo-evolutionary theories adopted the model of scientific explanation, which sought to identify causality (technology in White's view, and Steward's more diverse, but still causal, interaction between technology and environment).

In the next decade functionalist explanation was criticized as static and circular, thus inadequate; neo-evolutionary theories were also argued as inadequate on the grounds that they were overdeterministic or too narrow. Both of these theories were characterized as part of the "scientism" of the "anthropological mainstream" (Wolf 1972:234) in which science in general[4] as well as in Anthropology was increasingly seen by Wolf and others as an overregularization and overapplication of science, which they criticized in particular and in general.

In the anthropological mainstream is White's scientism, his postulate that cultural events have determinate causation and his insistence that one should look for material factors and material explanations before ascribing causation to a variety of spiritual entities. . . . Every point of view has in-built limitations as do the scientific categories that embody it. (ibid.)

Nearly twenty years later, fieldwork ethnographers themselves seldom used the term "scientism" in their work, instead using the term "science" and thus collapsing all scientific practice into a version considered marked by excess.

Other challenges to science throughout the 1960s and early 1970s included addressing aspects of the subject-object splits which fieldwork ethnographers later took as a primary problematic in their own work. Metzger (1965:1293), for example, in his review of Marvin Harris's *The Nature of Things* (1964), criticized Harris's cultural materialism less on the basis of his assumptions about ecological adaptation than on the grounds of his assumption that an observer can stipulate the meaning of cultural events without the input of those observed. According to Metzger, "Harris assumes that one can develop an observer-oriented analysis of behavioral events. This precludes the need to know the actor's goals, motives and meaning" (ibid.). Metzger's phrasing preceded and incorporated central interpretive views, including some aspect articulated by Geertz (in the early 1970s) and fieldwork ethnographers (later in the 1970s) as the "actor's point of view."

Meanwhile, theories based in European, especially German philosophy (i.e., Marx, Adorno, Marcuse, Habermas), were weaving their way more firmly into elements of American Anthropological thought and practice, in part due to the influx of refugee scholars from Europe during and after World War II (see, for example, Coser 1984). Many of these ideas encompassed aspects seen as missing from American theoretical perspectives—notions of change, history,[5] and the relationship of the observer to the observed. For example, Matson's *The Broken Image: Man, Science and Society* (1964) set forth as its thesis that social science was returning from a "fragmented and alienated" view of man, and called for "participant intersubjectivity" rather than participant observation. Matson also dealt with ideas borrowed from the "new physics" (e.g., Heisenberg [1927] and Kuhn [1962] directly referred to in Dwyer 1982), of the observer as intervener, arguing "man cannot observe without disturbing, and . . . because any act of observation is an act of participation all laws are a priori and subjective" (1964:69). Matson's "participant intersubjectivity" was similar to ideas later elucidated by fieldwork ethnographers in which they described their position in the field as one in which they "negotiated" meaning through their experiences with the "Other," and in which they created a split within the Other's subjectivity. While a review of Matson's work in the *American Anthropologist* (Franks 1965:197) critiqued Matson's model for fieldwork, arguing that it "promoted religion and an art of interpersonal therapy not a science," within but a few years these ideas were widespread in social science theory and practice, indicative of, as well as a manifestation of a further move down the road of interpretation in Anthropology. Crapanzano, in particular, among fieldwork ethnographers, described his role with Tuhami as consistent with "interpersonal therapy."

I prefaced the typed notes of our last interview with the words, as if I were rationalizing to some unknown interlocuter—to my own Lahadi: "This was the last interview I was to have with Tuhami, and I did not want to leave him dangling. I therefore let him tell me his dreams and interpret them himself. As he seemed quite encouraged, I pushed the positive elements in his interpretation and avoided all other insights." (Crapanzano 1980:101)

But the growth of interest in interpretive analysis was not confined to its appearance in professional works and discussions within and of them. Discussions of the discipline as part of professional activity also reflected such interest as evidenced in proposals for symposia and the development of new journals. When fieldwork ethnographers came home to write their dissertations in the late 1960s, a central turn to "experience" as the subject of interpretation had already emerged as a "category" of interest in the discipline, and been institutionalized as a focus through sessions at the AAA meetings. In 1970, when fieldwork ethnographers were newly returned from their fieldwork experience, an organized session entitled "The Anthropology of Experience" was held. Announced in the Newsletter prior to the meeting, the session was promoted as "as much a style of learning as a theoretical position." The "Anthropology of Experience" was aimed at "translating meanings between cultures and in so doing bring the symbols, experiences, feelings of other peoples into our world of meaning" (Ridington, Newsletter 1970[9]:8). There were significant similarities between the ideas articulated by Ridington, Geertz (1973), and later fieldwork ethnographers concerning "actor-oriented" method as part of the rejection of positivism (just as Dilthey had promulgated interpretively framed epistemological objections in the sciences). According to Ridington:

The symbolic transformation necessary to bridge a cultural gap seems to me fundamentally no different from the touching that symbols make possible between subjectivities regardless of culture, yet the traditional frame of reference that treats our
subjects as objects to be seen only from the perspective of our positivist construction
of reality, may destroy the very thing we seek to understand, the symbolic constructions within which *they* experience reality. (ibid.)

Yankelovich and Barrett (1970:12) offered a reformulation of the self
through construction of a "philosophy of experience." By merging the ideas
of Husserl, Wittgenstein, and Heidegger, these authors argued that "the
focal unit of analysis should be a human experience which interweaves the
psychic and physical, inner and outer worlds." Peacock's (1972a:840) review of Yankelovich and Barrett's work extended this experiential frame to
Freud's work with symbols, which, Peacock wrote, "provides one experiential base for elaborating a theory of meaning which is the aim of the
philosophy of experience." The philosophy of experience was thus seen as
an elaboration of a theory of meanings. These ideas were consistent with
formulations of culture itself as a system of meaning, and with an increased
emphasis on aspects of the self. The use of other works in Anthropology,
which discussed the field experience as "anti-examples," provided evidence
of their broad dissemination in the field.

They were sort of anti-examples. . . . I had read those books but I thought that they
were sort of what I didn't want to do, not because they were bad but because they
reinforced exactly the split that there was science and then there were reflections, or
personal experience. . . . That sort of science, versus the personal anecdotal split was
exactly what I was trying to eliminate. . . . I was trying to shift the genre. (Rabinow
1989)

This effort by Rabinow and other fieldwork ethnographers to "shift the
genre" was salient to other percolating interests in the field in broad scale
paradigmatic shifts as described by Kuhn for science and quickly usurped
for various uses in the social science.
In 1974, a symposium on "paradigmatology" was sponsored by the AAA,
revealing not only intellectual shifts but also the way in which anthropologists engaged ideas of change. The 1974 symposium used Kuhn's ideas
regarding change of paradigms within physics to engage ideas of cultural
change. Science and interpretation were increasingly reified as competing
epistemologies combined with new specializations and both revealed and
created widening gaps in communication among anthropologists as vocabularies of paradigms and practice diverged. Neologisms emerged which evidenced confounded categories and perspectives. The announcement of the
"paradigmatology" symposium itself used these neologisms at the same time
as it decried growing problems of communication between anthropologists:

As the industrial era begins, the traditional Western homogenistic, scientistic, competitive and hierarchal paradigm is challenged by the emerging heterogenistic, contextual, symbolic . . . paradigm. . . . The methodologies of social science are changing. Communication between disciplines and between . . . groups often fails not so much because perspectives are different but more basically because of paradigmatic differences, they may perceive one another to be illogical, unintelligent, insincere or deceptive. (Newsletter 1974[10]:6)

A year later (1975), the Center for Twentieth Century Studies sponsored an "International Symposium on Ethnopoetics" as parts of Anthropology moved further down the path of interpretation away from science and toward the humanities. According to its organizers:

Ethnopoetics is the confluence of anthropological sciences and the arts, especially poetry, in our age, and combines the talents of poets . . . historians, anthropologists and literary scholars. It is a new field of study going to the roots of oral and tribal traditions which have value for us today, for that which has survived may be what will assure our survival. (Newsletter 1975[9]:4)

New societies formed which also demonstrated the increased interest in interpretive and humanistic strategies and concerns. For example, the Society on Anthropology and Humanism was organized during this time to "discuss the common feeling of need for a humanistic orientation to anthropological research and understanding" (Newsletter 1975[9]:6). Associated journals emerged which spoke to an "interpretive audience" including *Humanistic Anthropology* (1976), *Ethos* (1972), and *Marxist Anthropology* (1974) (later changed to *Dialectical Anthropology*). Stanley Diamond, editor of *Marxist Anthropology*, announced its purpose in the first issue, a purpose which resonated with the claimed new interests of fieldworker ethnographers in their work (although as noted later, there is a political edge [through Marxist theory] in Diamond's work, that is not apparent in the work of fieldwork ethnographers). Diamond stated in part that the journal would make the Marxist perspective more relevant in the "conventional academy" than it had been before, and further, that conceived as a paradigm for "radical thought," the articles in the journal would explore "the relationship between dialectical, existential and related approaches. . . . (which) must serve as the ground for a critical anthropology, the ultimate aim of the journal." The tide had turned and successive waves of interpretation swamped the grounds of science.

Rabinow (1976), Crapanzano (1977), and Dwyer (1977, 1979) all contributed articles presaging their fieldworker ethnographies to *Dialectical Anthropology*. As these anthropologists began producing these articles following completion of their dissertations and first books (with the exception, as noted, of Dwyer) they had already spent years in New York working at part-time or temporary positions connected to each other through a series of experiences and through networks of individuals. For instance, Diamond, editor of the journal *Dialectical Anthropology* and head of the Anthropology department at the New School for Social Research, often hired these anthropologists for adjunct positions.

PARADIGMATIC EXPERIENCES

Starting in the late 1960s and through the middle of the 1970s, a group, primarily made up of recent graduates from the University of Chicago doctoral program in Anthropology, began meeting regularly in New York. Rabinow (1989) recalled:

When I got back from the field in 1969, I didn't go back to Chicago for a lot of reasons. I'm from New York and I wanted to go there. . . . At this point there was a large group of ex-Chicago people . . . Sherry Ortner, Bobby Paul, Steve Barnett, Kevin Dwyer, Karen Blu, Nancy Foner . . . I'm forgetting one or two others . . . in the New York area. We formed a group which went on for seven or eight years and was really very important. . . . Jean-Paul Dumont was eventually a sort of a part of the group. . . .
Stanley Diamond was the only one around who was advocating and encouraging people to be more critical, to be more adventurous . . . a sort of fringe character in the field but visible within the school and in the forum.[6]

In *Moroccan Dialogues* Dwyer's acknowledgments revealed links between Chicago anthropologists, a group at Princeton (including Geertz and Steve Barnett) and those at the New School.

I would particularly like to thank Daisy Dwyer . . . Steve Barnett and Tom Dichter . . . for the many hours we spent over several years discussing the arguments I put forward in part 2; Talal Asad, Stanley Diamond (who published two early versions of my theoretical argument and gave me the opportunity in a seminar he directed in 1977, to develop my ideas further), Clifford Geertz and Sidney Mintz, for their comments on various versions of "The Dialogic of Anthropology" (Part II of *Moroccan Dialogues*). (Dwyer 1982:v)

An intellectual network of sorts existed between the Chicago group and others at the New School, including Bob Scholte (a contributor to *Reinventing Anthropology*), who had been at Berkeley as a student when Berreman and Hymes were there on the faculty. Dumont (1989), a "latecomer" to the meetings of the Chicago group in New York, described his inclusion toward the end of the years in which the group met, "mainly because Bobby (Paul) who knew me as a colleague, liked me, and told the other guys 'well, he's not Chicago, but he might be all right.' " Dumont's more detailed recollections provide some insight into the breadth of the network of connections as they eventually moved across the country.

I was first hired at Fordham at a time when structuralism, the French version of it, was still very much in. A few years later it was a very different story. Spearheaded from Columbia, a hard-core version of the so-called cultural materialism had taken over the New York scene. It became increasingly difficult to find a job for those who did not toe the line. Embattled on the same side as myself were other demonized, "idealized" and otherwise "symbolists" who did not necessarily share the same ideology—some were Marxists, others just Weberians, some at ease with Freud's teachings, others committed phenomenologists, but most had in common their training at the University of Chicago. I had met Robert A. Paul at Queens College, and then I met Paul Rabinow at a party. With Edward Schieffelin I had shared the same office for two years in the Bronx, and we lived in the same neighborhood in Manhattan. Then I knew everybody once I knew the three of them. I thus met Sherry Ortner and Karen Blu, among others, in a discussion group in which I felt welcome and capable of being listened to with a relatively sympathetic ear. Suddenly I could be challenged without feeling attacked.

I found myself in Seattle in 1976 . . . (and went on a sabbatical the following year). . . . There was a post-doctoral program for some program in linguistics, for some training across disciplinary lines. I applied to that SSRC program and decided to go to Berkeley. Paul Kay and Brent Berlin said yes, and it worked out. . . . It was a productive year for me but it was a little by chance to fall upon old friends. Paul Rabinow came that year to do some post-doctoral work of his own. . . . Robert Paul was at Stanford that year visiting. Through them I met Shelly Rosaldo and Renato Rosaldo, who were each writing up their Philippine material. Robert Paul was rewriting his Sherpa thing, Paul Rabinow was putting the last touch to his *Reflections on Fieldwork,* and so it became very much a sort of fun action group. We were all writing our own monographs together; we saw each other a lot, read each other's chapters; in short, it was pleasantly effervescent.

During their early years in the discipline and then in the profession, fieldwork ethnographers were enmeshed in a particular intellectual milieu which was more a product than a process of the interpretive turn, as views argued earlier by others, in documents of the profession, were now asserted in fieldworker ethnographies as professional documents.

OBJECTIVITY-SUBJECTIVITY: THE RELATIONSHIP OF PERSON AND PRACTICE

A particular aspect of the interpretive turn in the 1960s and 1970s was the merging of epistemological and personal interests as intrinsic to the anthropological enterprise. Remember that historically, Boas (Stocking 1960) separated the scientist from the layman as part of establishing Anthropology as a profession. But in the 1960s and 1970s there had been collision and, to some extent, coalescence between roles of professional and person which reverberated in roles of (anthropologist as) scientist and citizen. These changes challenged the view of the scientist as objective in *both* contexts of discovery and validation. Anthropologists, specifically those in academia, took for granted that it was appropriate to hold certain values and in some cases explicitly teach them to students, rather than adopt the value-free objective perspective which research, in some versions of science, required.

The Newsletter published a "Teaching Anthropology" column, which became a forum for discussion of Anthropology as a way of life as much as a profession.[7] Ideas were exchanged as to how anthropologists could appropriately socialize neophytes, that is, provide students with a certain set of values which many professional anthropologists conceived of as intrinsic to, and inseparable from, the discipline. These values had an *a priori* existence[8] and were presented as professional values, which were personally held—a professional version of the "cultural self." Freed from the necessity to include the "trappings" of academia, contributors expounded personally held versions of Anthropology which they generalized as common and fundamental to the rest of the "tribe" of anthropologists, thus establishing the existence of a perceived "Anthropological self." This theme was often repeated throughout the column's existence and can be generally summed up as expressed by Fathauer (Newsletter 1966[9]:4):

After all, to most of us, anthropology is a way of life, not just a field of research. . . . We seem to assume that our knowledge and point of view are to some degree inseparable from the persons who teach them. . . . Most of us feel that the subject matter of anthropology cannot be effectively separated from the anthropologist. Thus the . . . major task of anthropology is to communicate our knowledge but especially values and attitudes of the anthropological viewpoint.

The absence of a description of the particular values which were to be taught to neophytes and the absence of questions from the membership as to what contributors were referring to (similar to social and some political resolutions passed within the Association) indicates that these terms, even if differentially shared, were taken for granted by the community of anthropologists. Just as in the resolutions passed by the Association, equality, opportunity, and human rights were held to ground Anthropology as a discipline, and anthropologists took for granted their position as "disseminators" of these values to students and others. Fieldwork ethnographers also made such generalized claims in their ethnographies but these claims differed in important ways from earlier ones. While Fathauer and others generalized a taken-for-granted (as common) set of values as an underpinning of practice, authors of fieldworker ethnographies generalized their (personal) experience as a given of practice. While Fathauer and others expounded culturally grounded and personally held values and tagged them as part of the discipline, fieldwork ethnographers generalized personal experience and tagged it as cultural.

By the end of the 1960s, president of the Association Sherwood Washburn (Newsletter 1969[12]:4) referred to shifts in the terms of practice, as he sought to acknowledge both the interests of science and interpretation as consistent with professional and person in his address to the membership of the AAA. The goals of Anthropology, he announced, were in the process of re-identification:

The goals of Anthropology have been changing . . . they are humanistic, personalist and scientific. The humanistic goals extend the student's world view beyond that of his own culture, its history and its limitations. Personal goals . . . help the student to see himself with some greater assurance, the purpose of which is to provide deeper insights so that an individual will act differently. Finally, anthropology could be used to help the student understand the use of science to help solve human problems. In anthropology, there are no "two worlds" but only human problems to be understood by any means possible.

Above, Washburn referred to and rejected the idea of science and the humanities as "two cultures" and re-articulated views consistent with older, more flexible notions of scientific practice. But in a shifting social and political world, the terms of the argued dissonance had also changed. In science, as understood in Old Science, American anthropologists used and accepted an array of analytic methods, including, for example, those of history (Kroeber), psychology (Mead), and literary criticism (Benedict). But issues of "fact and value" had become especially relevant in political contexts as anthropologists struggled not with unity of method claims per se, but the assumed and required objectivity of the scientist, no matter what method was being employed. The struggle, pressed by events in the public realm, shifted from the methods employed by the researcher to the researcher's viewpoint while employing methods. In the midst of, and linked to, political and social turmoil, questions of what was taken for granted as science rose to the forefront of Anthropological argument. Social and political crises were reflected in intellectual ones, as anthropologists grappled with what happened to science when objectivity was redefined or abandoned. In the cultural climate of the times, Washburn's "dual" conception of Anthropology was more argued over than agreed upon. Ideas that scientific and humanistic goals were equally appropriate and not adversarial were perhaps efforts to pull together what were emerging as significant gaps in conceptions of Anthropological practice; gaps which soon became wounds as social realities pressed on the terms of interpretation.

An exchange in the Newsletter between anthropologists Amsbury and Brugge, discussing the primary "obligation" of anthropologists, represented these divisions within the discipline. When Amsbury (Newsletter 1971[4]: 16) argued in the *American Anthropologist* that the anthropologist's primary obligation was to "do objective research," Brugge responded:

I wonder what he means by "objective." There are those who maintain that inward self-inspection cannot be objective because it is by definition "subjective." On the other hand there are those who argue that without such self-inspection one cannot be objective. This is no new thing. In 1928, it was already a cliche when I learned that "the anthropologist is part of his material."

At the Southwestern Anthropological Association meetings this past spring, it became obvious that we are again reaching a new level of demand for awareness. We are now not only being asked to be aware of our attitudes, values and fictions concerning the cultures we study, but also our attitudes, values and fictions concerning the people with whom we are working. (Newsletter 1971[5]:6)

Brugge's statement was significant in two ways. First, it pointed out that interest in and arguments about objectivity and subjectivity were as much a "return" as a turn.[9] They were "already a cliche in 1928," but newly raised in intellectual and practical discussion (see also two decades later, letters to the editor in the *American Anthropologist*, 1947–1953). Second, although these issues were not unique; they were being raised with increasing frequency and intensity and with different emphases. The Southwestern Association meeting Brugge referred to was just one among many professional settings in which objectivity, subjectivity, and the construction of ethnography were subjects of discussion. This time, however, anthropologists were not only discussing whether objectivity was possible, but whether it was actually inappropriate. From this point of view, neutrality was itself defined as activity—activity likened to that of German scientists in which refusal to speak out was viewed as complicity. A new group of "younger anthropologists," in the academic generation prior to fieldwork ethnographers, argued for the revision of the terms of science and with it, anthropological practice.

REVISING THE GROUNDS OF EPISTEMOLOGY

Reinventing Anthropology (1972b), advertised by its publisher as an "anti-text," was a compilation of essays written by anthropologists (some of them students) applying primarily critical philosophical perspectives to the study of their own discipline, profession, and society. Sections included "Studying Dominated Cultures," "Studying the Cultures of Power," and "The Responsibilities of Ethnography." These general themes were consistent with particular assertions which later run through fieldwork ethnographies, evidencing an intellectual milieu in which power, domination, self, and experience had become subjects for study and asserted as categories of significance.

As the 1960s and the education of fieldwork ethnographers began, the intellectual world was increasingly permeated by politicized interests and events which anthropologists, through positions of the AAA articulated in the 1950s and earlier, had declared off limits. By the later years of the 1960s into the 1970s, the charge of "scientism" in Anthropology was clearly an attack on objectivity as the foundation of scientific practice, as well as an attack on unreflective theoretical positions. This attack was primarily leveled from a "revisionist" position" held by anthropologists including Hymes, Berreman, Diamond, Scholte, Nader, Klein, Wolf, Dimen-Schein and others, most of whom were active in the politics of the Association especially as they related to the politics of the public realm. According to Hymes: "It should be clear that my position, intellectual and social, is more revisionist than revolutionary, regarding both anthropology and socialism, and regarding the tradition concerned with the general problem of the evolution of mankind, in which they share" (Hymes 1972b:57).

From a revisionist perspective,[10] theory and practice were held as inseparable. The work and activities of anthropologists were seen to appropriately merge in ways not dissimilar from those cited as part of the discussion in "Teaching Anthropology," and consistent with those claimed as appropriate by supporters of the Vietnam Resolution. What was different about this perspective was that it claimed for anthropologists a politically activist role as part of appropriate professional enactment.

Conversant with European philosophy (including critical theory and recent work by Habermas [1971]), and with the work of revisionist sociologists (i.e., Louis Wirth, Robert MacIver, and Robert S. Lynd), revisionist anthropologists continued to use the framework of science. However, they also argued that the generation before them (post–World War II Anthropology through the 1950s) had falsely separated fact and value, resulting in a *laissez-faire* bias, which aside from practical implications "was also not even good 'science' " (Berreman 1972:145).

The revisionist program for eliminating the "static" or "laissez faire" bias in the work of second-generation American anthropologists (e.g, structural functionalists, functionalists, neo-evolutionists) was similar to that in sociology, especially their interest in declaring their biases. Berreman (1989) articulated his position thus: "I don't think there's any such thing as value-free social science. No person can be value-free, but you can try to give at least a hint, or as good a description as you can, of what your biases are likely to be or what you're after." Revisionist anthropologists held that Anthropology was a science, but one which required change in the definition of its requirements. Although Crapanzano (1980:x), for example, denied wanting to follow in the path of *Reinventing Anthropology*, which he saw as a denial of Anthropology ("I do not wish to deny the anthropological enterprise, as some critics have tried to do [Hymes 1972b]"), there were cogent similarities in theme which run through fieldwork ethnographies and these earlier formulations, which were themselves the product of preceding broad discussion and debate. For example, in an article in *Reinventing Anthropology*, "Personal and Extrapersonal Vision in Anthropology" (1972) Robert Jay reflected then current concerns with research funding and prob-

lems of intervention in the affairs of those studied, and stated his own interests as starting "farther back . . . with a more radical and personal
rethinking of the problem, namely, how I relate myself to the subjects of
my work, what kinds of knowledge I look for, and how the problem becomes part of those relationships" (Jay 1972:368). Similarly, Hymes, in his
introduction to *Reinventing Anthropology* wrote:

Where Diamond calls for critical, dialectical and activist anthropology, Scholte calls
upon anthropology to turn criticism upon itself, through comparative study of its
own traditions and their role in the shaping of anthropological knowledge; through
reflection on the inescapable personal and emergent dimensions of ethnographic encounter, and through efforts to develop anthropology toward an emancipatory role.
(Hymes 1972a:60)[11]

Revisionist anthropologists argued politics in the professional setting of
the Association and in so doing critiqued science, especially positivist science, thus wrapping political arguments up with intellectual ones and vice
versa. Revisionists argued that the position of objectivity and its correlate,
neutrality (which grounded mainstream Anthropology), was neither possible
in the field away, nor desirable at home. In their view researcher "bias"
must be made as explicit as possible in the course of fieldwork, but their
real concentration was on the role of the anthropologist at home in his/her
own society. Rather than value-free, these anthropologists argued that Anthropology was not only inevitably value-engaged in the field at home, it
was appropriately so. In the tradition of German critical theory, revisionist
anthropologists cast themselves in the role of cultural critics, for whom
value-freedom and its correlate neutrality were not only unnecessary to science, but destructive. Klein (1972:317), for example, argued: "I do not
claim to be an 'impartial' observer or a 'value-free' social scientist. On the
contrary, I conceive my role as anthropologist in much the way as Adorno
conceived his, as "cultural critic"—with all the contradictions and difficulties this implies." (In the mid-1980s anthropologists as "cultural critics"
appear in postmodern work. See, for instance, Marcus and Fischer [1986];
Clifford and Marcus [1986c]. This later articulation differed in that science
was given up as part of the method, and replaced primarily by literary criticism.)
    From this point of view, science, as set out in the early 1970s, was to be
applied within the framework of a critical tradition in which self-knowledge
led to the revision of one's own practice (and ultimately one's own society)—to the development of *praxis* in which theory and practice merged.
As used in revisionist work, "praxis" referred to social and political theory
about what constitutes a "good life" turned into social and political policy,
furthering the development of the "good society." Fieldwork ethnographers

picked up the vocabulary of "praxis," but in their articulation its meaning shifted to a more individuated experience—to a theory about the way life should be lived (e.g., Crapanzano 1980) or a theory about their own practice in the field (e.g., Rabinow 1977 and Dumont 1978).

Revisionist anthropologists extended an interest in the history of the discipline in particular to an interest in history as a context for the discipline. In their view, it was important to examine their own modes of thinking and acting in relation to the disciplinary and cultural context in which they worked. According to these anthropologists, the absence of self-knowledge (the Anthropological self) threatened all other Anthropological knowledge. They argued for study and reflection of the foundations of the discipline and departments, situated in their cultural and academic contexts. For example, they examined the historical relationship between the development of Anthropology and colonialism (Hymes 1972a), Anthropology and imperialism (Caulfield 1972), Anthropology and race (Willis 1972; Szwed 1972), Anthropology and power (Wolf 1972; Nader 1972), and Anthropology's intellectual grounding (Diamond 1972; Scholte 1972).

Fieldwork ethnographers applied many of these ideas to their own experience as unchallenged assumptions of colonialism and imperialism and transformed them to assertions of power and domination. But revisionist anthropologists investigated these relationships (albeit often with an ideological overlay in which the United States was assumed to play a particular role, given revisionist interpretation of events in the United States and the role of American anthropologists in South America, Vietnam, and Thailand) while fieldwork ethnographers assumed them. For fieldwork ethnographers, the United States as the dominant partner in the colonialist encounter was, at least intellectually, re-enacted by the ethnographer in his encounter with the Other, as part of the ethnographer's own interpretation. In fieldworker ethnographies these relationships were not so much the subject of investigation as the subject of a circular assertion. That is, having assumed a colonialist framework they then interpreted relationships as rooted in colonialism. Evidence for Anthropology as a colonialist enterprise was less an intellectual argument (although it influenced such arguments and lent an appearance of cultural critique), than the residue of a political one. What was an assumption of colonialism in revisionist investigations turned into an assertion of it in fieldworker ethnographies.[12]

At base, in revisionist work, critiques of ideology were often rooted in ideology. When, for instance, revisionists argued that those who do not acknowledge assumptions about the course of history nevertheless make assumptions about its course, these assumptions, including those of theory and method, turned into a kind of transcendent truth. Science, it was argued, turns into "scientism"—an enactment not of an objective, value-free position, but an enactment of ideology. Scholte, for example, argued:

One can, and should go even further: the entire concept of a value-free social science (and the methods proper to such activity) is to a large extent the historical outcome and the cultural consequence of a normative and bourgeois ideology. . . . In the current context of academic social science, this ideology is further mediated and concretized in an occupational group which often seeks to merely maintain, justify and spread its own socio-economic interests in an ideological false consciousness under the protective rubric of scientific objectivity and technological efficiency. . . . If this is true (and the evidence seems overwhelming), the logical irony is readily apparent: a so-called value-free perspective in principle embodies and in fact perpetuates a normative ideology. (Scholte 1972:434)[13]

Influenced by intellectually powerful arguments articulated by Marx, Adorno, Habermas, C. Wright Mills, and others, revisionist thought itself was grounded in Enlightenment views consistent with American constructs, especially as part of the public realm. The assumption and exploration of power, ethics, and social responsibility were fundamental to the revisionist idea of what science should be. Ideology, power, and political domination as part of Anthropological work became a central subject of study as revisionists demanded that:

individual scholars be held accountable for their activities as scientists, for only thus will a humane science of man emerge rather than one which is simply adjunct to the inhumane, socially uninformed, and irresponsible goals of politicians, militarists and entrepreneurs. We ask that anthropological work be relevant in the sense that it address the issues facing people in their social existence and we ask that it reflect the quality of that social existence as it seeks to provide foundations and practical recommendations for improving it. (Berreman 1972:96)

Revisionist anthropologists, as part of social and professional networks when fieldwork ethnographers were in New York, were clearly conduits for the flow of intellectual ideas. But this site as an exchange of argument and discussion was a very different social and political terrain from that experienced by revisionist anthropologists through the AAA. In the late 1960s, many American anthropologists struggled to define themselves intellectually including politically, through their practice. This struggle included grappling with the appropriate role of the anthropologist not only during fieldwork but at home, as events in the public realm including the civil rights movement, the assassinations of John F. Kennedy and Martin Luther King, and the Vietnam War, rose to the forefront of concern for many Americans and were part of what has been widely recognized as remarkable activity in the American civic realm. The America to which fieldwork ethnographers returned was one of incipient "malaise"—a malaise which became more pronounced as the 1970s decade wore on.

The global dimensions of the 1960s shrunk both politically and intellectually in the 1970s. The dimensions of the critical and political roles of the anthropologist as described by Diamond and Scholte were "narrowed" in fieldworker ethnographies to a primarily individual project. Revisionist anthropologists engaged in a broad range of political activities within the Association and the broader American setting. Fieldwork ethnographers, consistent with the turning "inward" of Americans in general, reflected in the profession, "substituted" an intellectualized discussion of political activity for engagement in it. Berreman, when asked if he saw any connection between his own reflection on fieldwork in *Behind Many Masks* (1962) with fieldworker ethnographies, responded:

I think it's an intellectual connection. Being older, I tend to think there's nothing new. In fact now, this stuff with text and context . . . well, it was said so much better thirty years ago, not by people like me but by people ahead of me, C. Wright Mills and Stanley Diamond and others, but it's fine . . . people have to rediscover and say it again . . . so there's nothing wrong with it. But people are always announcing great new paradigms that are just not new at all and I think we're all very aware of the issues and the problems of doing fieldwork and the problems of value judgments and the problems of the whole issue of objectivity versus subjectivity. I was on the board of Anthropology and Humanism Quarterly. . . . When it started, the humanism I had in mind was a concern with the well-being of people and now the journal has become more literary—but originally it wasn't that. It was empathetic and sort of C. Wright Mills sociological imagination stuff—to be concerned about what's happening—his emphasis on what he called "the politics of truth."

The questions raised in fieldworker ethnographies no longer grappled with the possibilities and problems of value-free versus value-engaged social science. Instead anthropological work was assumed as inevitably and appropriately subjective. The question of "what kind of science" had no meaning when science had been wholly rejected. The concern was not with objectivity, but with subjectivity, and consistent with the postmodern turn, not with "How do I see this?" but with "How do I feel about this?" and its relationship with the "object" of study.

Fieldwork ethnographers did not argue the obligations of scientists or citizens at home and abroad. The substance of these "categories" disappeared in the pre-eminence of a presupposed, powerful Western self. The role for professionals in political and social movements as enacted in earlier crises in Association, national, and global venues was reduced to involvement in the professional realm, and in that realm from the politics of the Association to the politics of publications. Fieldwork ethnographers asserted the political implications of their practice but it was more an intellectual project than a practical one as it engaged the politics between persons rather than nations. Where many anthropologists of a generation before propelled themselves into the civic realm, the next generation of "philosophically informed" (Marcus and Cushman 1982) ethnographers propelled themselves

into the professional one. By the late 1970s, the civic realm was intellectualized and uninhabited.

NOTES

1. Geertz, Goodenough, and Schneider are included here as voices within the
interpretive model, although clearly their frames of reference were significantly different in specific respects. For example, Geertz drew on phenomenology and hermeneutics, while Goodenough and Schneider drew on linguistics, albeit differently.
Schneider borrowed explicitly from structural linguistics and structuralism familiar
through Levi-Strauss while Goodenough borrowed from ideas familiar in componential analysis. Interest in linguistics is consistent with the interpretive turn, although
insofar as linguistics is often seen (and announces itself) as the most scientific of the
social sciences, it may be argued that it straddles both frameworks. Levi-Strauss's
work, influenced by Freudian (and Levi-Strauss claims Marxist) as well as Durkhei-
mian ideas, is itself firmly situated outside the framework of positivist science. Ortner
(1984) put Geertz and Schneider in the category of "symbolic anthropologists" and
referred to Levi-Strauss's influence on Schneider. "The other major figure in the
Chicago school of symbolic anthropology has been David Schneider. Schneider, like
Geertz, was a product of Parsons and he too concentrated primarily on refining the
culture concept. But his efforts went toward understanding the *internal logic* of
systems and meaning, by way of a notion of 'core symbols' and also by way of ideas
akin to Claude Levi-Strauss's concept of culture."

2. In my interview with Berreman (1989) he said he was no longer able to use
that work successfully in his introductory classes as a means to present aspects of
being in the field. For Berreman, Goffman's framework was a means to analyze his
own presentation and position in the field. Students in the 1980s viewed "many
masks" as intentional (and unacceptable) manipulation of Berreman's presence in the
field and of the views of Others in relation to the anthropologist. Students in the
1960s did not interpret it in the same way.

3. Rabinow (1977:3), for example, wrote, "Perhaps the two books which ex-
pressed the ethos of that time (during his undergraduate education) for me were
Thomas Kuhn's *The Structure of Scientific Revolutions* (1962) and Claude Levi-
Strauss's *Triste Tropiques* (1955). Dumont (1978), as an undergraduate student of
Levi-Strauss's, also referred to *Triste Tropiques* as a particular influence on him.

4. For example, scientism was defined by Habermas (1973:4) in philosophy as
"science's belief in itself: that is, the conviction that we can no longer understand
science as *one* form of possible knowledge, but rather must identify knowledge with
science."

5. While history had been a central interest in Anthropology since Boas, the
"particularism" of its focus and the lack of theory generated by such work were part
of its decline. Eventually Boas's science was seen as insufficient science (e.g., Ray
1956 above).

6. Although outside the range of this particular research, this characterization of
Stanley Diamond as a "fringe character" in the field is interesting, in part because it
may reveal "historical" and perhaps traditional views (and in the view of some, ani-
mosities) between the University of Chicago and the New School for Social Research.

Coser (1984), for example, points out that during the Second World War refugee scholars coming to America met with different receptions (and offers) from different universities. Coser argued that Carnap (the "father of logical positivism") met with a welcome from the University of Chicago, since his views (consistent with American pragmatism) were more in keeping with those found at the University of Chicago. Critical theorists did not find such a welcome from Chicago, and were largely marginalized in the United States, where they found opportunities at the New School. The particular view of Diamond as marginal is interesting since, although he was not part of the faculty, for instance, at Columbia (also in New York, with the weight of the Boasian legacy behind it), he had authored a number of books and articles, was the editor of "his own" journal, was an active member of the American Anthropological Association (i.e., he was an active organizer of both the Anthropology of Experience and Ethnopoetics symposiums) both intellectually and in its internal politics, and was on the board of several other journals. He was, through these avenues, visible more than "within the school and the forum."

7. It is interesting to note that one of the studies of "ourselves" which Sorenson and others had suggested as a remediation for the problems within the Association found that the second occupation for which the largest percentage of anthropologists questioned were best suited was social work. The third was members of the clergy (Newsletter 1976:1).

8. I use the term "a priori" here ff. Apel (1977:187), in his discussion of "a priori communication" which he defines as "norms, standards, conventions, rules, goals, concepts, methods, and so forth that constitute scientific activity [which] presuppose intersubjective understanding within this community."

9. I find it interesting and perhaps significant that Brugge refers to this discussion being part of Anthropology in 1928, which was a year after Heisenberg's ideas on uncertainty were presented and which created a stir in the community of physicists and presumably beyond, perhaps similar to that stirred by physicist Thomas Kuhn following publication of *The Structure of Scientific Revolutions* (1962). This is not to suggest that these works were seminal in the sense of responsible for creating subsequent turmoil in definitions, but that they certainly contributed to discussion and engendered it.

10. In addition to following Hymes's own description of his position as "revisionist," I have borrowed the term "revisionists" from Leon Bramson in *The Political Context of Sociology* (1967), in which Bramson refers to Wirth, MacIver, and Lynd (among others) as students of the "scientific generation" who were exposed to European social theory and "imbibed along with their Weber, neo-Kantian theories of knowledge; and with their Marx and Mannheim a feeling for the problem of ideology in sociology itself" (145). According to Bramson, these sociologists also argued against what they saw as the false separation between fact and value in sociological work.

11. The interest in "emancipation" which Hymes argues for here is situated in German Hegelian and Marxist traditions and is one of Habermas's knowledge-constitutive interests. The critical sciences presuppose Enlightenment interests in truth, freedom, justice, and so on and are part of the achievement of autonomous adults. "Emancipatory knowledge" uses reason and rational knowledge, and leads to freedom from ideology. See Habermas, *Knowledge and Human Interests* (Boston: Beacon Press, 1971).

12. In either case, the relationship between colonialism and Anthropology is complex and none of these works makes much of an effort to sort it out in serious and less than ideological terms. At the meetings of the American Anthropology Association in 1986, anthropologists in their sixties and seventies addressed the audience at a session entitled "Looking Backward—Looking Forward: Remarks from some Old Codgers." In this forum, anthropologists including William Schwab, John Middleton, Arthur Vidich, and Aidan Southall, who had gotten funding through government agencies in the 1930s and 1940s, objected to being categorized by younger anthropologists as "agents of colonialism," a characterization they found somewhat laughable considering what they saw as their own marginality both at home and abroad during and following their research. According to these anthropologists, even those in the profession who were well-known in the discipline were seldom well-known outside it, or in a position of power in or out of the field setting. Also see, for instance, William Davenport's article in Helms's (1984b) collection of "ethnohistorical" studies in which he offers an interpretation of the Thailand study that differs sharply from that presented here from discussion gleaned from the AAA Newsletter; or Reining's (1962) article in which he presented documents to demonstrate that Anthropology began in Britain as part of an anti-racist movement. Anthropology as a product of colonialism, and Anthropology as a colonialist project have not sufficiently been disentangled. The visibility of certain anthropologists and their work during World War II was an exception. Even in that instance, given different viewpoints, diverse interpretations and conclusions can be drawn.

13. What Scholte failed to wrestle with is the persistent dilemma of interpretation and ideology. That is, if critique is undertaken and objectivity taken as itself the product of false ideology (making objectivity impossible), then all critique of ideology is undertaken from the standpoint of one ideology or another. Such a critique is already value-engaged and the critique itself is also the product of a "normative bourgeois ideology," albeit of a different type.

CHAPTER 12

Reflections on
Fieldworker Ethnographies

One of the aims of fieldworker ethnographies as stated by their authors was to reveal the "cultural self"—the publicly and socially constructed aspect of self. As written by individuals these works were unique. As symbolic works, taken together, their sum was greater than their parts. Embedded in and permeated by the upheavals in American culture, the works reflected the times from which they emerged and in which they were written. As fieldworkers struggled to make sense of their fieldwork experience in its immediacy and years later, at home, they did, as claimed, reveal aspects of the cultural self. But what they "say" is less available from the analysis *in* them than the analysis *of* them. What emerged in these works were not reflections *on* the cultural self, but reflections *of* it. Fieldworkers and the sense they made of their experiences were, in salient terms, cultural constructions.

THE CULTURAL CONSTRUCTION OF
ETHNOGRAPHY

> One of the consequences of the social and political unrest of the nineteen sixties was a series of attacks on, and radical critiques of the social sciences. . . . There was a growing skepticism (that) . . . the belief that increased systematic empirical understanding of how society and politics work would naturally lead to the intelligent formulation of policies, ameliorate social inequalities and injustices and enable us to solve the problems of society. (Dallmayr and McCarthy 1977:xi–xii)

Paradigm Shift

Dallmayr and McCarthy (above) tie intellectual shifts to crises which, in various and complex ways, create a loss of faith. Intellectualized as well as intellectual responses to crises are, in part, efforts to make sense of multiple, often conflicting events and activities in the "real world." Just as science rose as a powerful paradigm for explanation as empirical evidence came into conflict with theological explanation,[1] interpretation was turned to as science came into conflict with human experience. As Dallmayr and McCarthy (1977) implicitly remind us when they link political unrest to intellectual shifts, the ways in which we engage the world, including epistemologically, are significantly cultural.

Embedded in American sense-making of the value of science was its tie to the Enlightenment, and its promise as a means to solve society's problems, including "social inequalities and injustices." Science was to be used to build the "good society" (Bellah 1985) where egalitarian and individual *cum* "human rights" would bring about "liberty and justice for all." Americans as citizens shared this "creed" (Myrdal 1962). Disrupted in the 1960s, this aspect of the cultural self was disrupted as it, to paraphrase Rabinow (ff. Ricoeur), "confronted itself through the confrontation of the Other" in venues around the world and at home.

EXPERIENCE, CONFRONTATION, AND FRAGMENTATION

Within the paradigm shift, there was a further turn from observation to experience as a foundation of knowledge. In meetings, journals, published work, and discussions of them, the interpretive turn validated and encouraged knowledge of Others through the "I" of the self. This focus on experience was enacted and empowered in fieldworker ethnographies as the role of fieldworker as subjective participant replaced the objective observer.

When fieldworker ethnographers focused on fieldwork and more specifically on the *experience* of fieldwork, they thus reflected salient aspects of the Anthropological milieu in which they were working. While fieldwork as a method had long been a subject of discussion and interest in the community of anthropologists, by the mid-1970s the focus on fieldwork had taken on additional meaning. It had been newly emphasized within the Association as the common denominator of a discipline that had become seriously divided along lines of epistemology, theory, ideology, specialization, generation, ethics, and employment.

Yet as experience arose as a privileged category through which to construct meaning, in significant respects a central lesson available to Americans and anthropologists was that (at least, past) experience itself provided no lessons. The orientation to the present was celebrated, as Americans were urged by the voices of the "younger" generation to "Just do it." This was not itself novel nor necessarily negative in American conceptions, as apparent in American cultural views about the past. Rather than experiencing a lack of "history" as an absence of grounding, many Americans (especially new ones) have viewed past experience as irrelevant. Lack of historical grounding was actually a valued expectation by those in the first waves of immigration to American shores. Throwing off the "chains" of the past and declaring oneself born anew was part of what has drawn new populations to American shores. This "denial of history" (Chock 1991:285) was part of the means by which immigrant experience was mythologized into opportunity stories, as "no individual has a past that matters." Certainly, in American terms familiar in the 1960s, when fieldwork ethnographers were being educated in American universities, no past mattered.[2] In most fieldworker ethnographies, no past (practice) mattered. Among fieldwork ethnographers, it was only Dumont, the anthropologist born in France, who, rather than denying history and past practice, saw his work as continuous with it.

As part of the upheavals in American society in the late 1960s through the early 1970s, Americans in general were hard-pressed to understand themselves or their activities as connected to the past; as part of a chain of experience seemingly unconnected to the past, it also held no credible meaning for the future. In a time of widespread tumult and change, the self (variously constructed) was, in a variety of settings, "at risk" (Dwyer 1982). In the Association, the older generation saw their experience as members of a small, cohesive, professional society swept aside in the tide of tumultuous and divisive expansion in populations, committees, specializations, activities, opportunities, and arguments. Within the decade, younger members (and their students) saw a broadened, politically charged, and ethically engaged activist Association (and society), in which they experienced a heady sense of change, promise, and power (for themselves and their ideas), abruptly narrowed to an Association passing resolutions which sought jobs, not justice.

Turns and changes within the Association were repeatedly identified as "crises," and were inextricably linked to larger ones in the broader public realm. Events in South America (Project Camelot), the Vietnam War, the growth in population, the recession of the 1970s, challenged the conceptions and expectations of anthropologists as Americans and Americans as anthropologists. Civil rights and war protests, student demonstrations, the counterculture movement as a whole, encompassed a sense of hope in the future while secret research and the breakdown in trust in government policies and leaders provoked a series of challenges to authority. Confrontations in the public realm between the "Establishment" and "anti-Establishment" disrupted the social world, institutions, and the lives of individuals. These disruptions permeated the sense that Americans, including American anthropologists, made of themselves and each other, and reached into the sense that fieldwork ethnographers as Americans eventually made of encounters with Others.

CONFRONTING "OURSELVES"

Conceptualizing the field encounter as inevitable confrontation in which anthropologist and Other were caught as they enacted asymmetrical webs of power and domination employed terms that anthropologists and Americans used for events and interactions at home. The effects of these events on the life of the Association have been described. At home and away, breakdowns in communication regularly occurred and just as regularly, went unresolved. In the passage of resolutions and arguments over ethics, what looked like a "revolution in consciousness" to some represented a form of tyranny and oppression to others. Even as participants in the same events, anthropologists disagreed over their meaning. In reflections on their own experience in the field, fieldwork ethnographers were confronted with a self-asserted complicity in Western domination, a domination they claimed to reject. In such conditions ethnographers' confrontations with Others were permeated by contradictions within the anthropologist as he simultaneously asserted and rejected his participation in colonialist practice.

The conception of America and Americans as "neo-colonialist" was enacted, accepted, extended, and elaborated, not only away but at home, by Americans, including American anthropologists, who simultaneously asserted and took for granted their own dominance. Activities by agencies and academics were often equally castigated as intervention. Anthropologists depicted themselves as powerful Americans, enacting an "inevitable," "symbolic violence," even in the absence of confirmation by Others. While Dwyer struggled to assert his significance despite the denial by the Other, and heavily pondered final questions, the Faqir dozed off. The ethnographer's profession, his presence and his project, were clearly a matter of choice, not inevitability. Other countries and Others were understood as "given no choice" in the face of the powerful West(erner). "Power" itself had become a powerful construct, one not unique to fieldworker ethnographies, but demonstrated by them. Power and its "partner" domination dominated the interpretations of social analysts.

THE DOMINATION OF "POWER"

> We enter the period of the present, a period in which the phenomenon of power is uppermost in men's minds. This period, it seems to me is characterized by two opposing and yet interconnected trends. The first of these is the growth of the machine which is becoming the governing mechanism of our lives. . . . on the other hand, the pacific or pacified objects of our investigations . . . are ever more prone to define our field situation gun in hand. A new vocabulary is abroad in the world. It speaks of "imperialism," "colonialism," "neo-colonialism" and "internal colonialism." (Wolf 1972:258)

In 1972, anthropologist Eric Wolf described the tension and ambivalence of American life in the 1960s as permeated by issues of power, and argued that the dominant intellectual issue of the time was "the nature of public power" (ibid.). He linked the shift in intellectual frameworks and the terms of analysis within them to issues in the American socio-historical context. In this context, fieldwork ethnographers along with other Americans were reshaping their picture of reality and their common understandings of it. They adopted the "new vocabulary" to which Wolf referred and applied it to their understanding of themselves and Others, including the Other's understanding of the anthropologist. Just as the success of functionalism in the 1950s has been argued as, in part, a function of the perceived equilibrium of the times in which it served as a dominant mode of explanation,[3] terms of power, domination, and confrontation are themselves a function, in part, of the times in which they emerge—times during which the United States had become a world power, with no experience. In 1972, anthropologist Norman Klein offered this analysis:

A hegemonic spirit pervades our social sciences. Anthropology is no exception. The dictates of "structural functionalism" and various psychological approaches—all primarily interested in the mechanics of social equilibrium and harmony—virtually dominated the field until very recently. To focus on competition and conflict between different political economies, vested interests, as expressed in the ideology and social structure of peasant cultures, has indeed become more acceptable than it was a few years ago—even commonplace today. . . . I am arguing that we may be misled by the spectacles of conflict into granting appearance more substance than it actually has, and that such deception can be destructive to real chances of transformation. (Klein 1972:315)

Framed more broadly, Klein's concern speaks to this study directly. How much of the work of the anthropologist is the reflection of, put more strongly, the product of, culture? If functionalism's success was in part due to its resonance for the sense Americans made of their experience and society, so the "hegemonic spirit" pervading American society since the 1960s has made interpretations and explanations rooted in conflict, confrontation, domination, and most of all, power, more likely to arise and more likely to be convincing. This concentration on power has not been confined to Anthropology or the social sciences, but has also been part of the philosophical grounding of much recent work in these fields. Thus, for example, Foucault, Bourdieu, and Habermas all assume power as the pervasive construct in which social life is grounded and through which their analyses are themselves constructed.

Fieldworker ethnographies sought a dialogue but often through depersonalized interpretation, produced a monologue. Not only did these authors deny or fail to take into account the experience of Others, but they ignored the experience of other anthropologists as well. Despite the theoretical commitment in the interpretive framework to alternative interpretations, those of the Other were unavailable, and those of other fieldworkers were ignored or criticized. Interpretations of their own experience by anthropologists which did not show the sense of risk and separation described in fieldworker ethnographies were announced as "less sensitive." Differences in experience were not used as grounds for reflection on their own sensemaking, nor as an opportunity to reflect on differences.

While other anthropologists argued that an ethnographer's responsibility was *not* to ask questions which Others did not want to answer (Berreman 1989) (which I do not take here to mean that they were left unanswered), fieldwork ethnographers saw these kinds of questions as essential to their projects. The dissonant encounter was argued as inevitable and undeniable. Neither as part of a recollection of their original research program nor as part of their reconstruction of their experience were efforts to assess or question the authors' own interests or interpretation of their projects present in fieldwork ethnographies. Such an examination of differences in fieldworker experiences could have led to productive discussions of the experiential frames in which the ethnographies were cast. The failure to integrate or accept the experience of Others (however constructed) as equally legitimate inverted the claimed intent of these works to reflect on the cultural self.

Instead, fieldworker ethnographies "absolutized" the experience of fieldwork ethnographers, creating problems similar to those of scientism (cf. Habermas 1988).[4] On one hand, fieldworker ethnographies thus devolved into a privileging of particular (i.e., the ethnographer's) experiences. As Parkin (1991:161) has put it, "reflexivity has, in the hands of many, become a synonym for a creatively controlling 'I' which is every bit as essentialized as the impersonal structures it replaced." On the other hand, the cultural self was there, but revealed through its enactment rather than its exposition. It is in this absence of critical questioning of their assertions and the assumption of their own personal experience in the field as a generalized prototype that the "cultural self" surfaces. Whatever its relation to the personality, psychology, or biography of these anthropologists, this lack of examination is also linked to aspects of the American experience itself, aspects which these anthropologists took for granted.

Thus, for example, presuppositions and assumptions of fieldwork ethnographers related to constructs of power and experience were embedded in their own experience and that of the nation. Doxa was held as truth and ideologically[5] asserted. Earlier generations of American anthropologists took for granted Enlightenment values wrapped up in activities and resolutions in which justice, freedom, equality, democracy, and human rights were to be universally applied to the poor, disenfranchised, gays, women, racial groups, and an array of ethnic groups, among others. Claims of Western hegemony became hegemonic. The generation of fieldwork ethnographers were socialized into a profession and, in some respects, in an American milieu of fragmented meanings. In the turmoil of the American experience of the 1960s, the unresolved dilemma for many Americans was "what does it mean?" Geertz's program for Anthropology, itself a product of its times, asked the salient question.

WHO'S THERE?

In the "next generation" the question of "what does it mean?" was further "refined." "What does it mean to whom?" The struggle to redefine the Anthropological enterprise as a means to resolve the gap between Anthropology and Other in fieldworker ethnographies resulted in a narrowing of the project. While their authors drew on a critical vocabulary, including that used by revisionists, and asserted Anthropology as inevitably involved in a political and ethical project, the venue in which such claims were enacted was narrowed from engagement in broad public venues (already "accomplished" by Geertz, whose work was apolitical)[6] to private interactions between individuals. This was also marked in the civic realm as enacted through the profession. There is a marked absence of civic engagement in any but intellectual terms. While using a critical, often politicized vocabulary, these anthropologists drew from an interpretive frame of reference which was itself disengaged from political and social life. These terms were part of interpretive philosophical constructions (e.g., Husserl and Schutz in phenomenology, Ryle in analytic philosophy) relevant to fieldworker ethnographies, but were themselves a narrowing of other philosophical discussions of public and private realms in society (e.g., Arendt 1958:28).

While fieldwork ethnographers abandoned observer objectivity, they held to this practice of extending objectivity as neutrality in the public realm. These tendencies were also trends in the wider social landscape to which these ethnographers returned, and in which they wrote their fieldworker accounts. The "blurring of genres" (Geertz 1983) in the intellectual realm was mirrored by the blurring of private and public realms, noted by analysts of American life (Jacobs 1990), exacerbating a larger trend in American society—a "constrictive individualism" in which there is a marked absence of civic consciousness (ibid.:266).

DON'T TAKE THIS PERSONALLY

In fieldworker ethnographies the terms of experience as power and domination, and efforts at establishing identity, were relevant to individual (and sometimes personal) struggles, not public (as social and political) ones. Fieldwork interactions described by fieldwork ethnographers were part of individual, and to that extent, personal politics and ethics. When Crapanzano, for example, personalized these realms by asserting that politics and ethics were part of all choices an individual makes, his project was fundamentally an individual one. What was his responsibility (as he saw it) to the "people we study?" How did his interpretive strategy, including its Freudian and literary "conceits," play out in ethical and political ways? While Crapanzano's position was theoretically arguable, such an argument was fundamentally abstract and part of an intellectualized rather than practical engagement in matters of human interaction.

Fieldwork ethnographers often disengaged themselves from the public realm, phrased as a concern with the failure of such practice, as part of their reconstructed cultural and academic past. Here, for them, was the past that mattered.

There may be situations in which the anthropologist can directly aid the community, but my guess is that they are rare. I have heard aid advocated most fervently by those who have never done fieldwork. This position seems more justifiable within one's own society, where thought, actions and responsibility are more closely connected. Having thought about the problems over the years, however, it is unclear to me what I could have done to aid villagers which would not have been the kind of blatant interference in their affairs for which we criticized A.I.D. programs. If the ethical status of the anthropologist is ambiguous, then the do-gooder, whatever his cause, would seem to be even more profoundly disqualified. (Rabinow 1977:8)

In this instance, Rabinow expressed the view argued in the Association debate over the Vietnam Resolution, that taking action within one's own society was acceptable, but taking action outside it was questionable. Fieldwork ethnographers did not in fact claim neutrality, but activity and ethical responsibility. But how was such activity to be carried out?

Even the claimed dialogue between anthropologist and Other had devolved to a monologic assertion of understanding. As Rabinow made clear, the sense of the time was that any interaction was an intervention, and any intervention carried with it the taint of colonialism. The Enlightenment project as enacted by America had turned it from the world's "savior" in World War II to the world's villain in Vietnam, a scant generation later. The cultural dissonance that was part of the turning upside down of American conceptions of themselves permeated American experience and the sense they made of themselves. What started out in fieldworker ethnographies as a "global" project—a meeting of the West and the non-West—was projected inward, and the series of inversions in fieldworker accounts take on a quality of involution—they end up turning in on themselves. But this too was part of other American experience, as the preoccupation with the personal self was "endemic." According to Yankelovich:

The task that preoccupied many Americans in the seventies was rethinking their personal goals. Such basic rethinking is a rare event. It involves a form of reflection that has not been a notable part of our cultural heritage . . . in the late 70's surveys showed 72% of Americans spending a great deal of time thinking about themselves. . . . a high point for introspection as a mass phenomenon.

Inevitably when they try to answer introspective questions people make mistakes. They go to extremes, become self-occupied—so much so that clever observers take note and apply labels like the "me decade" and the "culture of narcissism." By definition, introspective thinking is oriented toward the self and the nature of the project makes self concern inevitable. (Yankelovich 1981:192)

This focus on the individual, on personal experience, on a sense of self-importance which was, ironically, simultaneously powerful and at risk, significantly permeated and constructed American self-understanding in the 1970s. The patterns of experience in the small world of fieldworker ethnographies were those of the Association and the broader context of American life. When fieldworker ethnographies were written, even the most visible activists had begun their retreat from the civic realm, which was left largely uninhabited. Fieldwork ethnographers came home, and stayed there.

"I AIN'T MARCHIN' ANYMORE" (PHIL OCHS)

The antiwar movement declined early in the Nixon presidency, but it regrouped to mount massive demonstrations in the fall of 1969. Exhausted and fragmented . . . it was unable to capture or mobilize the widespread public protest evoked by the administration's invasion of Cambodia the following spring. The politics of confrontation seemed to have played out, despite a brief resurgence in the spring of 1971. (DeBenedetti 1990:1–2)

The description (above) of the energy, expansion, fragmentation, and exhaustion of events is recognizable as part of the total American experience and of the Anthropological one as well. "Domestic disorder" was apparent in the disarray and dysfunction in the AAA. Within the Association it was not Cambodia but Thailand, not the U.S. presidential campaign but that of Berreman in the Association that marked the end of the "politics of confrontation." Even the brief resurgence, in the form of the release of the Principles of Professional Responsibility, produced by activist anthropologists, occurred "in the Spring of 1971." These patterns were part of, to differing degrees, the experience of all Americans, not peculiar to the experience of American anthropologists nor the experience of fieldworker ethnographers. "By the early Seventies the upheaval was over—as mysteriously as it had appeared, and as worldwide" (Gitlin 1993:3).

"... LATE MODERN" (RABINOW 1991)

> "Tis all in peeces, all cohaerence gone." When the world comes to us
> in pieces, in fragments, lacking any overall patterns it is hard to see how
> it might be transformed. (Bellah 1985:12)

For much of the history of Anthropology in the United States, American anthropologists have worked and argued for a discipline that was scientific. They extended the definitions of science not only through an assortment of analytic strategies, but often through an assortment of statements validated not through positivism, but "Americanism" (Samson 1935). In the framework of the Cold War and a cold political climate at home, anthropologists temporarily stepped out of the fray and sought the safety of pure science. During World War II, they set their neutrality (and in some instances their objectivity) aside. In the 1960s, revisionist anthropologists argued in the Association for an interpretive and critical Anthropology, committed to social justice and ethical practice. In public they argued for an America committed to the same ideals.

These ideals, in various ways and to different degrees, served and clung to those rooted in the Enlightenment and defined a project which was "public, heroic, collective and universal.... Precisely (the) qualities that postmodernization theory has condemned as the very embodiment of modernity itself" (Alexander 1995:25). In contrast, postmodernists have "coded privacy ... subjectivism, individuality, particularity and localism as the embodiments of the good" (ibid.). It is also precisely these latter qualities which have been identified as hallmarks of fieldworker ethnographies, and accounts in part for their identification by some readers as postmodern. It is this set of qualities which I have emphasized in understanding the works in question and their meanings. Yet if these ethnographies represent the particular, isolated, personal, local, and individual—the question remains: Why have they been so regularly cited, copied, and criticized—in short, so significant for two decades?

A paradox of postmodern life[7] is that it is *because* of the elevation of the personal and subjective and the abandonment of the collective and the universal, rather than despite it, that it speaks to so many. Fieldworker ethnographies, as early examples of postmodern works, made (cultural) sense to a particular (significantly) American audience, and particularly to those in Anthropology who had been engaged not in the crises of political life, but in, for example, the "crisis of representation" (Clifford and Marcus 1986c; Marcus and Fischer 1986). From a critical perspective, what is interesting about this project is that it concerns itself not with the crisis and experience of everyday life, but with the ways in which everyday life is represented. This significantly literary project serves as a reminder that there is more than one way to create distance between anthropologists and their subjects, and Anthropology and its subject. It serves as a reminder that denying the authority of the past (as fieldwork ethnographers denied the authority of past practice, and those interested in the critique of ethnography questioned the ethnographer's authority) simultaneously denies its security. We are left with a salient feature of American events and Anthropological practice as traced here—the paradox of perpetual crisis.

LEGITIMATE MALAISE

In *Legitimation Crisis*,[8] Habermas (1975:75–91) discusses the problems of postindustrialist society and the formation of "crises."[9] These crises engender breakdowns and shifts in cultural values which ordinarily allow members of society to make sense of contemporary social, economic, and political conditions. According to Habermas, the evolution of society includes social integration as the means by which social life "makes sense" once power and authority are transferred to the State. Social integration is in turn dependent on the extent to which worldviews can legitimate and rationalize social institutions. In the late stage of capitalism (a stage to which the United States and other societies are "assigned" by Habermas), deficits pile up in both legitimation and motivation (a version of Weber's "disenchantment"). Institutions once guaranteed to ensure social reproduction and integration, (i.e., church and education) disintegrate along with what is left of traditional worldviews. Collective self-representations, which once easily evoked and sustained politically effective legitimations, lose their power. The boundaries of the political system shift and are called into question and there is widespread frustration and suspicion.[10]

In the period of growth, energy, and promise following World War II through the 1960s, the American dream became an expectation. Fieldwork ethnographers matured in a political, economic, and professional world turned upside down; a world in which collective symbols of meaning were fragmented, fragmenting the social integration upon which society depends. Civic agendas were lost and individual agendas rose as the psychological and social costs of crises created a culture of malaise (discussed by other theorists as anomie, meaninglessness, alienation, and lack of purpose). Berreman had already described his own and others' sense of malaise in the early 1970s (as Rabinow had on his return from Morocco). Berreman wrote:

I felt moved to say something here about the malaise that is affecting our discipline, our professional association, our department, our students, our faculty—in short ourselves—because I think that the malaise is . . . close to the heart of the troubles faced by intellectuals in America today. Those troubles threaten to tear us away from each other and from any possibility of realizing the hope that many of us have cherished for a viable, responsible and useful study of mankind. . . . There is something happening around here, and it isn't just at Berkeley. And I don't suppose it's just in

anthropology, but that is where we see it. It is variously described as anomie, alienation, anti-intellectualism, unscientific attitude, disrespect, laziness, know-
nothingism, narcissism, being stoned, or being on the forefront of a new era.
(Berreman 1972: 83–84)

It *was* in many ways the "forefront of a new era," but not the one that
Americans had traditionally envisioned. The sense of malaise permeated and
surrounded American lives, and it wasn't just intellectuals who felt it. So
profound was this sense of things that Jimmy Carter, then president of the
United States, referred to it in a nationwide address. This malaise, personally
felt, was part of national experience, and part of the complex and ongoing
experience of the generation who, "coming of age in America," produced
fieldworker ethnographies. Their works are in part the product of an American experience. They spoke, and continue to speak to an American audience, an experience, a cultural self of half-formed and half-forgotten
legitimacy.

NOTES

1. Dallmayr and McCarthy (1977:2) explain the inception of modern natural
science as itself the result of a "crisis of understanding," and the rupture between
man and nature "or a certain metaphysical-theological conception of nature)."
"When man was no longer able to view himself as an integral part of creation and
when the divine 'book of nature' . . . was no longer intelligible to him as a direct key
to the workings of the universe, he began to investigate nature as a set of empirical
processes in accordance with strict logical-mathematical canons . . . and later in accordance with the method of experimental replication."

2. This is also consistent with characteristic American constructions in which
history itself has no authority. Klein (1972:325) called this ahistorical attitude "typically American." Other American observers and analysts of American life agree, including, paradoxically, some American historians of the 1960s, who as professional
historians denied the "pastness of the past" (Susman 1964:251). In the 1960s, Lynd,
the leading spokesman for the group of "radical" historians to which Susman referred, wrote:

The historian need not be embarrassed if he concerned himself more with the present and the
future than with the past . . . the past is ransacked, not for its own sake, but as a source of
alternative models of what the future might become. (Lynd 1968:107)

3. When functionalism was toppled from the position it held in the 1950s as the
dominant theoretical perspective, it was in part on the basis of (what were considered)
its intellectual limits. But some anthropologists argued that functionalism was itself
a function of its own political and social context. From this point of view, the pop-
ularity of functionalism's premise of culture as a homeostatic mechanism seeking
equilibrium was argued as a product and reflection of its own cultural milieu. Functionalism viewed as part of the relatively quiet time following World War II, was seen
as consistent with that time, that is, ahistorical, apolitical, conservative, and static.

Coupled with and further limited by the synchronic viewpoint of the fieldwork method (limited by the slice of time in which the anthropologist was in the field), functionalism and its "sidekick" structuralism could not account for change. In the face of the volatile national and international social and political climate of the 1960s, the inability to address change was seen by some critics as a central intellectual failing, insofar as it meant that explanation, as the aim of such practice, was beyond Anthropology's own terms of analysis. In "keeping with the times" such critiques were part of discussions in letters and other documents by professionals rather than professional documents. When included in professional documents such comments were "buried." For example, the following comment by Evon Vogt (1965:367) appeared in a footnote:

One of the central tendencies of our United States international policy is to try to maintain or to restore homeostatic states or conditions—to keep things in equilibrium. The Communist world, on the other hand, operates with the opposite premise in mind—that social and cultural systems are continually changing. Since they expect change, the Communists can look forward to, and take advantage of economic, social and political upheavals as they occur. They seize the *initiative* while we continually find ourselves in the awkward position of *reaction* to Communist programs and policies. (emphasis in original)

4. In *On the Logic of the Social Sciences* (1988), Habermas comments on the problems of an extreme swing in hermeneutics in the absolutizing of interpretation. In the unquestioned grounds of taken-for-granted "categories" of interpretation, it seems that interpretation runs the same risk as scientism.

5. I use "ideology" here, following Habermas, as ideas that either hide or legitimate arbitrary power.

6. In an interview published in the *New York Times* (April 9, 1995), Geertz affirmed this apolitical (seen as neutral) stance. "I hold democratic values, but I have to recognize that a lot of other people don't hold them. So it doesn't help much to say 'This is the truth,' that doesn't mean I don't believe anything" (Geertz in Berreby 1995:47). Berreby underlines this later in the interview. "Still, Geertz acknowledges that life often enough requires a bottom line, a decision between one set of values and another. After all the rug-pulling, zigzagging and otoh-botoh, somebody has to choose. Geertz would say that's not the anthropologist's job. His job is simply to facilitate negotiation by making people's belief systems intelligible to each other (Berreby 1995:47).

7. This should not be confused with postmodernism, or postmodern theory.

8. Even as I find evidence for the "crisis of legitimation" predicted by Habermas, I am aware that the call of "crisis" is familiar and may itself be situated in culturally based perceptions about the nature of change.

9. Habermas's analysis here is primarily rooted in Marxist theory, which he applies to four basic types of crisis. Although there is much of interest in these ideas, I am leaving aside much of the central elements of his argument. I do not see this as violating the sense of his argument nor weakening its relevance for the present analysis.

10. I am not here drawing on some central aspects of Habermas's work, that is, part of Habermas's detailing here relies on the "irreducible" dependency on the provisions of the welfare state (here he draws heavily on German experience). I leave this (and other) aspects of Habermas out, not because it is irrelevant, but because it seems to have less relevance to the particular population focused on here.

Appendix

The following synopses are not intended as formal summaries, but as an indication of the variations between and among these works. They are presented in order of year of publication.

REFLECTIONS ON FIELDWORK IN MOROCCO

Reflections on Fieldwork in Morocco (1977) is a reconstruction of Rabinow's fieldwork experience in Morocco (1968–1969), and is intended as an essay about anthropology itself (Rabinow 1977:4). (Rabinow had already produced what he described as a "complementary" and "traditional" ethnography based on his fieldwork in Morocco, *Symbolic Domination* [1975]). Drawing primarily on Geertz (1973), Ricoeur (1969), and sources in phenomenology (Schutz 1971; Berger and Luckmann 1967), Rabinow argued that the strategy of the anthropologist in conventional Anthropological writing represented a positivist view of the Anthropological project on the part of its practitioners. Arguing that theory and practice should be a continuous integrated enterprise, Rabinow found it anomalous that the process of participant observation in Anthropological fieldwork was separate from the mainstream of theory in Anthropology, that "the enterprise for enquiring is essentially discontinuous from its results" (1977:5). Rabinow sought to dissolve this separation by offering a nonpositivistic account of his fieldwork experience, one informed by an interpretive epistemology. In particular, Rabinow drew on hermeneutics as articulated by French philosopher Paul Ricoeur, who had defined hermeneutics as "the comprehension of the self by the detour of the other" (ibid.). Further, Rabinow argued that Anthropological analysis must incorporate two facts: (1) anthropologists themselves

are historically situated—the questions asked and the ways in which understanding is sought are part of the historical situation, and (2) information
which anthropologists gather from their subjects is also mediated by culture
and history. Rabinow contended then that the self under investigation in
his work was not the Cartesian or Freudian self but the "culturally mediated
and historically situated self which finds itself in a continuously changing
world of meaning" (1977:6).

Reflections on Fieldwork in Morocco begins with the anthropologist leaving
Chicago (where he was a student) for a brief stopover in Paris on the way
to his destination in the field. Succeeding chapters focus on a series of encounters (sometimes condensed) with particular informants through which
Rabinow reflected on the anthropological project and the role of the ethnographer. The plan of the book is such that each chapter is designed to
build as well as further illuminate the chapter which preceded it. The book
ends with Rabinow's account of his return from the field and his troubled
re-adjustment to the American setting.

THE HEADMAN AND I

In *The Headman and I* (1978), Dumont re-interpreted his fieldwork experience among the Panare undertaken for his dissertation research, and the
basis for his first book-length ethnography *Under the Rainbow: Nature and
Supernature among the Panare Indians* (1976). Dumont broke with what
he identified as positivist traditions in Anthropology, arguing that his work
and others', including Rabinow's, were situated between confessional and
positivist anthropological work.

Dumont situated *The Headman and I* in a tradition of other anthropological works which sought to reveal central aspects of anthropological practice, in particular the fieldwork experience. While Dumont placed his own
interest as consistent with these earlier works in Anthropology, he specifically
sought to investigate the "I" in the fieldwork experience as a self-conscious
and critical tool engaged in an interpretive and dialectical effort to grasp the
fieldwork encounter. Even as he drew on Levi-Straussian dialectics, Dumont
pushed them further to investigate the relationship between theory and practice and between anthropologist and informant. "My effort will be directed
toward perceiving, apprehending and interpreting the 'and' of the relationship which my fieldwork built between an 'I' and 'they' " (Dumont 1978:
1).

Following his description of the nature and purpose of *The Headman and
I*, Dumont framed his work in three parts, set out as a series of encounters
with informants placed in an ethnographic context focused on conditions
of life and social organization among the Panare. The work ends with Dumont's brief return to the Panare (as part of a television project in January
and February of 1970), where he re-encountered his informants outside the

framework of the fieldwork experience and completed the dialectic of his encounter with them.

Revisiting the Panare under these conditions was more an escape than anything else. Chatting with my "brother" and the other people of the settlement was no longer fieldwork as I had undertaken it before. It was sheer involvement. I had the impression that I was visiting old friends, and the news and the gossip were only a pretext to maintain the flow of communication. Data collecting had now become epiphenomenal to the reality of my social experience. At the same time, revisiting Turiba Viejo as an old acquaintance rather than as an anthropologist was my way of demystifying my fieldwork. The revisiting soon came to an end. Then, and only then, could I begin to emerge from the opacity of the anthropological experience, upon which I could now begin to reflect with more serenity. (Dumont 1978:211)

TUHAMI

Tuhami (1980) is a life history of a Moroccan tile maker described by Crapanzano as married to a *jinniyya*, A'isha Qandisha—a Moroccan she-demon. Constructed from interviews with Tuhami (conducted with his assistant Lhacen who acted as interpreter), Crapanzano drew on Freudian constructs and various, sometimes conflicting theoretical perspectives in order to "illuminate the space of the encounter" in the field (Crapanzano 1980:xiii). Crapanzano further described his use of these viewpoints as more consistent with the work of a literary critic interpreting a specific text than the work of a social scientist whose effort it was to develop theory (ibid.).

Crapanzano first met Tuhami while he (Crapanzano) was in Morocco doing fieldwork for his dissertation on the religious practices of the 'Hamadsha. (Published as *The Hamadsha: A Study in Moroccan Ethnopsychiatry* [1973].) Through his interviews with Tuhami (which were not included as part of the Hamadsha ethnography), Crapanzano engaged a series of questions about Anthropological practice, including the "impress" of the anthropologist on the accumulation and presentation of material (Crapanzano 1980:ix). In *Tuhami*, Crapanzano argued that the field experience cannot be successfully separated from theory and the writing of ethnography in Anthropology. In Crapanzano's view, as part of the process of writing the ethnographer affirms a sense of self through his subject—a self which (ff. Devereaux 1967) Crapanzano argued as inevitably disrupted in the field as a result of the confrontation between the ethnographer and the native. Described as an "experiment" (Crapanzano 1980:ix), Crapanzano used his interviews with Tuhami to illustrate the means by which the ethnographer learned to take on the standpoint of the subject in a process of "self-dissolution and reconstitution" (Crapanzano 1980:70).

Tuhami is presented in five parts. Parts One, Three, and Five are records of Tuhami's "recitations" (Crapanzano 1980:ix), and include Crapanzano's questions and explanations of references which he assumed were unfamiliar to the readership, and which he stated "reveal at least my own bias" (ibid.) Parts Two and Four are reflections on the nature of constructing cultural sense in Morocco as well as sense of the Anthropological enterprise itself.

MOROCCAN DIALOGUES

Moroccan Dialogues: Anthropology in Question (1982) was the product of several fieldwork experiences in Morocco by Kevin Dwyer. In particular, Dwyer focused on interviews conducted in the summer of 1975 with a Moroccan cultivator, Faqir Muhammed, who had been Dwyer's informant during his earlier doctoral research. Dwyer explored issues he had previously identified as problems of Anthropological practice ("Dialogic of Fieldwork" [1977]; "Dialogic of Ethnology" [1979]), and argued that the comprehension of the self may be a necessary step in any attempt to transcend the self. However, he asserted that anthropologists must then move beyond this point to engage "further questions concerning the kind of objectification of other and of ourselves that we as anthropologists create" (Dwyer 1982: 143).

Dwyer rejected ethnographic accounts based on scientific or personal and unique aspects of the fieldwork encounter, instead presenting dialogues between himself and the Faqir focused on various events. Concerned with what he viewed as the inequality of partners in the ethnographic encounter, Dwyer drew on philosophers Goldmann and Lukacs to interpret the fieldwork encounter as a wager in which both participants took risks. While these risks and the relationship in which they were enacted were personally experienced, Dwyer interpreted these interests as tied to the larger interests of societies.

Moroccan Dialogues (1982) is divided into two main parts and includes a postscript in which Dwyer reflected on the "completed" project. A detailed table of contents includes prepared questions posed to the Faqir. The work begins with Dwyer musing on his early discomfort with the constraints of Anthropology as an academic enterprise in his first fieldwork, and then moves to a description of events and the discussions, which formed the subject matter of his interviews with the Faqir. Part Two includes a critique of the Anthropological enterprise in which Dwyer argued that fieldwork should be understood as a wager—a risk-taking enterprise in which confrontation and negotiation frame the interaction. "All this taken together, would permit, at least in principle, an anthropology that is able to challenge not only its practitioners' specific actions and its own theoretical formulations (a limited challenge that even science prides itself on making) but also to challenge both the discipline itself and the society within which that discipline developed" (Dwyer 1982:275).

Bibliography

Aijmer, Goran. 1988. Response to Sangren. *Cultural Anthropology* 29(3):424–425.

Alexander, Jeffrey C. 1995. *Fin de Siecle Social Theory: Relativism, Reduction and the Problem of Reason*. New York: Verso.

Anderson, Jon W. 1986. Reinventing the Shape of Meaning: Ambiguities in the Ontology of Ethnography. *Anthropological Quarterly* 59(2):64–74.

Apel, Karl Otto. 1977. The *A Priori* of Communication and the Foundation of the Humanities. In *Understanding and Social Inquiry*, edited by Fred R. Dallmayr and Thomas A. McCarthy, 292–315. Notre Dame, IN: University of Notre Dame Press.

Appadurai, Arjun. 1991. Global Ethnoscapes: Notes and Queries for a Trans-national Anthropology. In *Recapturing Anthropology*, edited by Richard G. Fox, 191–210. Santa Fe, NM: American School of Research Press.

Arendt, Hannah. 1958. *The Human Condition*. Chicago: University of Chicago Press.

Asad, Talal. 1973. *Anthropology and the Colonial Encounter*. New York: Ithaca Press.

Avruch, Kevin. 1981. *American Immigrants in Israel: Social Identities and Change*. Chicago: University of Chicago Press.

Barzun, Jacques. 1961. *Classic, Romantic and Modern*. Boston: Little, Brown.

Becker, Howard. 1986. *Writing for Social Scientists*. Chicago: University of Chicago Press.

Behar, Ruth and Deborah Gordon (eds.). 1995. *Women Writing Culture*. Berkeley: University of California Press.

Bellah, Robert et al. 1985. *Habits of the Heart: Individualism and Commitment in American Life*. New York: Harper and Row.

Benedict, Ruth. 1934. *Patterns of Culture*. New York: Houghton Mifflin.

———. 1946. *The Chrysanthemum and the Sword: Patterns of Japanese Culture*. Boston: Houghton Mifflin Co.

————. 1948. Anthropology and the Humanities. *American Anthropologist* 50:585–593.

Bennett, John A. 1946. The Interpretation of Pueblo Culture: A Question of Values. *Southwestern Journal of Anthropology* 2(4):361–374.

————. 1954. Interdisciplinary Research and the Concept of Culture. *American Anthropologist* 56:169.

————. 1996. Reply to Rowe: "The Renaissance Foundations of Anthropology." *American Anthropologist* 68:215–220.

Berger, Bennett. 1981. *The Survival of a Counterculture: Ideological Work and Everyday Life Among Rural Communards.* Berkeley: University of California Press.

Berger, Peter and Thomas Luckmann. 1967. *The Social Construction of Reality: A Treatise in the Sociology of Knowledge.* New York: Doubleday.

Bernstein, Richard J. 1978. *The Restructuring of Social and Political Theory.* Philadelphia: University of Pennsylvania Press.

Berreby, David. 1995. Unabsolute Truths: Clifford Geertz. *New York Times Magazine*, April 9, Sec. 6:44.

Berreman, Gerald. 1962. *Behind Many Masks: Ethnography and Impression Management in a Himalayan Village.* Ithaca, NY: The Society for Applied Anthropology.

————. 1966. Anemic and Emetic Analyses in Social Anthropology. *American Anthropologist* 68:349–354.

————. 1968. Is Anthropology Alive? Social Responsibility in Social Anthropology. *Current Anthropology* 9(5):391–396.

————. 1972. Bringing It All Back Home. In *Reinventing Anthropology*, edited by Dell Hymes, 83–97. New York: Random House.

————. 1980. *The Politics of Truth.* Berkeley: University of California Press.

————. 1989. Interview with author, April 17.

Bidney, David. 1975. Culture as Praxis. *American Anthropologist* 77:344–347.

Boorstin, Daniel J. 1958. *The Americans: The Colonial Experience.* New York: Vintage Books.

————. 1987. *The Image: A Guide to Pseudo-Events in America.* Toronto: Random House.

Borofsky, Robert. 1994. *Assessing Cultural Anthropology.* New York: McGraw-Hill.

Bottomore, Tom B. 1974. *Sociology as Social Criticism.* New York: Random House.

————. 1984. *The Frankfurt School.* New York: Tavistock Publications.

Bourdieu, Pierre. 1988. *Homo Academicus.* Cambridge: Polity Press.

————. 1990a. *In Other Words.* Cambridge: Polity Press.

————. 1990b. *The Logic of Practice.* Cambridge: Polity Press.

————. 1990c. *Reproduction in Education, Society and Culture*, 2nd ed. London: Sage.

Bowen, Elenore Smith (pseudonym of Laura Bohannan). 1954. *Return to Laughter.* New York: Harper and Row.

Braaten, Jane. 1991. *Habermas's Critical Theory of Society.* Albany: State University of New York Press.

Bramson, Leon. 1967 (1961). *The Political Context of Sociology.* Princeton, NJ: Princeton University Press.

Casagrande, Joseph. 1960. *In the Company of Man: Twenty Portraits by Anthropologists.* New York: Harper.

Caulfield, Mina Davis. 1972. Culture and Imperialism: Proposing a New Dialectic. In *Reinventing Anthropology*, edited by Dell Hymes, 182–212. New York: Random House.

Chapple, Eliot D. and Edward Spicer. 1979. Shaping the Anthropologist: The Crucible of the Field. *Anthropology Newsletter* 20(1):9–11.

Chock, Phyllis Pease. 1986. Irony and Ethnography: On Cultural Analysis of One's Own Culture. *Anthropological Quarterly* 59(2):87–95.

———. 1989. The Landscape of Enchantment: Redaction in a Theory of Ethnicity. *Cultural Anthropology* 4:163–181.

———. 1991. The "Illegal Alien Crisis" and American Public Speech. *American Ethnologist* 18:279–294.

Clifford, James. 1986. On Ethnographic Self-Fashioning: Conrad and Malinowski. In *Reconstructing Individualism: Autonomy and Individuality and the Self in Western Thought*, edited by Thomas C. Heller. Stanford, CA: Stanford University Press.

——— and George E. Marcus. 1986a. Introduction: Partial Truths. In *Writing Culture: The Poetics and Politics of Ethnography*, edited by James Clifford and George E. Marcus. Berkeley: University of California Press.

———. 1986b. On Ethnographic Allegory. In *Writing Culture: The Poetics and Politics of Ethnography*, edited by James Clifford and George E. Marcus. Berkeley: University of California Press.

———. 1986c. *Writing Culture: The Poetics and Politics of Ethnography*. Berkeley: University of California Press.

Colson, Elizabeth. 1984. Defining American Ethnology. In *Social Contexts of American Ethnology*, edited by June Helm, 177–182. Washington, DC: American Anthropological Association.

Conkling, Robert. 1975. Expression and Generalization in History and Anthropology. *American Ethnologist* 2(2):239–250.

Coser, Louis. 1984. *Refugee Scholars in America: Their Impact and Their Experiences*. New Haven, CT: Yale University Press.

Crapanzano, Vincent. 1970. *The Hamadsha*. Unpublished doctoral dissertation, Columbia University.

———. 1973. *The Hamadsha: A Study in Moroccan Ethnopsychiatry*. Berkeley: University of California Press.

———. 1977. The Writing of Ethnography. *Dialectical Anthropology* 2:69–73.

———. 1980. *Tuhami: Portrait of a Moroccan*. Chicago: University of Chicago Press.

———. 1981. Text, Transference and Indexicality. *Ethos* 9(2):122–148.

———. 1986. Hermes' Dilemma: The Masking of Subversion in Ethnographic Description. In *Writing Culture*, edited by James Clifford and George E. Marcus. Berkeley: University of California Press.

Dallmayr, Fred and Thomas A. McCarthy. 1977. *Understanding and Social Inquiry*. Notre Dame, IN: University of Notre Dame Press.

DaMatta, Roberto. 1994. Some Biased Remarks on Interpretivism: A View from Brazil. In *Assessing Cultural Anthropology*, edited by Robert Borofsky. New York: McGraw-Hill.

D'Andrade, Roy et al. 1975. Academic Opportunity in Anthropology 1974–1990. *American Anthropologist* 77(4):753–773.

Darnell, Regna. 1974. *Readings in the History of Anthropology*. New York: Harper and Row.

Davenport, William. 1984. The Thailand Controversy in Retrospect. In *Social Contexts of American Ethnology, 1840–1984*, edited by June Helm, 65–72. Washington, DC: American Anthropological Society.

DeBenedetti, Robert. 1990. *American Ordeal: The Antiwar Movement of the Vietnam Era*. Syracuse, NY: Syracuse University Press.

DeLaguna, Federicka. 1967. Presidential Address. *American Anthropologist* 70:469–476.

Devereux, George. 1967. *From Anxiety to Method in Behavioral Sciences*. The Hague: Mouton.

Diamond, Stanley. 1964. On the Origins of Modern Theoretical Anthropology. *American Anthropologist* 66:127–136.

———. 1972. Anthropology in Question. In *Reinventing Anthropology*, edited by Dell Hymes, 401–429. New York: Random House.

———. 1974. *In Search of the Primitive: A Critique of Civilization*. New Brunswick, NJ: E. P. Dutton.

———. 1979. *Toward a Marxist Anthropology: Problems and Perspectives*. The Hague: Mouton.

———. 1981. *Culture in History: Essays In Honor of Paul Radin*. New York: Octagon Books.

Dimen-Schein, Muriel. 1977. *The Anthropological Imagination*. New York: McGraw-Hill.

DuBois, Cora. 1955. The Dominant Value Profile of American Culture. *American Anthropologist* 57:1232–1239.

Dumont, Jean-Paul. 1972. *Under the Rainbow: A Structural Analysis of the Concept of Nature, Culture and Supernature*. Unpublished doctoral dissertation, University of Pittsburgh.

———. 1974. Book Review: Paul Rabinow (1975). *Symbolic Domination: Cultural Form and Historical Change in Morocco*. *Homme* 17(2–3):139–140.

———. 1976. *Under the Rainbow: Nature and Supernature among the Panare Indians*. Austin: University of Texas Press.

———. 1978. *The Headman and I: Ambiguity and Ambivalence in the Fieldworking Experience*. Austin: University of Texas Press.

———. 1989. Interview with author.

———. 1993. *The Headman and I: Ambiguity and Ambivalence in the Fieldworking Experience*. Prospect Heights, IL: Waveland Press.

Dunn, Stephen. 1974. Rejoinder to LaBarre. *American Anthropologist* 76:332–333.

———. 1976. Book Review: Paul Rabinow (1975). *Symbolic Domination: Cultural Form and Historical Change in Morocco*. *American Anthropologist* 78(4):916.

Dwyer, Kevin. 1974. *The Cultural Bases of Entrepreneurial Activity: A Study of a Moroccan Peasant Community*. Unpublished doctoral dissertation, Yale University.

———. 1977. On the Dialogic of Fieldwork. *Dialectical Anthropology* 2:143–151.

———. 1979. The Dialogic of Ethnology. *Dialectical Anthropology* 4:205–224.

———. 1982. *Moroccan Dialogues: Anthropology in Question*. Baltimore: Johns Hopkins University Press.

Edgerton, Robert B. and L. L. Langness. 1974. *Methods and Styles in the Study of Culture*. San Francisco: Chandler and Sharp.

Evans-Pritchard, E. E. 1981. *The History of Anthropological Thought*. New York: Basic Books.

Fabian, Johannes. 1983. *Time and the Other: How Anthropology Makes Its Object*. New York: Columbia University Press.

Fish, Stanley. 1980. *Is There a Text in This Class? The Authority of Interpretive Communities*. Cambridge, MA: Harvard University Press.

Forman, Shepard (ed.). 1995. *Diagnosing America: Anthropology and Public Engagement*. Ann Arbor: University of Michigan Press.

Fox, Richard G. 1991a. Working in the Present. In *Recapturing Anthropology*, edited by Richard G. Fox, 1–16. Santa Fe, NM: American School of Research Press.

———. 1991b. For a Nearly New Culture History. In *Recapturing Anthropology*, edited by Richard G. Fox, 93–114. Santa Fe, NM: American School of Research Press.

———. (ed.). 1991c. *Recapturing Anthropology*. Santa Fe, NM: American School of Research Press.

Franks, Lawrence. 1967. Book Review: Floyd Matson (1966). *The Broken Image*. *American Anthropologist* 69:415.

Frantz, Charles. 1968. The Current Milieu and the Immediate Future of U.S. Anthropology. *Anthropology Newsletter* 9(5):7–12.

———. 1984. Relevance: American Ethnology and the Wider Society 1900–1940. In *Social Contexts of American Ethnology, 1840–1984*, edited by June Helm. Washington, DC: American Anthropological Association.

Friedrichs, Robert W. 1970. *A Sociology of Sociology*. New York: The Free Press.

Gadamer, Hans-Georg. 1960. *Truth and Method*. New York: Seabury Press.

Geertz, Clifford. 1973. *The Interpretation of Culture*. New York: Basic Books.

———. 1983. *Local Knowledge: Further Essays in Interpretive Anthropology*. New York: Basic Books.

———. 1988. *Works and Lives: The Anthropologist as Author*. Stanford, CA: University of California Press.

Gitlin, Todd. 1993. *Sixties: Years of Hope, Days of Rage*. New York: Bantam.

Glaser, Barney and Anselm L. Strauss. 1967. *The Discovery of Grounded Theory*. Chicago: Aldine.

Goldmann, Lucien. 1964. *Pour une Sociologie du Roman*. Paris: Gallimard.

Goldschmidt, Walter. 1959. The Anthropology of Franz Boas: Essays on the Centennial of His Birth. *American Anthropologist* 61(5):Part 2.

———. 1976. Anthropology as Context. *American Anthropologist* 78:519–528.

———. 1977. Anthropology and the Coming Crisis: An Autoethnographic Appraisal. *American Anthropologist* 79:293–308.

———. 1984. The Cultural Paradigm in the Post-War World. In *Social Contexts of American Ethnology*, edited by June Helm, 164–174. Washington, DC: American Anthropological Association.

Goodenough, Ward. 1956. *Componential Analysis and the Study of Meaning*. Indianapolis, IN: Bobbs-Merill.

———. 1957. *Componential Analysis and the Study of Meaning*. Indianapolis, IN: Bobbs-Merrill.

———. 1961. Book Review: George Peter Murdock (1960). *Social Structure in Southeast Asia. American Anthropologist* 63:421.

———. 1970. *Description and Comparison in Cultural Anthropology.* Chicago: Aldine.

Goody, Jack. 1994. Culture and Its Boundaries: A European View. In *Assessing Cultural Anthropology,* edited by Robert Borofsky. New York: McGraw-Hill.

Gorer, Geoffrey. 1943. Themes in Japanese Culture. *Transactions of the New York Academy of Sciences* (Social Sciences Series II) 5:106–124.

Gouldner, Alvin. 1964. Anti-Minotaur: The Myth of a Value-Free Sociology. In *The New Sociology: Essays in Social Science and Social Theory in Honor of C. Wright Mills,* edited by Irving Horowitz, 196–217. New York: Oxford University Press.

Habermas, Juergen. 1971. *Knowledge and Human Interests,* translated by Jeremy J. Shapiro. Boston: Beacon Press.

———. 1973. A Postscript to *Knowledge and Human Interest. Philosophy of the Social Sciences* 3(2):157–185.

———. 1975. *Legitimation Crisis,* translated by Thomas McCarthy. Boston: Beacon Press.

———. 1977. A Review of Gadamer's *Truth and Method.* In *Understanding and Social Inquiry,* edited by Fred R. Dallmayr and Thomas A. McCarthy. Notre Dame, IN: University of Notre Dame Press.

———. 1984. *The Theory of Communicative Action. Volume One: Reason and the Rationalization of Society,* translated by Thomas McCarthy. Boston: Beacon Press.

———. 1988. *On the Logic of the Social Sciences,* translated by Shierry Weber Nicholsen and Jerry A. Stark. Cambridge, MA: M.I.T. Press.

Hallowell, A. Irving. 1956. *Culture and Experience.* Philadelphia: University of Pennsylvania Press.

———. 1965. The History of Anthropology as an Anthropology Problem. *Journal of the History of the Behavioral Sciences* 1:24–38.

Hartsock, Nancy. 1987. Rethinking Modernism. *Cultural Critique* 7:187–206.

Hatt, D. G. 1983. Book Review: Kevin Dwyer (1982). *Moroccan Dialogues: Anthropology in Question. Canadian Review of Sociology* 20:378.

Heisenberg, Werner. 1927. *Zs.f.Phys.* 33:879–893.

Helm, June. 1984a. Toward the Ethnohistory of American Ethnology. In *Social Contexts of American Ethnology, 1840–1984,* edited by June Helm. Washington, DC: American Anthropological Association.

———. (ed.). 1984b. *Social Contexts of American Ethnology, 1840–1984.* Proceedings of the American Ethnological Society. Stuart Plattner, Proceedings Editor. Washington, DC: American Anthropological Association.

Henley, John. 1980. Book Review: Jean-Paul Dumont (1978). *The Headman and I: Ambiguity and Ambivalence in the Fieldworking Experience. American Ethnologist* 7(1):205–206.

Herskovits, Melville. 1949. Some Problems of Training Graduate Students in Anthropology. *American Anthropologist* 51:517.

———. 1953. *Franz Boas: The Science of Man in the Making.* New York: Scribner.

———. 1959. Past Developments and Present Currents in Ethnology. *American Anthropologist* 61:389–398.

———. 1960. On Accuracy in Scientific Controversy. *American Anthropologist* 62:1050–1051.

Hoffman, Michael A. 1973. The History of Anthropology Revisited—A Byzantine Viewpoint. *American Anthropologist* 75:1347–1357.

Honigman, John J. 1976a. *The Development of Anthropological Ideas.* Homewood, IL: Dorsey Press.

———. 1976b. The Personal Approach in Cultural Anthropological Research. *Current Anthropology* 17(2):243–261.

Honneth, Axel et al. 1989. The Dialectics of Rationalization: An Interview with Jurgen Habermas. *Telos* 49:4–31.

Horkheimer, Max. 1937. Philosophy and Critical Theory. In *Critical Theory: Selected Essays,* edited by Alfred Schmidt, 236–268. New York: Herder and Herder, 1972.

Horowitz, Irving L. 1967a. Social Science and Public Policy: Implications of Modern Social Research. In *The Rise and Fall of Project Camelot: Studies in the Relationship Between Social Science and Practical Politics,* edited by Irving Horowitz, 339–376. Cambridge, MA: M.I.T. Press.

———. (ed.). 1967b. *The Rise and Fall of Project Camelot: Studies in the Relationship Between Social Science and Practical Politics.* Cambridge, MA: M.I.T. Press.

Hsu, Francis L. K. 1973. Prejudice in Anthropology. *American Anthropologist* 75: 1–19.

Hughes, Everett C. 1970. Teaching as Fieldwork. *American Sociologist* (5):13–18.

———. 1974. Who Studies Whom? *Human Organization* 33:327–334.

Hymes, Dell. 1968. Review of Roszak 1968. *Bulletin of the Atomic Scientists.* 1–2.

———. 1972a. The Use of Anthropology: Critical, Political and Personal. In *Reinventing Anthropology,* edited by Dell Hymes, 3–61. New York: Random House.

———. 1990. Interview with author, May 3.

———. (ed.). 1972b. *Reinventing Anthropology.* New York: Random House.

Jacobs, Mark. 1990. *Screwing the System and Making It Work: Juvenile Justice in the No Fault Society.* Chicago: University of Chicago Press.

Jarvie, I. C. 1975. Epistle to the Anthropologists. *American Anthropologist* 77:253–266.

Jay, Martin. 1973. *The Dialectical Imagination: A History of the Frankfurt School and the Institute of Social Research 1923–1950.* Boston: Little, Brown.

Jay, Robert. 1972. Personal and Extrapersonal Vision in Anthropology. In *Reinventing Anthropology,* edited by Dell Hymes, 367–381. New York: Random House.

Joseph, Roger. 1980. Behind the Wall of Meaning. *American Ethnologist* 7:774–778.

Kammen, Michael. 1997. *In the Past Lane: Historical Perspectives on American Culture.* New York: Oxford University Press.

Kaplan, David. 1974. The Anthropology of "Authenticity," Everyman His Own Anthropologist: An Essay Review. *American Anthropologist* 76:824–883.

Kardiner, Abram and Edward Preble. 1962. *They Studied Man.* Cleveland: World Publishing Company.

Kelly, Lawrence C. 1984. Why Applied Anthropology Developed When It Did: A Commentary on People, Money and Changing Times, 1930–1945. In *Social Contexts of American Ethnology, 1840–1984,* edited by June Helm, 122–138. Washington, DC: American Anthropological Association.

Klein, A. Norman. 1972. Counter Culture and Cultural Hegemony: Some Notes on the Youth Rebellion. In *Reinventing Anthropology*, edited by Dell Hymes, 312–334. New York: Random House.

Kroeber, Alfred L. 1935. History and Science in Anthropology. *American Anthropologist* 37:539–569.

———. 1956. The Place of Boas in Anthropology. *American Anthropologist* 58:151.

———. 1959. History of Personality of Anthropology. *American Anthropologist* 61:398.

——— et al. 1943. *Franz Boas: 1858–1942*. Memoir series no. 61. Washington, DC: American Anthropological Association.

Kuhn, Thomas. 1962 (1970). *The Structure of Scientific Revolutions*. Chicago: University of Chicago Press.

Kuper, Adam. 1973. *Anthropology and Anthropologists: The Modern British School*. London: Routledge and Kegan Paul.

———. 1995. Objectivity and Militancy Debate. *Current Anthropology* 16(3):424–426.

LaBarre, Weston. 1945. Some Observations on Character Structure in the Orient: The Japanese. *Psychiatry* 8.

———. 1974. On Dunn's Review of *The Ghost Dance*. *American Anthropologist* 76:332.

Lantis, Margaret. 1955. Introduction to "The U.S.A. as Anthropologists See It." *American Anthropologist* 57:113.

Latour, Bruno. 1983. Give Me a Laboratory and I Will Raise the World. In *Science Observed: Perspectives on the Social Study of Science*, edited by Karin D. Knorr-Cetina and Michael Mulkay, 141–170. Beverly Hills, CA: Sage Publications.

——— and Steve Woolgar. 1979. *Laboratory Life: The Social Construction of Scientific Facts*. Beverly Hills, CA: Sage Publications.

Leaf, Murray. 1979. *Man, Mind and Science: A History of Anthropology*. New York: Columbia University Press.

Lears, T. J. Jackson. 1981. *No Place of Grace: Anti-Modernism and the Transformation of American Culture 1880–1920*. New York: Pantheon Books.

Leland, Donald. 1974. Book Review: Dell Hymes (1972). *Reinventing Anthropology*. *American Anthropologist* 76:857–861.

Levi-Strauss, Claude. 1966. Anthropology: Its Achievements and Its Future. *Current Anthropology* 7:124–127.

———. 1955 (1967). *Tristes Tropiques*. New York: Atheneum Press.

Lipset, Seymour Martin. 1991. *Continental Divide: The Values and Institutions of the United States and Canada*. New York: Routledge, Chapman and Hall.

———. 1996. *American Exceptionalism: A Double-Sword*. New York: W. W. Norton.

Lowie, Robert. 1949. Science and Racialism. *American Anthropologist* 51:664.

———. 1953. Ethnography, Cultural and Social Anthropology. *American Anthropologist* 55:527–534.

———. 1956a. Boas Once More. *American Anthropologist* 58:159.

———. 1956b. Reminiscences of Anthropological Currents in America Half a Century Ago. *American Anthropologist* 58:995.

Lukacs, Gyorgy. 1971. *Essays uber Realismus*. Neuwied: Luchterhand.

Lynd, Staughton. 1968. *Intellectual Origins of American Radicalism*. New York: Vintage Books.

MacIntyre, Alasdair. 1978. The Idea of a Social Science. In *Philosophy of Social Explanation*, edited by Alan Ryan, 15–32. Oxford: Oxford University Press.

Macquet, Jacques. 1964. Objectivity in Anthropology. *Current Anthropology* 5:47–55.

Magnarella, Paul. 1983. Book Review: Kevin Dwyer (1982). *Moroccan Dialogues: Anthropology in Question. American Anthropologist* 85:981–982.

Magubane, Bernard. 1973. The "Xhosa" in Town Revisited. *American Anthropologist* 75(5):1701–1715.

Makkreel, Rudolph A. 1969. Wilhelm Dilthey and the Neo-Kantians: The Distinction of the *Geistewissenschaften* and *Kulturwissenschaften. Journal of the History of Philosophy* 7 (4):423–440.

Malinowski, Bronislaw. 1961. *Argonauts of the Western Pacific.* New York: E. P. Dutton.

———. 1967. *A Diary in the Strict Sense of the Term.* New York: Harcourt, Brace and World.

Marcus, George. 1986. Afterword: Ethnographic Writing and Anthropological Careers. In *Writing Culture: The Poetics and Politics of Ethnography*, edited by George Marcus and James Clifford. Berkeley: University of California Press.

———. 1994. After the Critique of Ethnography: Faith, Hope and Charity. In *Assessing Cultural Anthropology*, edited by Robert Borofsky. New York: McGraw-Hill.

——— and Dick Cushman. 1982. Ethnographies as Texts. *Annual Review of Anthropology*, Vol. 11. Palo Alto, CA: Annual Reviews Inc.

——— and Michael J. Fischer. 1986. *Anthropology as Cultural Critique.* Chicago: University of Chicago Press.

Mark, Joan. 1980. *Four Anthropologists: An American Science In Its Early Years.* New York: Neale Watson Academic Publishers.

Mascia-Lees, Frances E., Patricia Sharpe, and Colleen Ballerino-Cohen. 1989. The Postmodernist Turn in Anthropology: Cautions from a Feminist Perspective. *Signs* 15(11):7–33.

Matson, Floyd. 1966. *The Broken Image: Man, Science and Society.* Garden City, NY: Doubleday.

Mead, Margaret. 1952. Training of the Cultural Anthropologist. *American Anthropologist* 54:343.

———. 1956. Rejoinder to Steward. *American Anthropologist* 58:560.

———. 1961. Anthropology Among the Sciences. *American Anthropologist* 63:475.

Metzger, Duane. 1965. Book Review: Marvin Harris (1964). *The Nature of Cultural Things. American Anthropologist* 67:1293–1294.

Mills, C. Wright. 1959. *The Sociological Imagination.* New York: Oxford University Press.

Miner, Horace. 1956. Body Ritual Among the Nacirema. *American Anthropologist* 58:503.

Murdock, George. 1948. *Science* (AAA correspondence).

———. 1949. *Social Structure.* New York: Macmillan.

Myrdal, Gunnar. 1962. *An American Dilemma: The Negro Problem and Modern Democracy.* New York: Harper and Row.

Nader, Laura. 1972. Up the Anthropologist—Perspectives Gained from Studying

Up. In *Reinventing Anthropology*, edited by Dell Hymes, 284–311. New York: Random House.

Needham, Rodney. 1975. *Structure and Sentiment: A Test Case in Social Anthropology*. Chicago: University of Chicago Press.

Ohnuki-Tierney, Emiko. 1984. Native Anthropologists. *American Ethnologist* 11: 584–586.

Ortner, Sherry. 1984. Theory in Anthropology Since the Sixties. *Comparative Studies in Society and History* 26(1):126–166.

———. 1992. Reading America Preliminary Notes on Class and Culture. In *Recapturing Anthropology*, edited by Richard Fox, 163–190. Santa Fe, NM: American School of Research Press.

Parkin, David. 1991. *Sacred Void: Spatial Images and Ritual Among the Griama of Kenya*. Cambridge: Cambridge University Press.

Peacock, James. 1972a. Book Review: Daniel Yankelovich and William Barrett (1970). *Ego and Instinct: The Psychoanalytic View of Human Nature. American Anthropologist* 74:839–840.

———. 1972b. Three Fallacies of Scientific Materialism. *American Anthropologist* 74:839–840.

Piaget, Jean. 1962. *Play, Dreams and Imitation in Childhood*. New York: W. W. Norton.

Powdermaker, Hortense. 1964. *Stranger and Friend: The Way of an Anthropologist*. New York: W. W. Norton.

Rabinow, Paul. 1971. *The Social History of a Moroccan Village*. Unpublished doctoral dissertation, University of Chicago.

———. 1975. *Symbolic Domination: Cultural Form and Historical Change in Morocco*. Chicago: University of Chicago Press.

———. 1976. Sartre as Marxist Anthropologist. *Dialectical Anthropology* 1:96–97.

———. 1977. *Reflections on Fieldwork in Morocco*. Berkeley: University of California Press.

———. 1978. Working in Paris: Review. *Dialectical Anthropology* 3(4):361–364.

———. 1979. Masked I Go Forward. *Philosophy and Culture* 6(2):227–242.

———. 1989. Interview with author, April 16.

———. 1991. For Hire: Resolutely Late Modern. In *Recapturing Anthropology*, edited by Richard Fox, 163–190. Santa Fe, NM: American School of Research Press.

Radin, Paul. 1933. *Method and Theory of Ethnology: An Essay in Criticism*. New York: McGraw-Hill.

Ray, Verne. 1955. Book Review: Melville Herskovits (1953). *Franz Boas: The Science of Man in the Making. American Anthropologist* 57:128–140.

———. 1956. Rejoinder (to "Boas Once More"). *American Anthropologist* 58:164.

Read, Kenneth. 1965. *The High Valley*. New York: Charles Scribner & Sons.

Redfield, Robert. 1953. *The Primitive World and Its Transformations*. Ithaca, NY: Cornell University Press.

Reich, Charles. 1970. *The Greening of America*. New York: Bantam.

Reining, Conrad C. 1962. A Lost Period of Applied Anthropology. *American Anthropologist* 64:593.

Richardson, Miles. 1975. Anthropologist—The Myth Teller. *American Ethnologist* 2(3):517–533.

Ricoeur, Paul. 1970. *Freud and Philosophy: An Essay on Interpretation*, translated by Denis Savage. New Haven, CT: Yale University Press.

———. 1971. The Model of the Text: Meaningful Action Considered as a Text. *Social Research* 38(4):539–562.

Rosen, Lawrence. 1984. Book Review: Kevin Dwyer (1984). *Moroccan Dialogues. American Ethnologist* 11:597–598.

Rosenau, Pauline. 1992. *Postmodernism and the Social Sciences: Insights, Inroads and Intrusions.* Princeton, NJ: Princeton University Press.

Rowe, William. 1965. The Renaissance Foundations of Anthropology. *American Anthropologist* 67:21–30.

Ruby, Jay (ed.). 1982. *Crack in the Mirror: Reflexive Perspectives in Anthropology.* Philadelphia: University of Pennsylvania Press.

Ryan, Alan. 1978. *The Philosophy of the Social Sciences.* New York: Pantheon Books.

Ryle, Gilbert. 1949. *The Concept of Mind.* New York: Hutchinson's University Library.

Samson, Leo. 1935. *The New Humanism.* New York: Washburn.

Sangren, P. Steven. 1988. Rhetoric and the Authority of Ethnography. *Current Anthropology* 29(3):405–424.

Scholte, Bob. 1966. Epistemic Paradigms: Some Problems in Cross-Cultural Research on Social Anthropological History and Theory. *American Anthropologist* 68:1192–1201.

———. 1971. Discontents in Anthropology. *Social Research* 38:777–807.

———. 1972. Toward a Reflexive and Critical Anthropology. In *Reinventing Anthropology*, edited by Dell Hymes. New York: Random House.

———. 1976a. On the Function of Scientific Discourse. *American Anthropologist* 78:74–78.

———. 1976b. Dwelling on the Everyday World: Phenomenological Analysis and Social Reality. *American Anthropologist* 78:585–594.

Schneider, David. 1968. *American Kinship: A Cultural Account.* Englewood Cliffs, NJ: Prentice-Hall.

Schutz, Alfred. 1963. Common-sense and Scientific Interpretation of Human Action. In *Philosophy of the Social Sciences*, edited by Maurice Natanson, 302–346. New York: Random House.

———. 1971. The Social World and the Theory of Social Action. *Social Research* 38:203–221.

———. 1977. Concept and Theory Formation in the Social Sciences. In *Understanding and Social Inquiry*, edited by Fred R. Dallmayr and Thomas A. McCarthy, 225–239. Notre Dame, IN: University of Notre Dame Press.

———. 1978. Problems of Interpretive Sociology. In *Philosophy of Social Explanation*, edited by Alan Ryan, 203–220. Oxford: Oxford University Press.

Statement on Human Rights. 1947. Submitted to the Commission on Human Rights, United Nations by the Executive Board of the American Anthropological Association. *American Anthropologist* 49:539–543.

Stein, Howard F. 1976. Ideology in the Study of American Racism, Ethnicity and Poverty. *American Anthropologist* 76:834–844.

Steward, Julian. 1955. Irrigation Civilization: A Comparative Study. A Symposium on Method and Result in Cross-Cultural Regularities. Washington, DC: Social Science Section, Department of Cultural Affairs, Pan American Union.

Stocking, George. 1960. Franz Boas and the Founding of the American Anthropological Association. *American Anthropologist* 62(1):1.

———. 1982. Afterword: A View from the Center. *Ethnos* 47:173–186.

Strathern, Marilyn. 1987. Out of Context: The Persuasive Fictions of Anthropology. *Current Anthropology* 28(3):251–270.

Susman, Warren I. 1964. History and the American Intellectual: Uses of the Usable Past. *American Quarterly* 16(92):243–263.

Szwed, John F. 1972. An American Anthropological Dilemma: The Politics of Afro-American Culture. In *Reinventing Anthropology*, edited by Dell Hymes, 153–182. New York: Random House.

Tannen, Deborah. 1997. *The Argument Culture: Moving from Debate to Dialogue*. New York: Random House.

Taylor, Charles. 1979. Interpretation and the Sciences of Man. In *Interpretive Social Science: A Reader*, edited by Paul Rabinow and William M. Sullivan. Berkeley: University of California Press.

Thompson, John B. 1981. *Critical Hermeneutics: A Study in the Thought of Paul Ricoeur and Jurgen Habermas*. Cambridge: Cambridge University Press.

———. 1984. *Studies in the Theory of Ideology*. Cambridge: Polity Press.

———. 1990. *Ideology and Modern Culture*. Cambridge: Polity Press.

Toth, John. 1983. Book Review: Kevin Dwyer (1982). *Moroccan Dialogues: Anthropology in Question. Middle East Journal* 8:280.

Toulmin, Stephen. 1961. *Foresight and Understanding: An Enquiry into the Aims of Science*. New York: Harper and Row.

Trouillot, Michel Rolph. 1991. Anthropology and the Savage Slot: The Poetics and Politics of Otherness. In *Recapturing Anthropology*, edited by Richard G. Fox, 17–44. Santa Fe, NM: American School of Research Press.

Turner, Victor. 1967. *Forest of Symbols: Aspects of Ndembu Ritual*. Ithaca, NY: Cornell University Press.

Varenne, Herve. 1984. Collective Representation in American Anthropological Conversations: Individual and Culture. *Current Anthropology* 25(3):281–291.

Vincent, Joan. 1991. Engaging Historicism. In *Recapturing Anthropology*, edited by Richard G. Fox, 17–44. Santa Fe, NM: American School of Research Press.

Voget, Fred W. 1975. *A History of Ethnology*. New York: Holt, Rinehart and Winston.

Vogt, Evon. 1965. Water Witching: An Interpretation of a Ritual Pattern in a Rural American Community. In *Reader in Comparative Religion*, edited by William A. Lessa and Evon Z. Vogt, 346–376. New York: Harper and Row.

Wallace, Anthony F. C. 1978. *Rockdale: The Growth of an American Village in the Early Industrial Revolution*. New York: Knopf.

Washburn, Sherwood. 1963. The Study of Race. *American Anthropologist* 65:521–531.

Watson, Graham. 1987. Make Me Reflexive But Not Yet. *Journal of Anthropological Research* 43:29–41.

Wax, Murray. 1956. The Limitation of Boas' Anthropology. *American Anthropologist* 58:63.

———. 1957. Boas in Anthropology. *American Anthropologist* 58:151, 159, 164, 734.

————. 1958. Comment on Matson's "The Broken Image: Man, Science and Society." *American Anthropologist* 67:156.

Wax, Rosalie, Solon T. Kimball, and James Watson. 1976. Crossing Cultural Boundaries: The Anthropological Experience. *American Anthropologist* 78:46–57.

Weber, Max. 1977. Objectivity in Social Science and Social Policy. In *Understanding and Social Inquiry*, edited by Fred R. Dallmayr and Thomas A. McCarthy, 24–37. Notre Dame, IN: University of Notre Dame Press.

Webster, Steven. 1982. Dialogue and Fiction in Ethnography. *Dialectical Anthropology* 2:91–114.

White, Leslie. 1945. The Ethnography of Franz Boas. *Bulletin of the Texas Memorial Museum No. 6*. Houston: Texas Memorial Museum.

————. 1949. *The Science of Culture: A Study of Man and Civilization*. New York: Farrar, Strauss.

————. 1959. *Evolution of Culture: The Development of Civilization to the Fall of Rome*. New York: McGraw-Hill.

Whitten, Norman. 1982a. Book Review: Jean Paul Dumont (1978). *The Headman and I: Ambiguity and Ambivalence in the Fieldworking Experience*. *American Ethnologist* 9(1):259.

———— and Emiko Ohnuki-Tierney. 1982. When Paradigms Collide: Introduction to Symbolism and Cognition II. *American Ethnologist* 9:635–643.

Williams, Elgen. 1951. Anthropology for the Common Man. *American Anthropologist* 49:84–90.

Willis, William S. 1972. Skeletons in the Anthropological Closet. In *Reinventing Anthropology*, edited by Dell Hymes, 121–152. New York: Random House.

Wilson, Edward O. 1998. *Consilience: The Unity of Knowledge*. New York: Alfred A. Knopf.

Winch, Peter. 1977. The Idea of a Social Science. In *Understanding and Social Inquiry*, edited by Fred R. Dallmayr and Thomas A. McCarthy, 159–188. Notre Dame, IN: University of Notre Dame Press.

Wittgenstein, Ludwig. 1953. *Philosophical Investigations*, translated by G. E. M. Anscombe. New York: Macmillan.

Wolf, Eric R. 1964. *Anthropology*. Englewood Cliffs, NJ: Prentice-Hall.

————. 1970. Anthropology on the Warpath in Thailand. *New York Review of Books*, November 19:26–35.

————. 1972. American Anthropologists and American Society. In *Reinventing Anthropology*, edited by Dell Hymes, 251–263. New York: Random House.

————. 1980. They Divide and Subdivide and Call It Anthropology. *New York Times*, November 30.

————. 1984. Culture: Panacea or Problem. *American Antiquity* 49:393–400.

————. 1990. Distinguished Lecture: Facing Power—Old Insights, New Questions. *American Anthropologist* 92:586–596.

Yankelovich, Daniel. 1981. *New Rules: Searching for Self-Fulfillment in a World Turned Upside Down*. New York: Random House.

———— and William Barrett. 1970. *Ego and Instinct: The Psychoanalytic View of Human Nature*. New York: Random House.

Index

About the Author

SUSAN R. TRENCHER is Assistant Professor of Anthropology at George Mason University.

ISBN 0-89789-673-4

EAN

9 780897 896733

90000>

HARDCOVER BAR CODE